IMAGES
of America

PLAISTOW,

WESTVILLE, AND THE NORTH PARISH

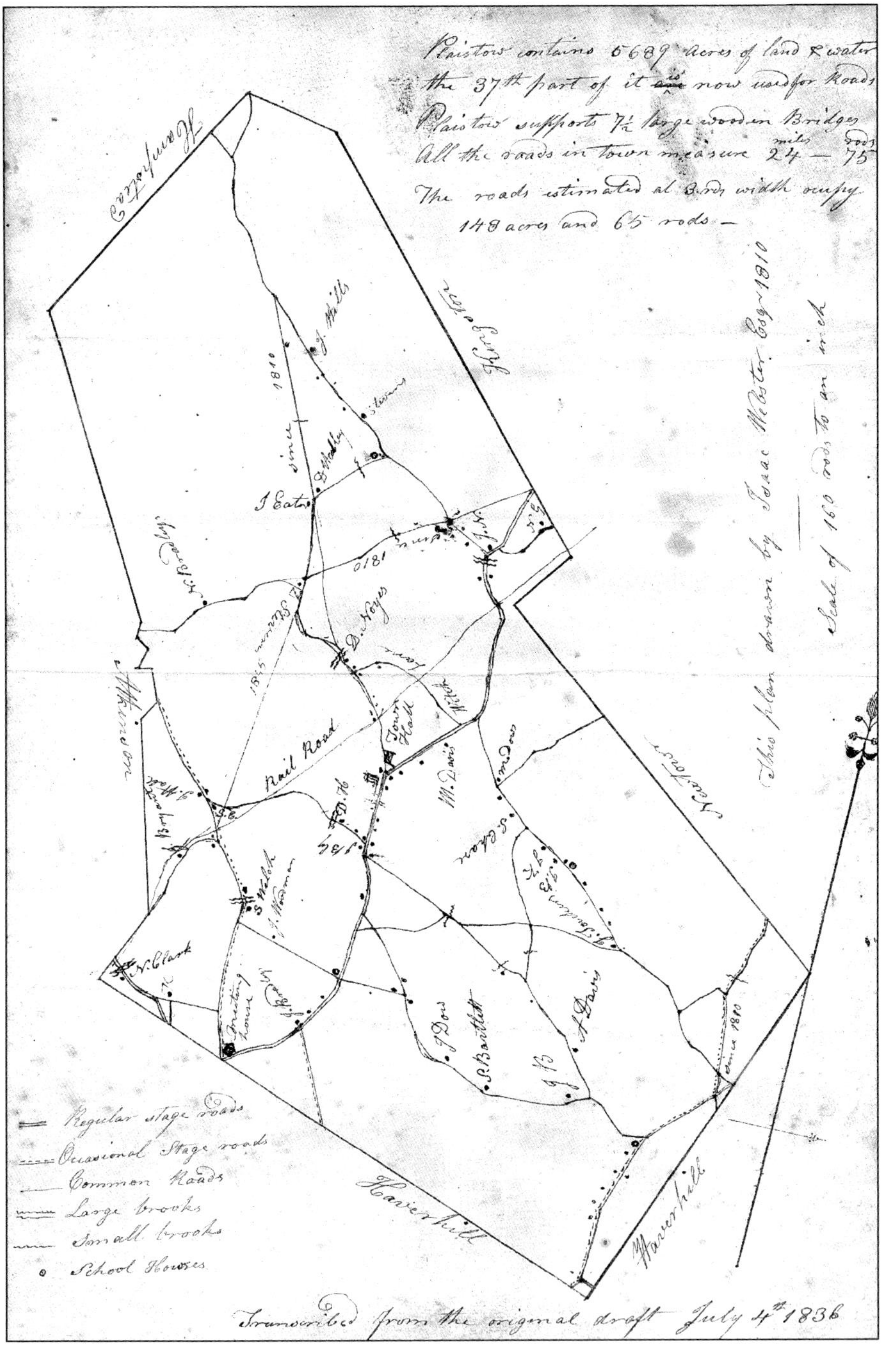

This July 4, 1836 map of Plaistow, based on a plan created in 1810 by Isaac Webster, shows the extant roads, bridges, and houses in town. The larger squares in the center of the map show the locations of the old town hall and the Baptist church. The squiggly lines transversing the roads show the locations of bridges. The inscription on the top right reads: "Plaistow contains 5689 acres of land & water, the 37th part of it is now used for roads. Plaistow supports 7½ large wooden bridges. All the roads in town measure 24 miles—75 rods. The roads estimated at [illegible] width occupy 148 acres and 65 rods." The map's scale is 160 rods to an inch.

IMAGES
of America

PLAISTOW,
WESTVILLE, AND THE NORTH PARISH

Mark C. Foynes

ARCADIA
PUBLISHING

ISBN 978-0-7385-0943-3

Published by Arcadia Publishing
Charleston, South Carolina

Printed in the United States of America

Library of Congress Catalog Card Number: Applied For

For all general information contact Arcadia Publishing at:
Telephone 843-853-2070
Fax 843-853-0044
E-mail sales@arcadiapublishing.com
For customer service and orders:
Toll-Free 1-888-313-2665

Visit us on the Internet at www.arcadiapublishing.com

In memory of Donald C. Foynes,
Plaistow native, history lover, and father.

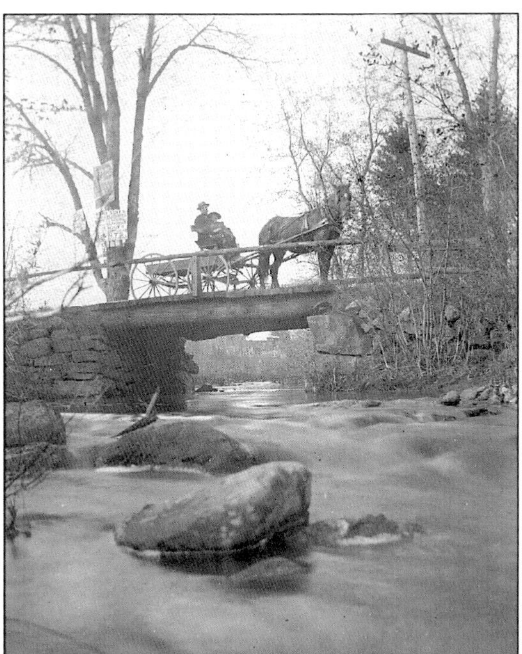

This bridge spanned Pollard Brook in the late 1800s. The bottom sign on the tree advertises a clothier called Blaisdel's, which specialized in men's and boys' clothes.

Contents

ACKNOWLEDGMENTS

The author would like to extend his heartfelt appreciation to the following organizations and individuals without whose assistance this work would not have been possible:

The Plaistow Historical Society, whose visual history collection provided the bulk of images included in this volume; specifically, I would like to thank Bernadine FitzGerlad, Mildred Ilsley, Nancy Marston, Paul Holmes, Connie Cullen, Bill Hubbard, and the rest of the society's memberships. Were it not for their cooperation, this history could never have come to be.

J. Alden and Ruth Palmer of Plaistow, who supplied images, expertise, and moral support to the author over the course of this project.

Gregg Laing of the Haverhill Public Library's Special Collections Department, who was extremely supportive of this project through his generous permission to use a large number of rare photographs of the North Parish, which straddles the Plaistow-Haverhill line. He was also instrumental in helping the author acquire this volume's Newton Road resources.

Catherine "Katie" Rowell, née Catherine Yawnitz, who made the Westville section of this book possible.

Wayne Gallup, Bill Copeley, David Smolen, and Phillip Abbot of the New Hampshire Historical Society's Tuck Library.

Charlene and Patrick Foynes for their love and support in this endeavor.

Sarah M. Ricker, herself an Arcadia author of a history of her native Milton, for her loving support and technical assistance on this project.

The late Donald C. Foynes, to whom this volume is dedicated. Foynes instilled within the author an abiding love of history and the town each called home.

Key to photograph credits:

AC	Courtesy of the author's collection
CYR	Courtesy of Catherine Yawnitz Rowell
CHC	Courtesy of Constance Holmes Cullen
HPL	Courtesy of Haverhill Public Library Special Collections
KV	Courtesy of Ken Veroneau
NHHS	Courtesy of New Hampshire Historical Society
PF	Courtesy of the Palmer family
PH	Courtesy of Paul Holmes
PHS	Courtesy of Plaistow Historical Society

INTRODUCTION

This collection of images offers a unique glimpse into the lives of the people of Plaistow and offers insights into the town's changing built environment. Since I delved into the history of this small town a few years ago, I have concluded that a pictorial history of Plaistow is useful and worthwhile for two reasons: opportunity and necessity.

Surviving images of historical Plaistow offer modern readers a unique opportunity. To be sure, photographs have a tremendous ability to educate. Pictures can make the remote more immediate, tangible, and relevant. I hope that this work will be useful and enjoyable to longtime residents of Plaistow, new arrivals, grade school students and their teachers, casual passers-through, and anyone with an interest in local history.

A pictorial history of Plaistow is also something of a necessity. While working on an earlier project, I was frustrated by the lack of traditional written documentary sources. There is no record of the first town meeting of 1749; few, if any, sermons survive from 18th-century ministers of the town's Congregational church; no functional equivalent of the diaries of Martha Ballard or Stratham's Samuel Lane illuminates the domestic life of the town's women and men; no account books survive from the town's brickyards or shoe shops. Nor is there a Colonial Revival or Depression-era history of the town that describes the minutia of the goings-on of Plaistow from the arrival of the first settlers onward.

However, there are images—photographs, drawings, doodles, paintings, maps, and more. These images illustrate many aspects of small-town life: work, worship, getting from place to place, and the celebrations and diversions that enriched the lives of the town's men, women, and children. As a result of having spent the past year studying these images, I have developed a fuller and more complete sense of what life in Plaistow was like for previous generations.

As much as I have sought to include, this volume contains many omissions. These omissions are not by choice or bias but are a matter of the historical record. No one saw it fit to capture and preserve any images of the hearthside labors of housewives or the French Canadians who toiled at the brickyards that thrived in the late 1800s. The images that do survive of work are of machines and buildings that stand as monuments to the ingenuity and hard work of proprietors. When laborers' images were captured, they stood at attention for posed photographs.

Perhaps it is fitting that even a pictorial history of Plaistow should be so incomplete. Plaistow itself is, to an extent, an exercise in subtraction.

Originally there was the land, wild and forested. Local tribes established camps here and migrated through this area in search of game. In 1642, Englishmen claimed this land and tamed the landscape by supplanting the wilderness with pastureland.

In 1741, the king of England redrew the provincial boundary three miles north of the Merrimack River; eight years later, Gov. Benning Wentworth carved Plaistow out of land previously claimed by the settlers of Haverhill.

A hundred years later, in the mid-1800s, many of the town's best and brightest heeded the advice of Horace Greeley, who urged a new generation to stake its future in the lands out West.

Following World War II, the town experienced an identity crisis as residential and commercial development challenged the town's rural character. Concurrently, the fraternal and religious-based organizations that supplemented and sustained the everyday lives of townsfolk before the war began to erode. It was during this time that Plaistow's only National Register site—the old trolley barn—was razed. Plaistow, once an idyllic New England village with ample outlying pastureland, began to feel the growing pains that it is still coming to terms with.

To focus on these "subtractions," however, is to overlook the obvious: Plaistow is a town that adapts to new realities. New people, whether they be the French-Canadian or Armenian immigrants of a century ago or today's exurbanites from greater Boston, have settled within the town's borders and have created a new dynamic within the community. Each group in turn has brought its own expectations and has created its own niche within the town while contributing to the development of its ever-evolving character.

This evolutionary character is reflected in Plaistow's geographical divisions, which lend themselves to several of this volume's chapter titles.

The North Parish section, located ironically on the town's southern boundary, owes its name to the fact that it was the northernmost district in Haverhill in the early 1700s; the traditional name was retained after the provincial boundary was redrawn in the 1740s. For about a century, the town's activity centered on the North Parish meetinghouse, which was the location of the first town meeting in 1749.

The coming of the railroad in the 1830s and trolley service in 1903 spurred growth and created the conditions that allowed for the development of Plaistow Village. With the erection of a town hall in 1831, the center of the town's activity became truly central. The growing importance of the village can be seen in the decidedly 19th-century character of this section's vernacular architecture, which is distinctly late Federal, Greek Revival, and Gothic in style.

The railroad also spurred development in Westville, whose brick industry thrived in the mid-1800s. The railroad permitted brick producers to more easily ship their goods to market and gave French Canadians the opportunity to migrate from their failing farms in Quebec to new opportunities here.

While some sections of town developed as a result of increased access to rail transportation, outlying areas such as the Newton Road and Kelly Town were bypassed. The reversion of Old County Road's pastureland to forest in the 1900s and the dilapidation of homes around Brandy Brow in the late 1800s partially speak to these areas' social and economic isolation.

Through surviving images, I have attempted to collect, preserve, and occasionally interpret the visual record of Plaistow's evolving human landscape. I hope that by seeing where we have come from, we can proceed into the future with a stronger sense of who we are as a community.

I write these lines from Concord but still consider Plaistow my home.

One

North Parish and Atkinson Depot

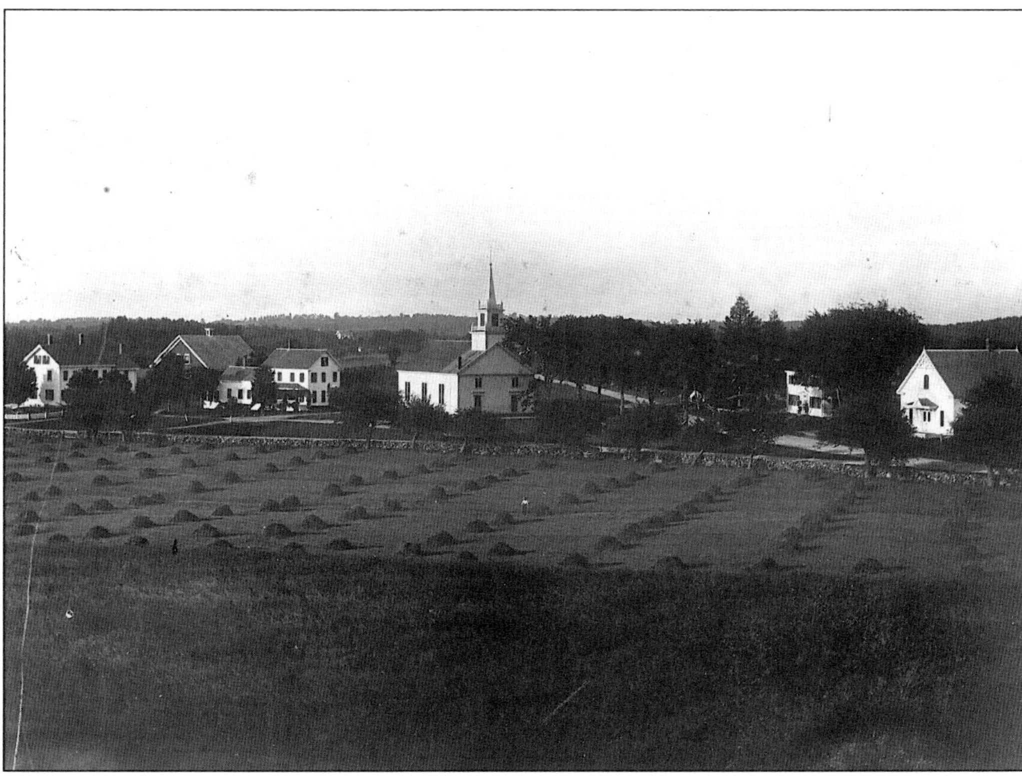

This is the view of the North Parish that James C. Merrill saw from his cupola in 1900. Buildings, from left to right, are Sawyer Farm, the Charles Hazeltine House, the North Parish meetinghouse, the parsonage, and the vestry. (HPL.)

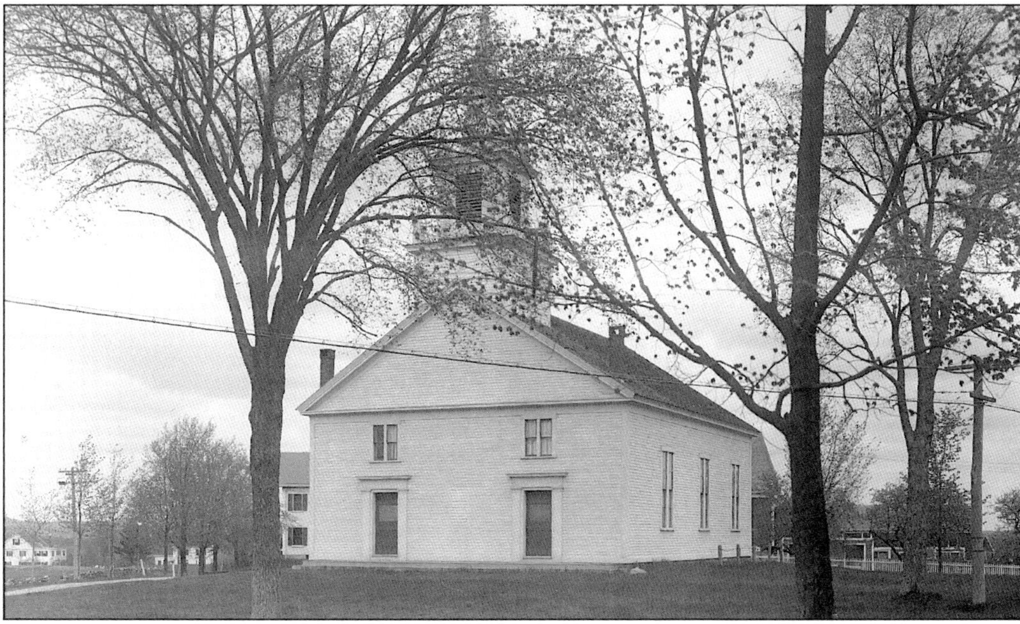

The present North Parish meetinghouse, shown here in 1916, was built in 1837. Organized in the 1730s, when the first meetinghouse was erected, Congregationalists met at this site until the 1950s. Prior to the construction of this building, which is solely in Plaistow, the old meetinghouse straddled the state line that was established in 1741. Consequently, New Hampshire couples exchanging vows in the original church were wed in the New Hampshire section of the building, while their Massachusetts counterparts did the same in the section to the south of the provincial boundary. (HPL.)

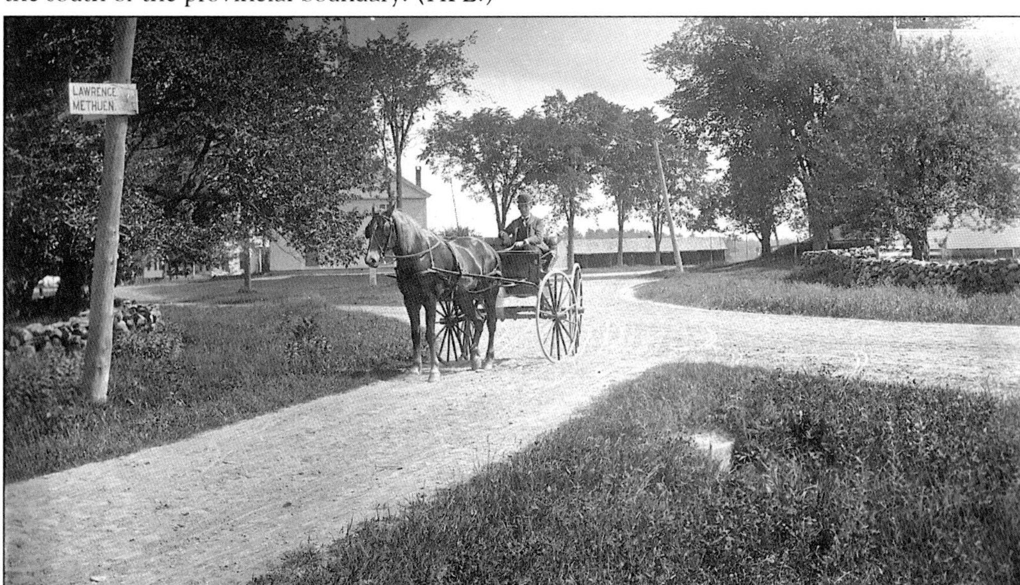

This late-1800s view of the North Parish, beyond Cushing Avenue, looks northeast. The building at right is the vestry. Beneath the horse's snout is the 1880s marker delineating the state boundary. Note the horse shed in the distance; after religious meetings, horse sheds were popular gathering spots for parishioners to gossip and discuss business. (HPL.)

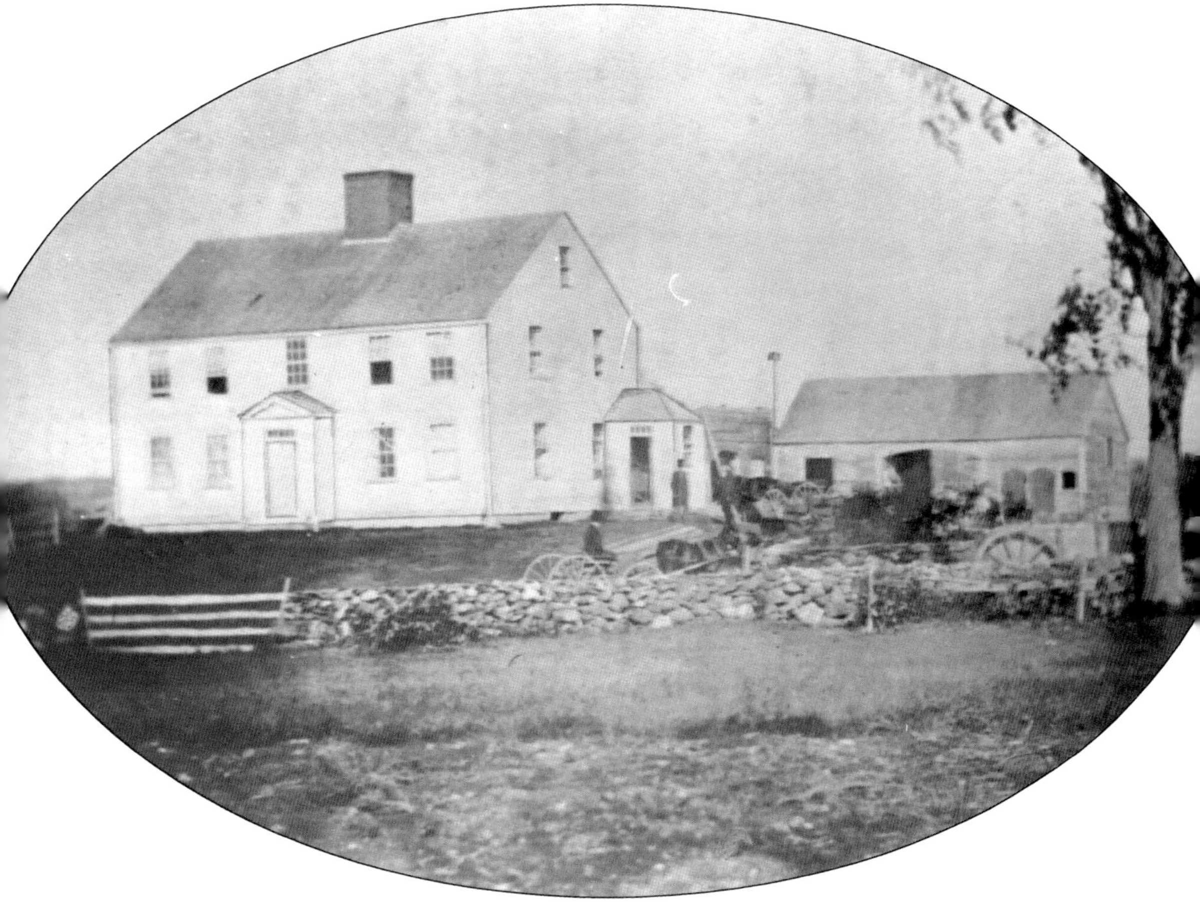

The parsonage was built in 1731 and was the home of the Reverend James Cushing, the first minister of the North Parish. Cushing's son-in-law, the Reverend Gyles Merrill, purchased this house in 1771, and the parsonage remained in the Merrill family for at least four generations until 1925. (HPL.)

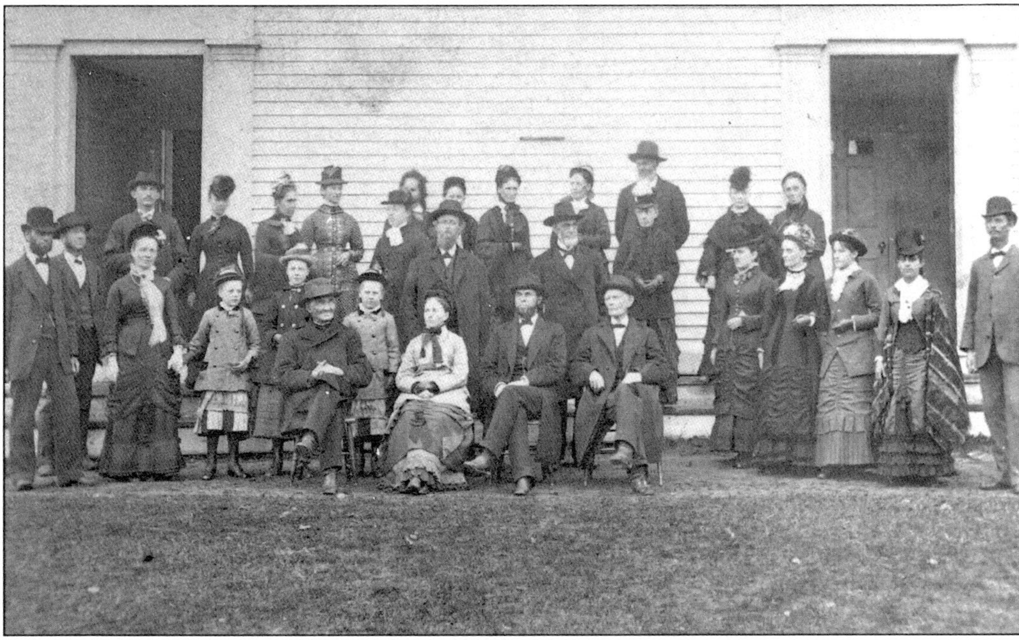

Congregants celebrating the 150th anniversary of the North Parish assemble in front of the meetinghouse on November 4, 1880. (HPL.)

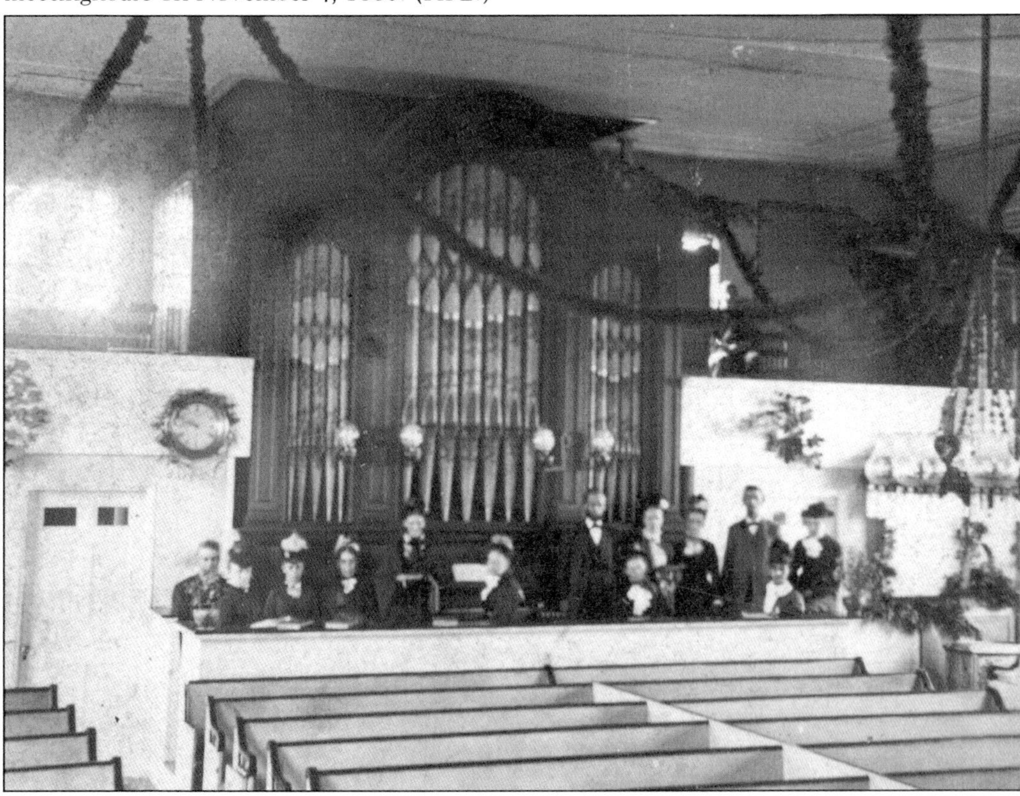

This interior view of the rear of the church shows the parish choir posing for a picture during the congregation's sesquicentennial celebration, in 1880. (HPL.)

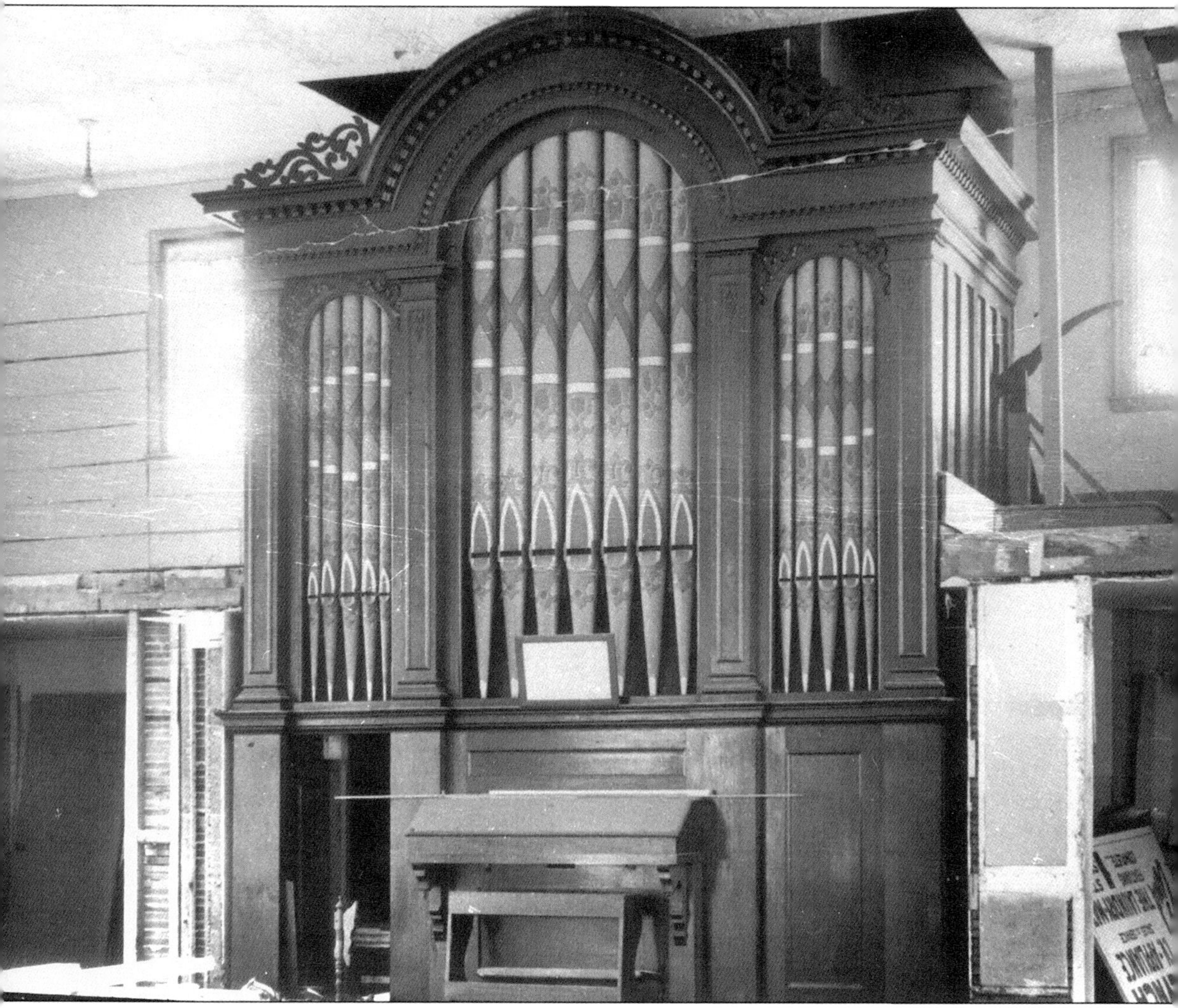

Edward D. Kimball of Salem, Massachusetts, donated this pump organ in honor of his parents, Nathaniel and Sarah Kimball of Plaistow. In 1953, the ecclesiastical use of the meetinghouse came to an end when the building was sold to the family of Herbert J. Lynch, who converted the building into a television and appliance store. The building was later used as a chiropractic clinic and is now the home of a loan company. (HPL.)

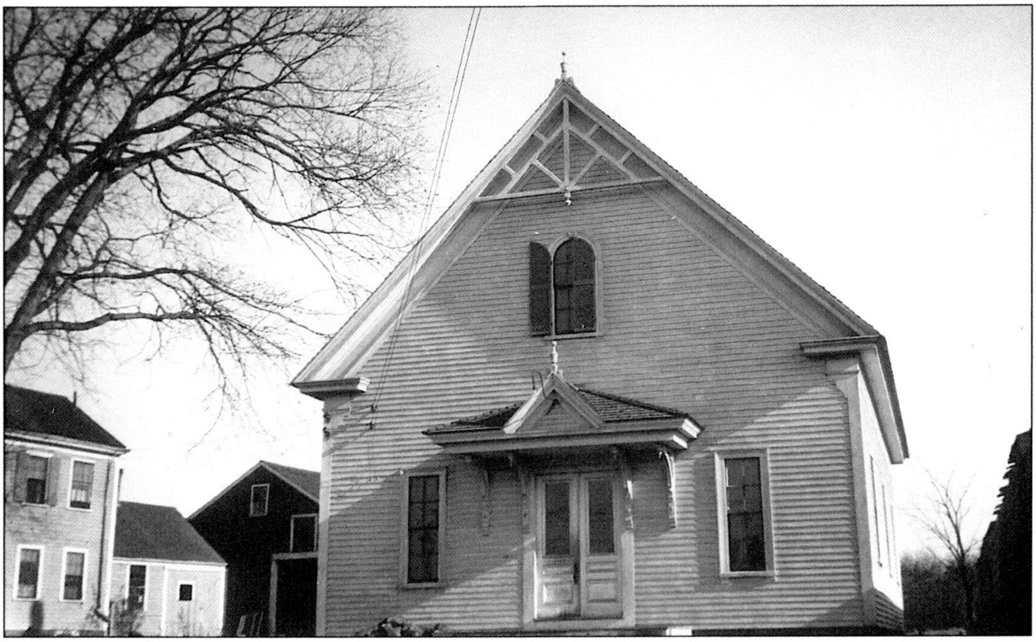

The vestry and Grange Hall are shown *c.* 1900. The building was torn down in 1978, and this is now the site of a Pizza Hut restaurant. (HPL.)

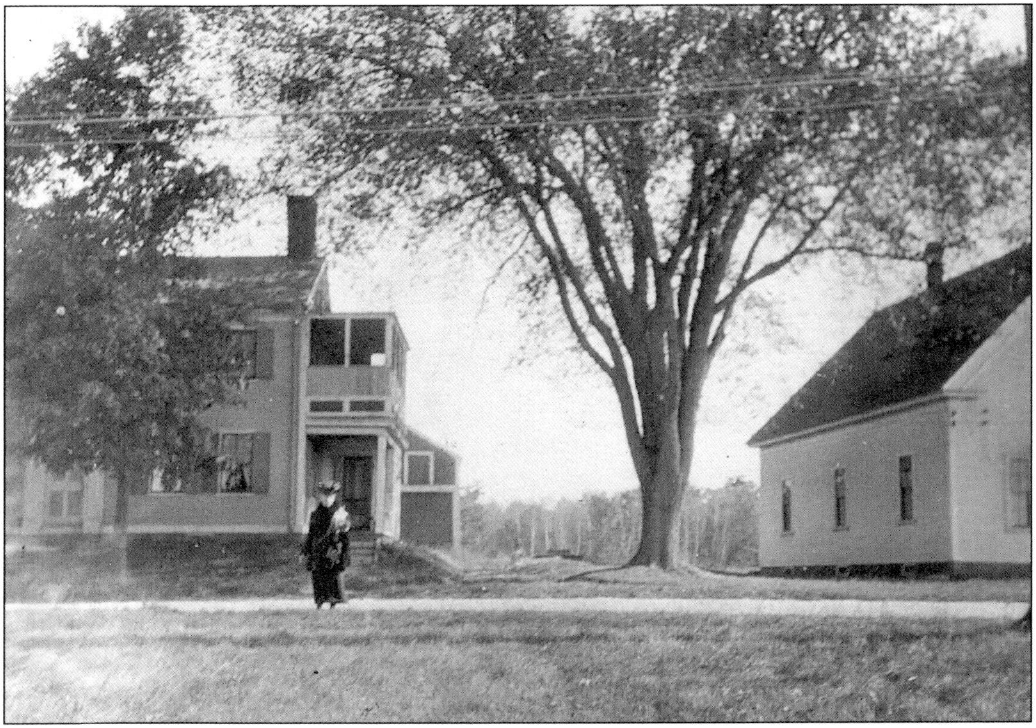

This early-1900s view looks south from the meetinghouse green into Haverhill. On the right is the vestry; on the left is the parsonage. Mary Oliphant Carleton Watson, who lived in the parsonage, is shown here in the foreground. (HPL.)

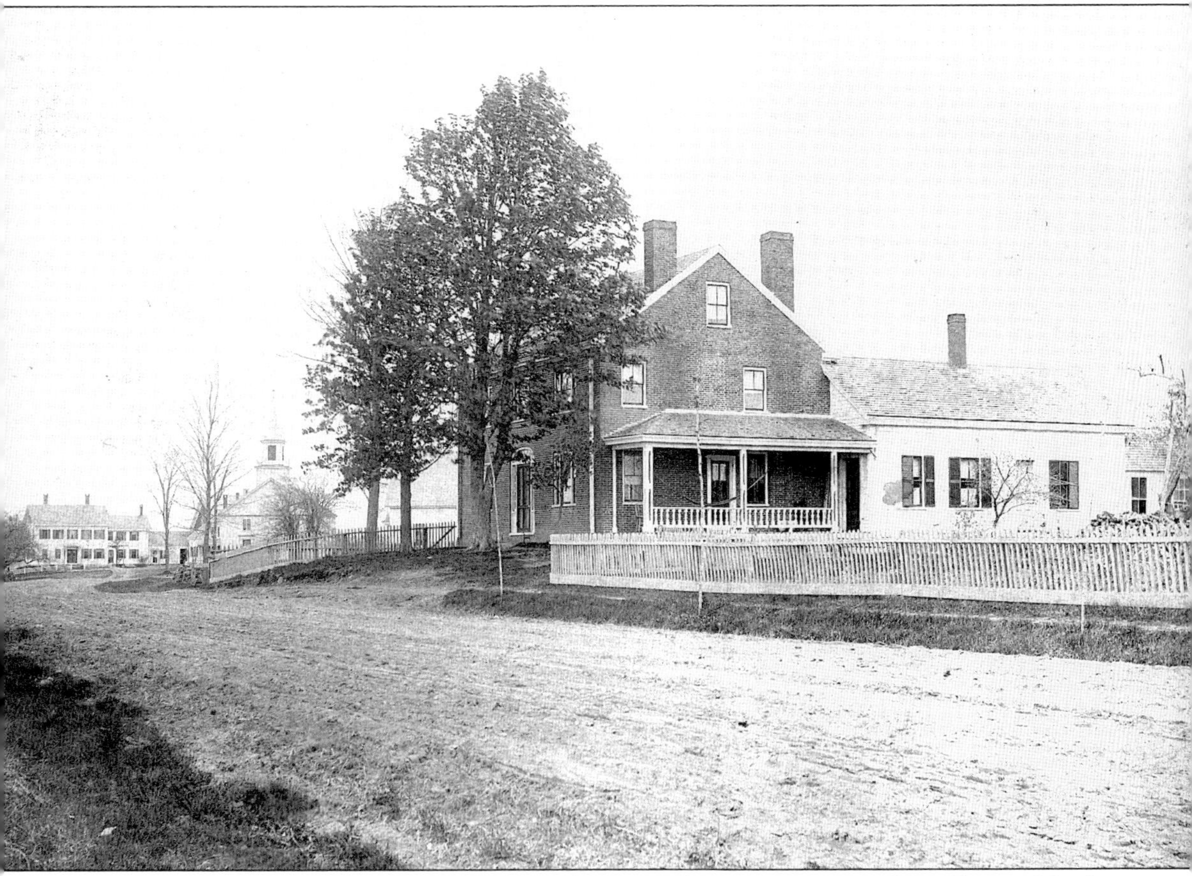

The Isaac Merrill House was built in 1824 and is shown here *c.* 1890. Isaac Merrill was a North Parish shoemaker, who, through his diary, recorded a half-century of change in Haverhill and Plaistow. On March 21, 1839, Merrill noted, "A Catholic priest from Lowell celebrates or performs a Mass at the Townhouse in Plaistow for the benefit of the Irishmen." These Irish presumably helped build the rail line, the completion of which Merrill noted on October 28 of that year. (HPL.)

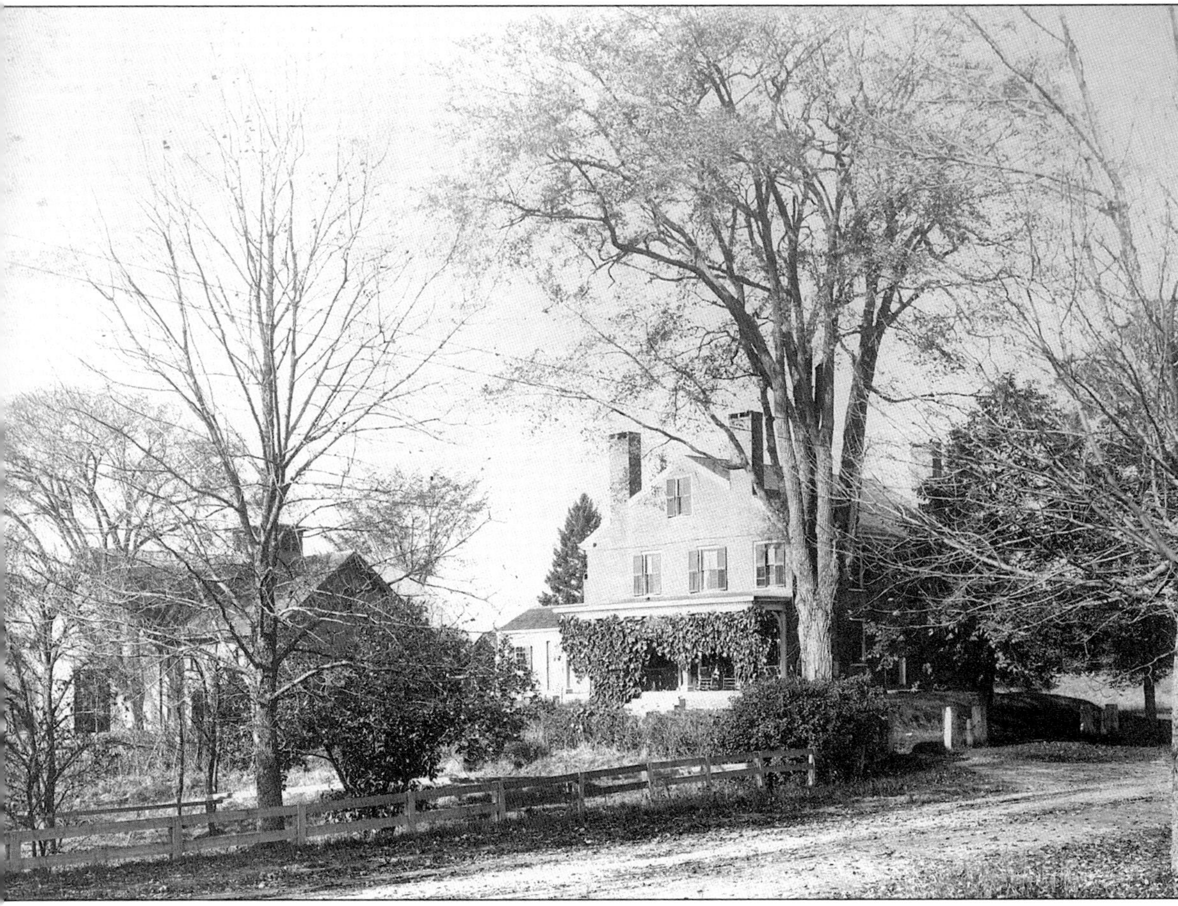

The Jesse Clement House, shown here in 1916, is located a stone's throw from Plaistow. Now the home of the American Legion, this house was built in 1824 and served as the center of Plaistow's temperance movement. The Temperance Society of Plaistow & Vicinity began meeting here in 1831 and worked for 10 years to ebb the flow of liquor into the area. Although Haverhill was often dry, the number of taverns near the border on Newton Road attests to the persistence of strong drink in Plaistow. (HPL.)

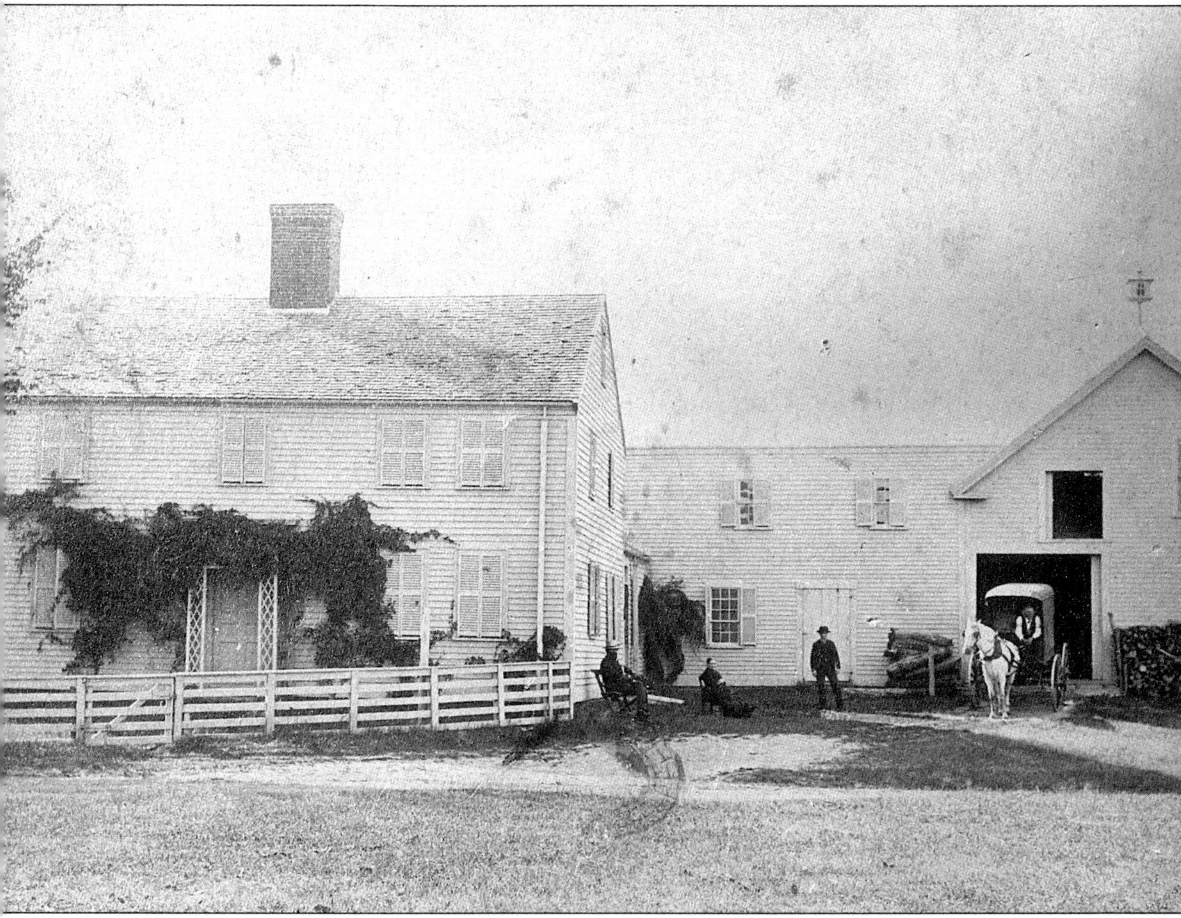

The Jesse Bradley House, shown here in the 1880s, was built in the late 1700s or the early 1800s. This house is located at the intersection of North Avenue, South Main Street, and Chandler Avenue, known as Bradley's corner. The structure's breezeway no longer exists and is now the location of the end of Chandler Avenue. This is now the home of Dr. and Mrs. John Walsh. (PHS.)

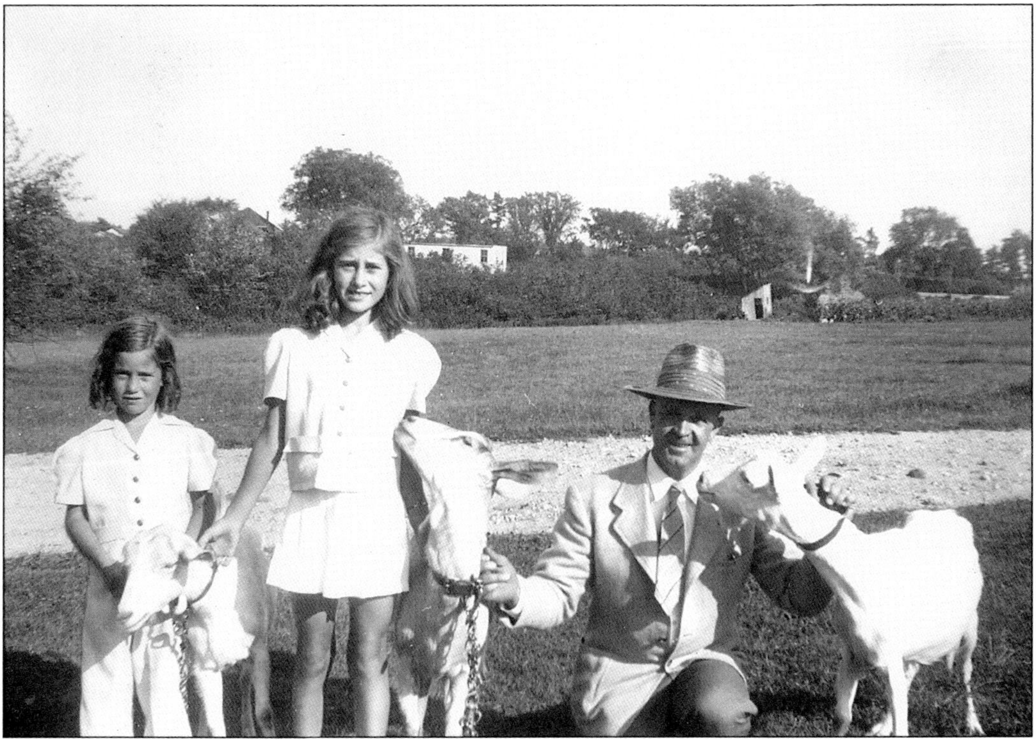

This Spinney Avenue scene dates from *c.* the early 1940s. The two girls are Lois and Joan Hardy with their father, Earl Hardy. (AC.)

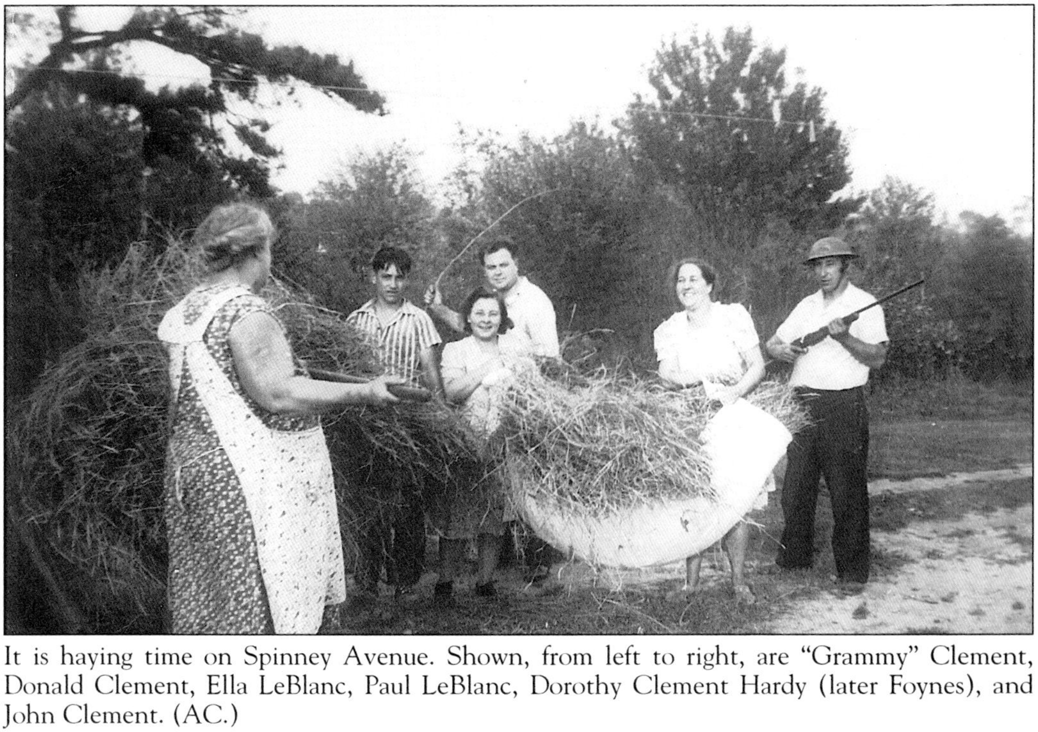

It is haying time on Spinney Avenue. Shown, from left to right, are "Grammy" Clement, Donald Clement, Ella LeBlanc, Paul LeBlanc, Dorothy Clement Hardy (later Foynes), and John Clement. (AC.)

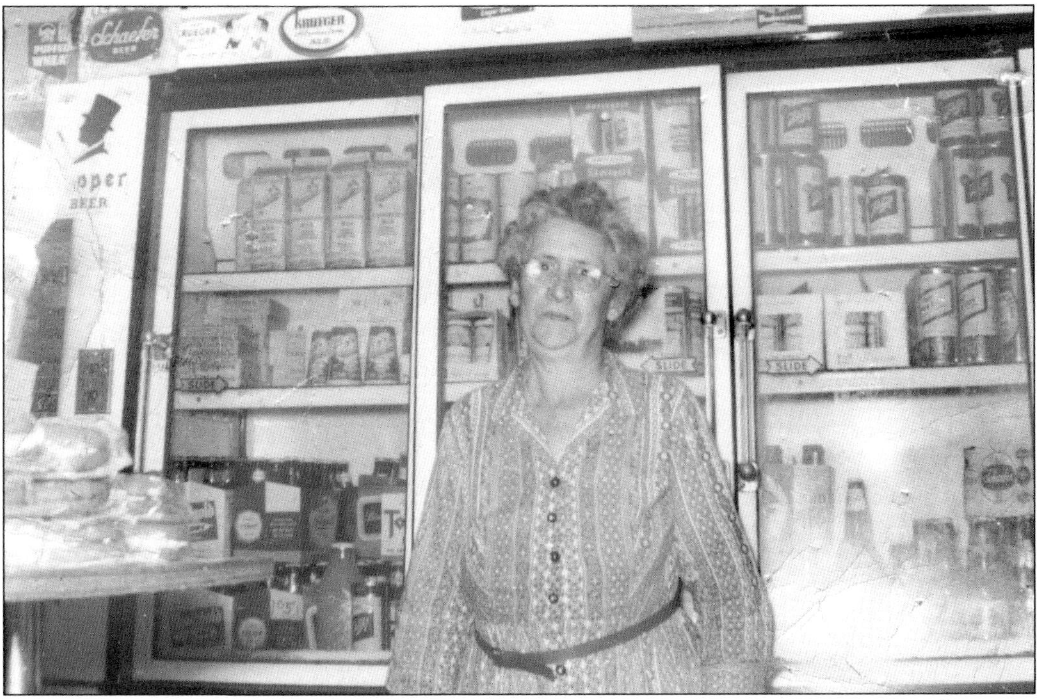

Mary Walsh, who died in 1971, operated a store in Plaistow's North Parish section for many years with her husband and son. Before being demolished to make room for an expanded D'Angelo's plaza, Walsh's store doubled as a farm stand, where Wally Leszciska sold corn and other produce from his East Haverhill farm. (PHS.)

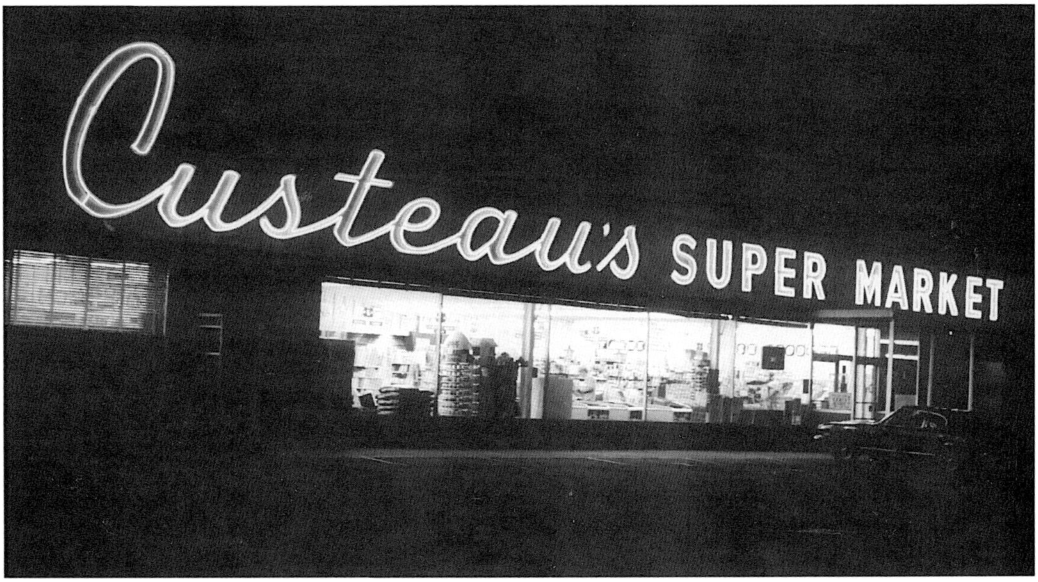

Custeau's Supermarkets were located in Plaistow and East Hampstead. The Plaistow store replaced the town's first supermarket, Glenn's, which was located in Hoyt's City Plaza. Prior to Glenn's, Plaistow residents who favored the selection supermarkets offered used to travel to Demoulas in Haverhill. Hoyt's City was refurbished, renamed, and greatly expanded recently to accommodate a new Shaw's Supermarket. (PHS.)

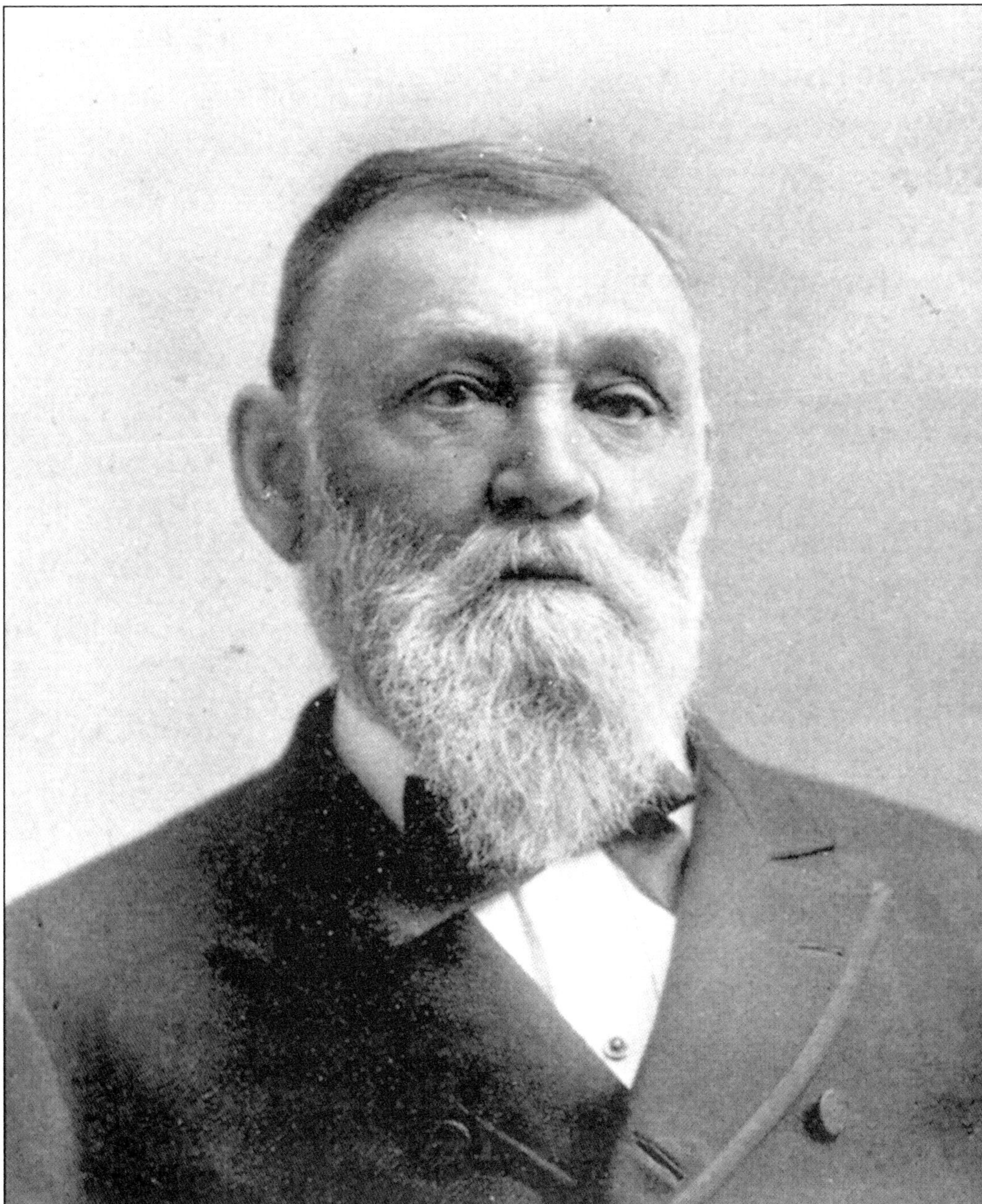

Hon. Nathaniel Haven Clark was a farmer-statesman who was born in 1826. A member of both houses of the state legislature, Clark also participated in the 1876 Constitutional Convention. As a member of the executive council, Clark "sternly forb[ade] his friends to work for his own political advancement." In 1885, Governor Currier appointed Clark to a commission that defined New Hampshire's southern boundary. (NHHS.)

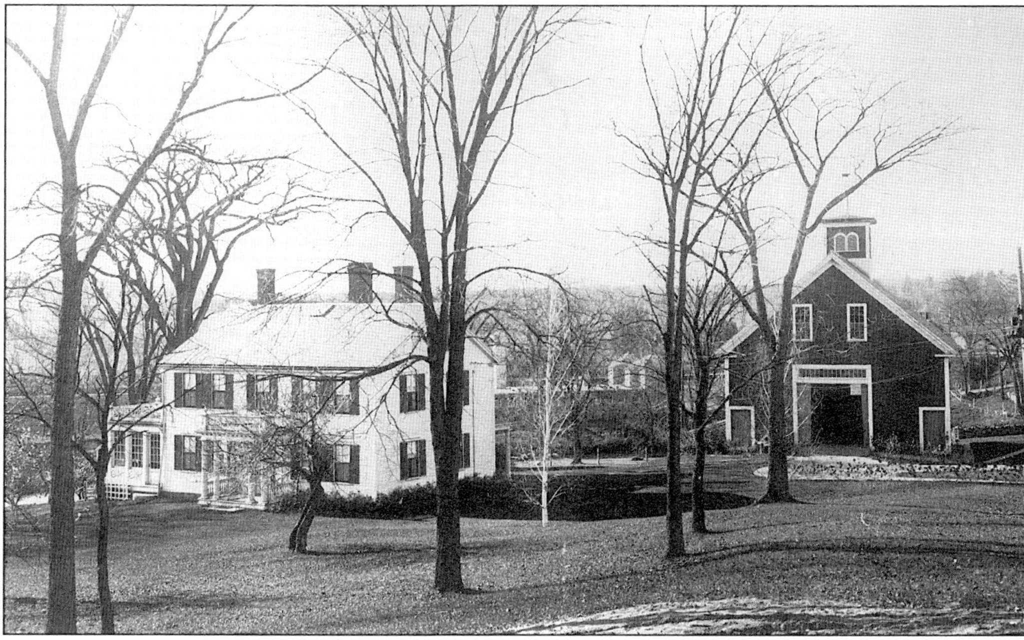

This is a 1919 view of the Nathaniel Clark House, in Atkinson Depot. For a century, the property was the subject of a dispute between New Hampshire and Massachusetts. The boundary dispute was settled in Plaistow's favor, in part due to Nathaniel Clark's efforts on a special commission. (HPL.)

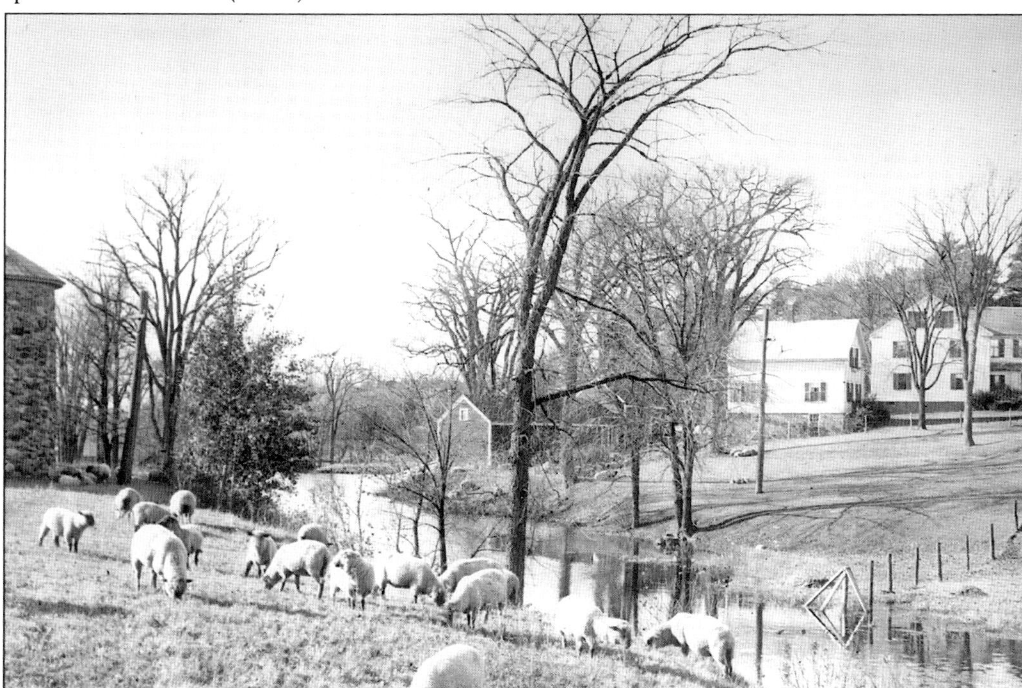

Here is another view of the Clark House, dating from the period between 1915 and 1925. At that time, the property was being used by the Inter-State Sheep Farms Company. On the left is a stone silo built by A.C. Barrows. In the center is the Little River. (HPL.)

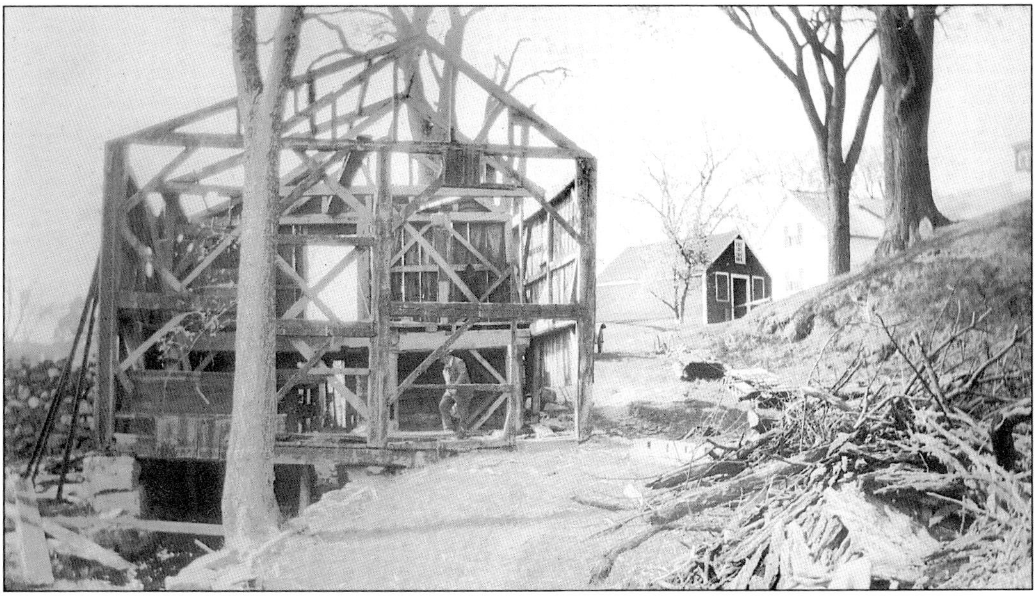

The Clark gristmill was disassembled in 1926. Following Henry Ford's 1915 visit to Plaistow, the auto manufacturer became enamored with this relic of New England's industrial past. After a decade of negotiations, Ford's representatives convinced the Barrows family to allow him to reconstruct the mill at an Americana museum he was creating in Dearborn, Michigan. Among the other artifacts Ford acquired from Plaistow were a Native American stone mortise and an early carriage, both from the Day family of Newton Road. (HPL.)

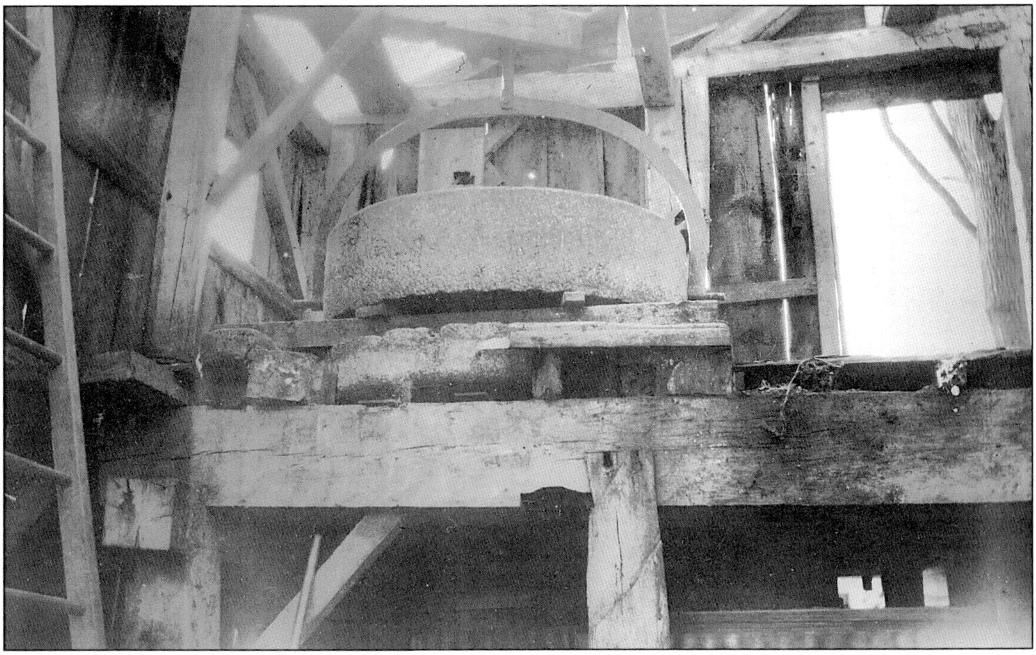

This interior view shows the grindstone of the Clark gristmill, built c. 1798. According to some accounts, the machinery in this mill was among the oldest in New Hampshire still in use in 1915. Note the giant cogs beneath the grindstone that transferred power from the Little River to the task of grinding grain. (HPL.)

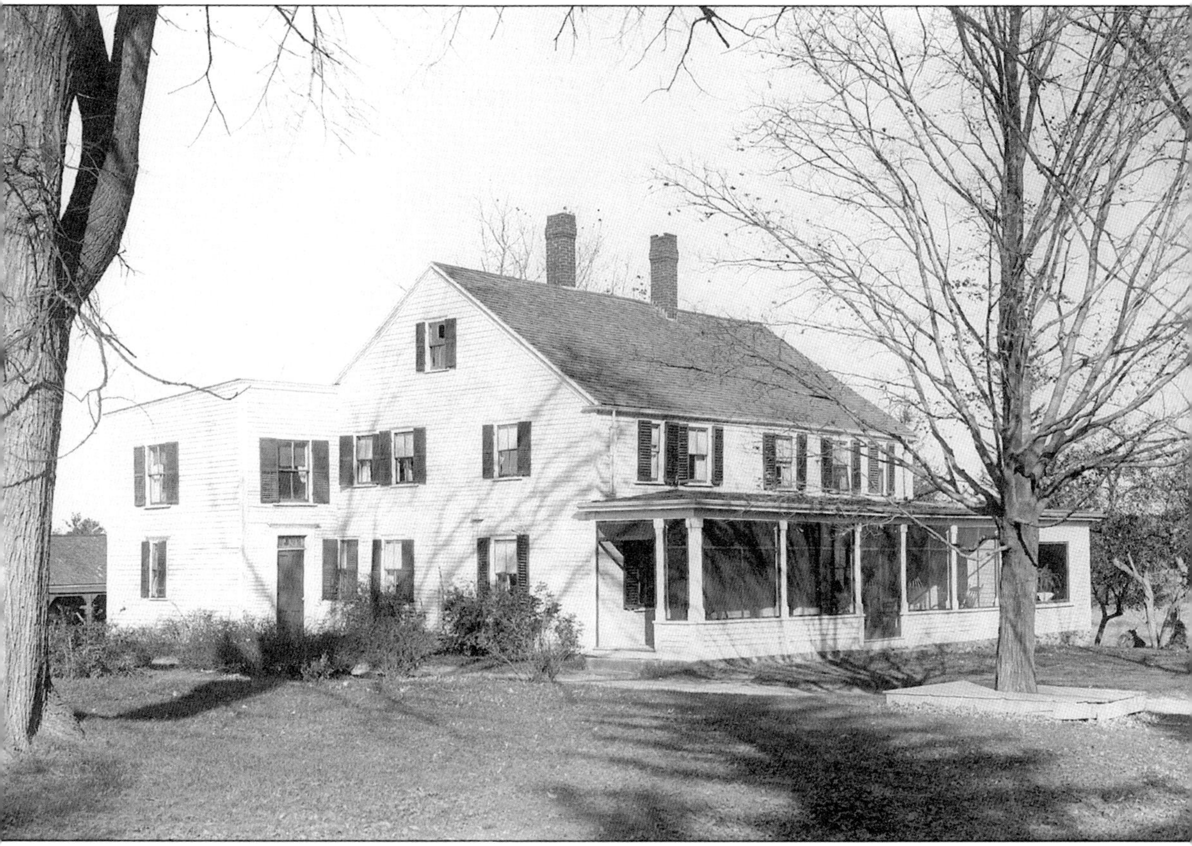

The Wentworth House was located behind the North Parish burying yard in Atkinson Depot. This view dates from 1919. (HPL.)

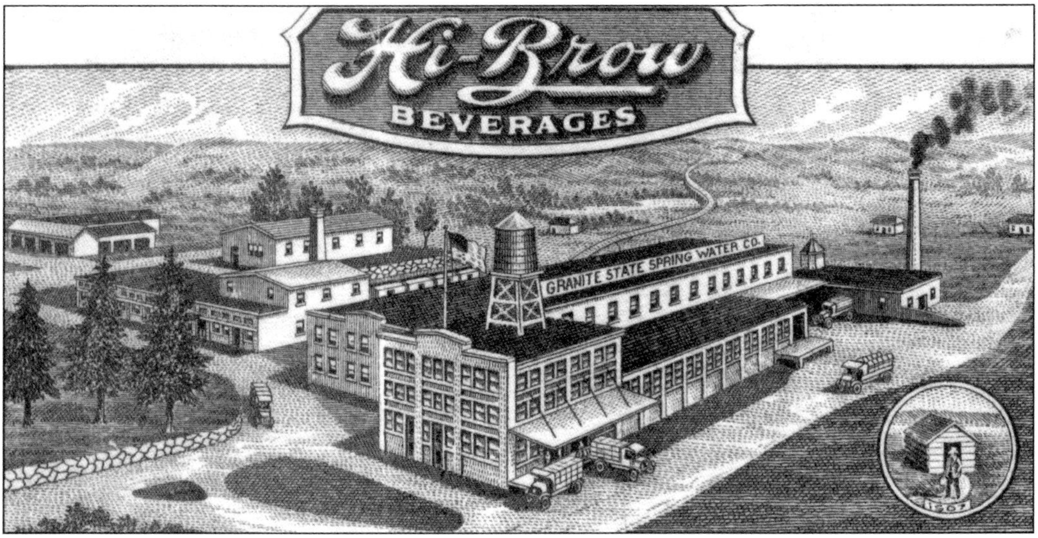

In 1896, M. Kimball Wentworth of the North Parish established the Granite State Spring Water Company in Atkinson Depot, near the present Holy Angels Church. Bottlers of carbonated soft drinks that were shipped nationally, the company thrived through the 1920s. The Leary Company of Newburyport acquired the plant before mid-century. Note the railroad spur track at the rear that connected the factory to the Boston & Maine Railroad. (PHS.)

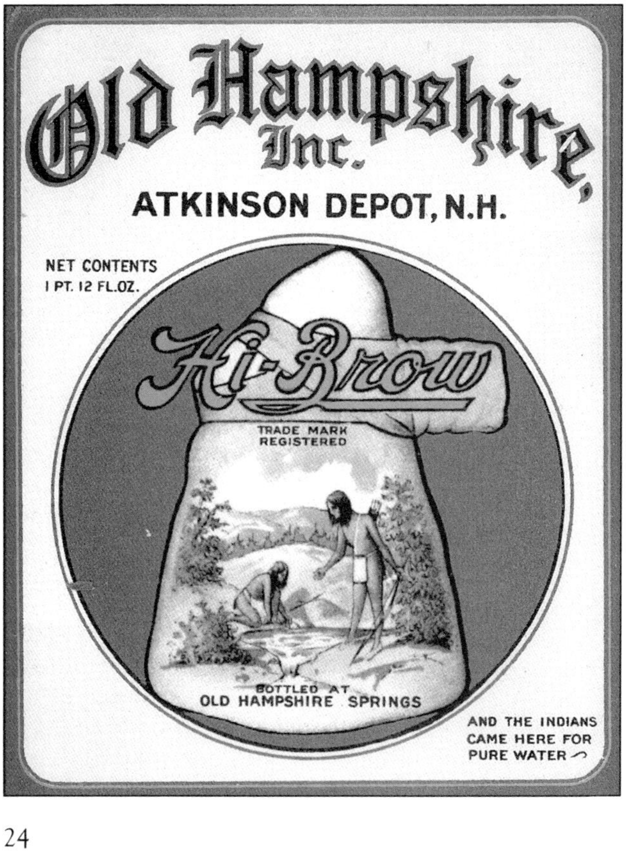

This label is from one of Granite State Spring's soft drinks. The company's motto was "And the Indians came here for Pure water." (PHS.)

Two

Plaistow Center and Elm Street

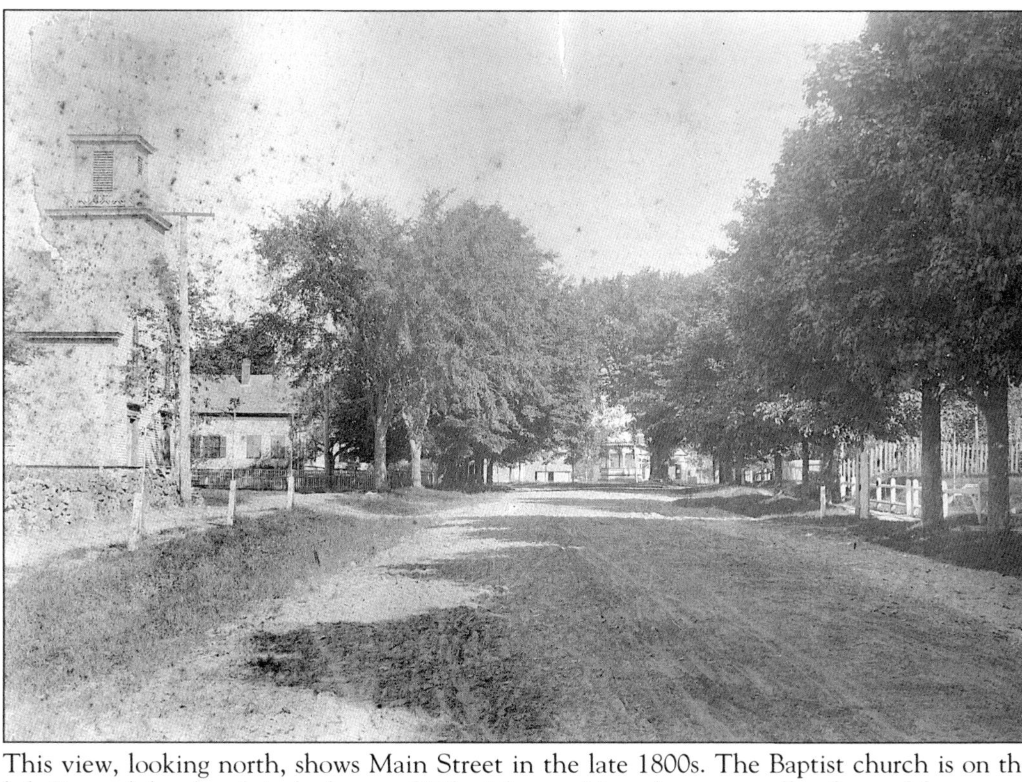

This view, looking north, shows Main Street in the late 1800s. The Baptist church is on the left. Beyond the church is the home of Giles Cheney. Note the stone wall in front of the present location of Pollard School and the bandstand in the distance. To the right of the bandstand, the big elm obscures the District No. 1 Schoolhouse. (PHS.)

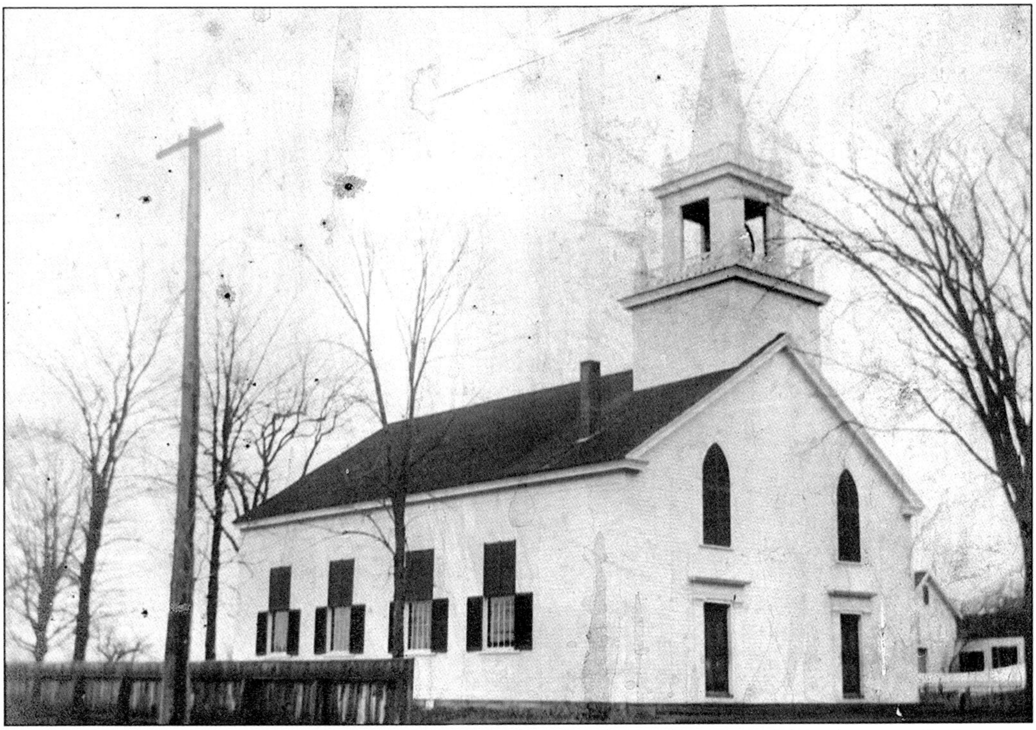

Prior to the construction of the First Baptist Church, shown here *c.* 1900, the town's Baptists gathered at the old town hall. The church was dedicated in 1837 and was built on land donated by John Pollard and Dustin Cheney. (PF.)

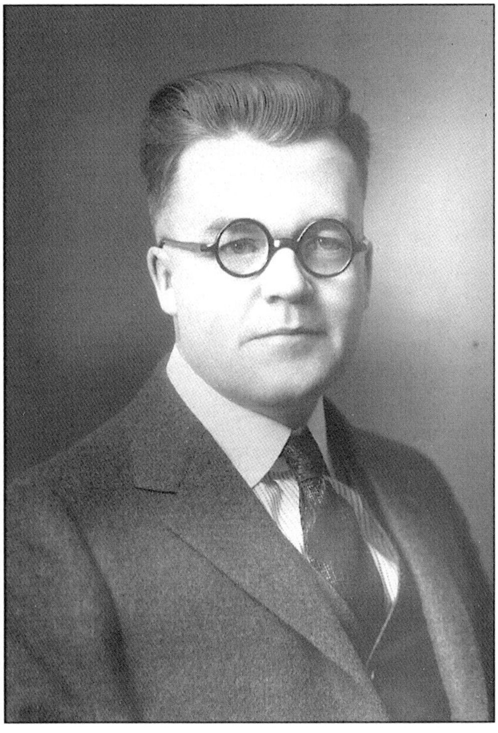

Reverend and church historian Ernest A. McKenzie ministered to Plaistow's Baptists from 1920 to 1926. (PF.)

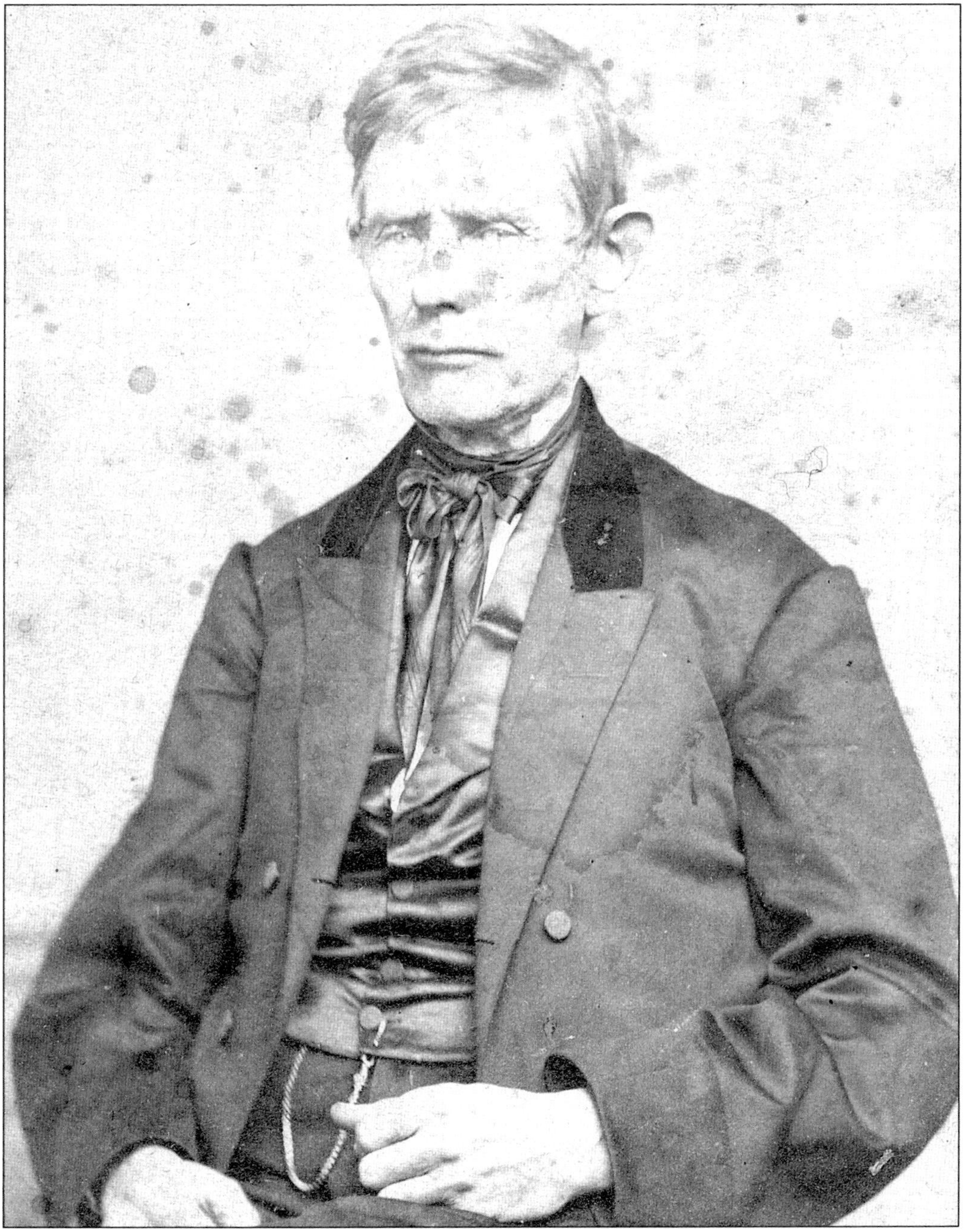

Dr. Nathaniel Knight Kelley, born in 1800 and shown here in 1866, practiced medicine in Plaistow after graduating from Bowdoin College in 1828. In Kelly's words, "I always determined that my patients should get well, cost *me* what it would. I never left a patient because he was poor." He noted in a biographical sketch, "During the war of the Rebellion, I never charged returned sick soldiers anything." Kelly also served in the state legislature in 1859. Despite his hefty workload and the fact that he lived two miles from the Congregational church, he noted, "I have no sympathy with those who have so much business that they cannot attend church." (PF.)

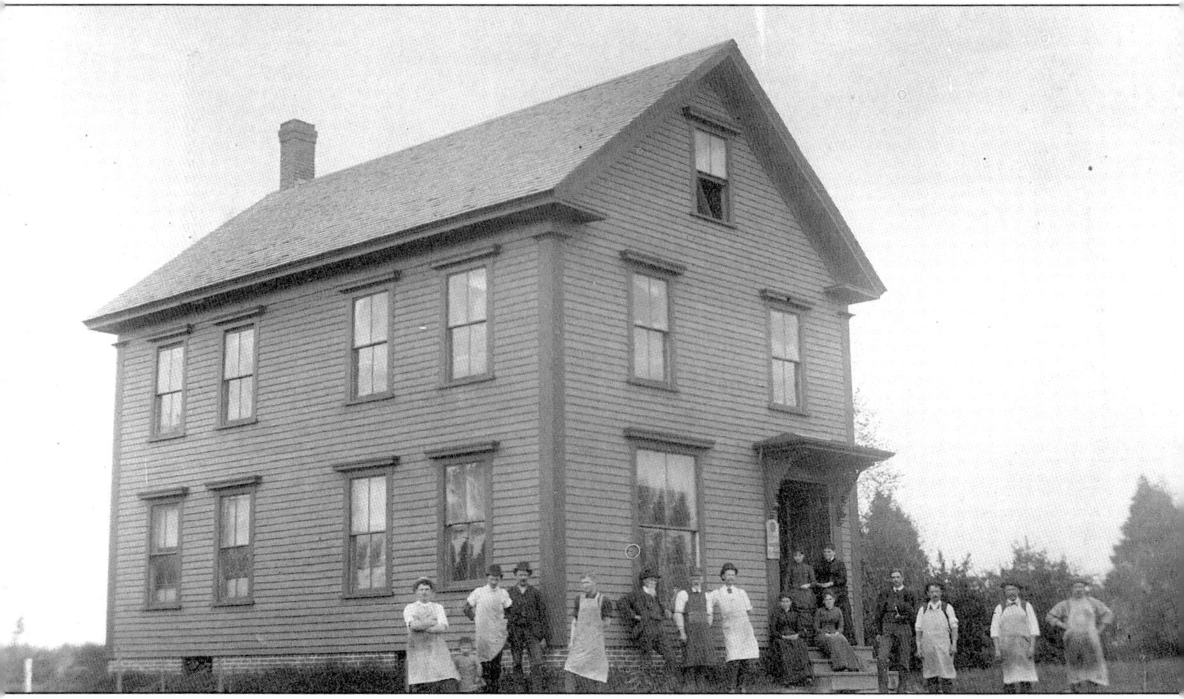

Sleeper's shoe shop is shown here *c.* the later 1800s. It was located on Park Lane, the third building on the left off Main Street. The shop was converted to apartments, according to local tradition, "during the War." (PHS.)

According to local tradition, the story of Plaistow's "Big Elm" began in 1791 when Samuel Cheney and two friends went fishing one day. Each brought home an elm sapling to plant. The fates of the other two trees are not known, but Cheney's elm continued to grow in size and stature for nearly 200 years. By the mid-1900s, sadly, the elm succumbed to Dutch elm disease and was cut down in 1975. It has been immortalized on the town's seal, and a cross section was preserved by the Plaistow Historical Society. (PHS.)

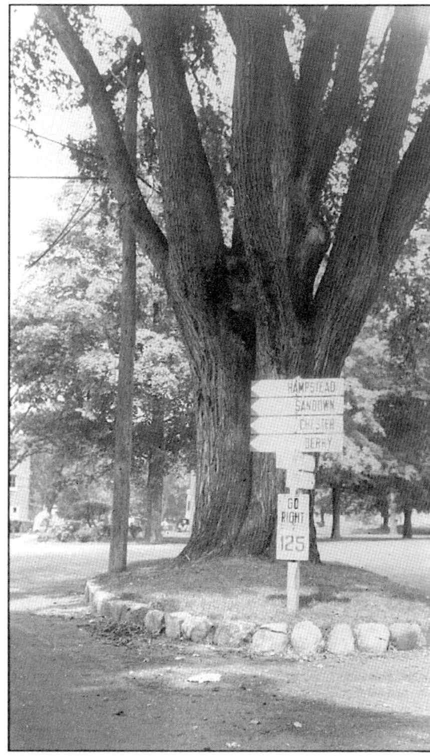

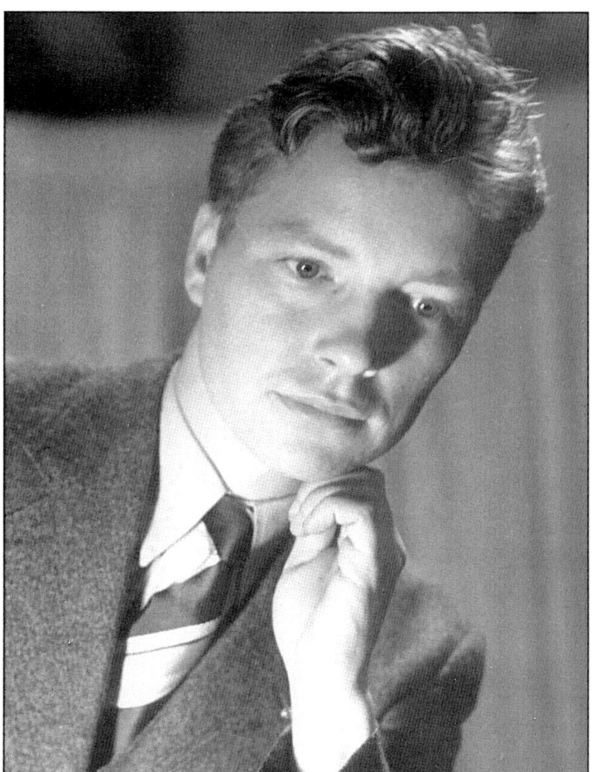

Plaistow native Daniel Smythe was raised in his family's home on North Avenue on the Plaistow-Haverhill line. By temperament he was urban and urbane and therefore considered himself a native of Plaistow's neighbor to the south. Nonetheless, rural Plaistow's Big Elm inspired his well-liked poem "Tree against Sky." Smythe later taught at Bradley University. (HPL.)

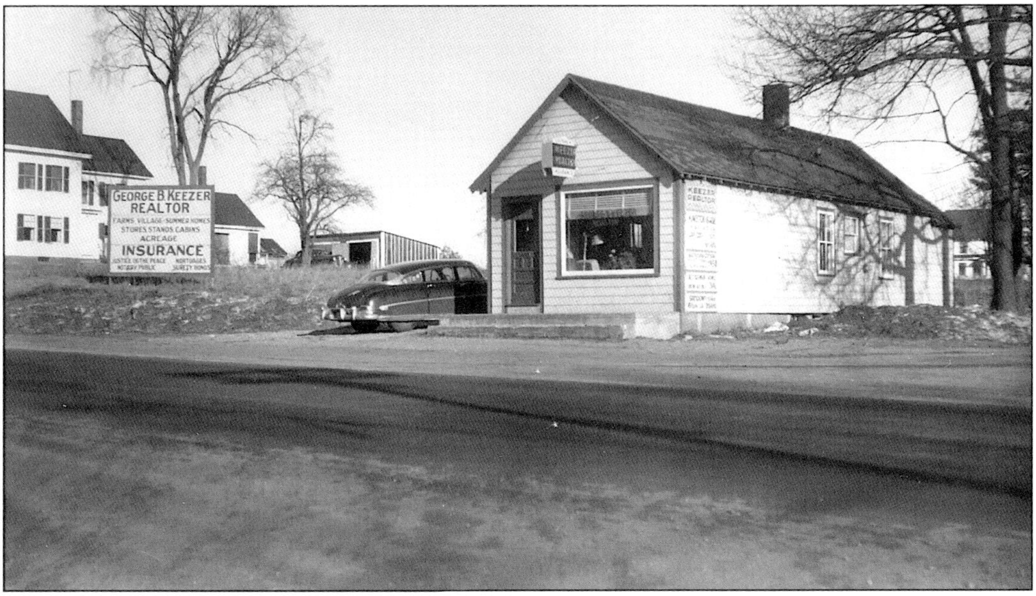

Located in the shadow of the Big Elm was the office of George B. Keezer, shown here in the 1940s. A realtor and insurance agent, Keezer offered a variety of services. His sign, on the left, reads, "George B. Keezer, Realtor, Farms, Village, Summer Homes, Stores, Stands, Cabins, Acreage, Insurance, Justice of the Peace, Mortgages, Notary Public, Surety Bonds." (PHS.)

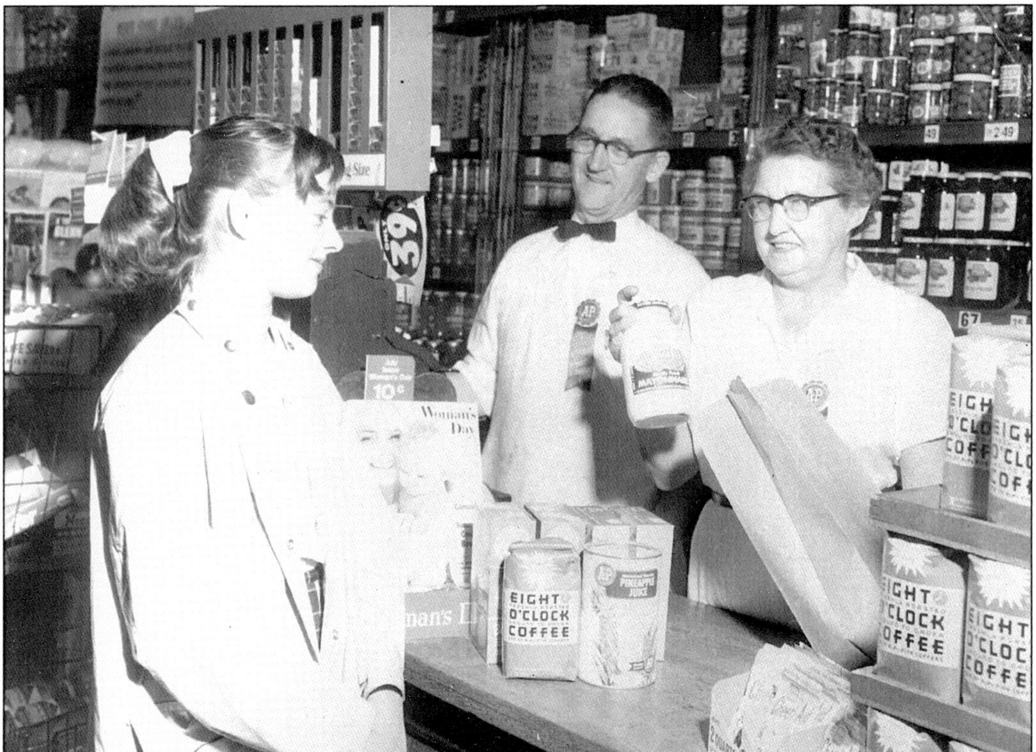

The A & P was located on Elm Street. Shown, from left to right, in 1958 are Donna Gilman, Albert Davis, and Mabel Davis. (PHS.)

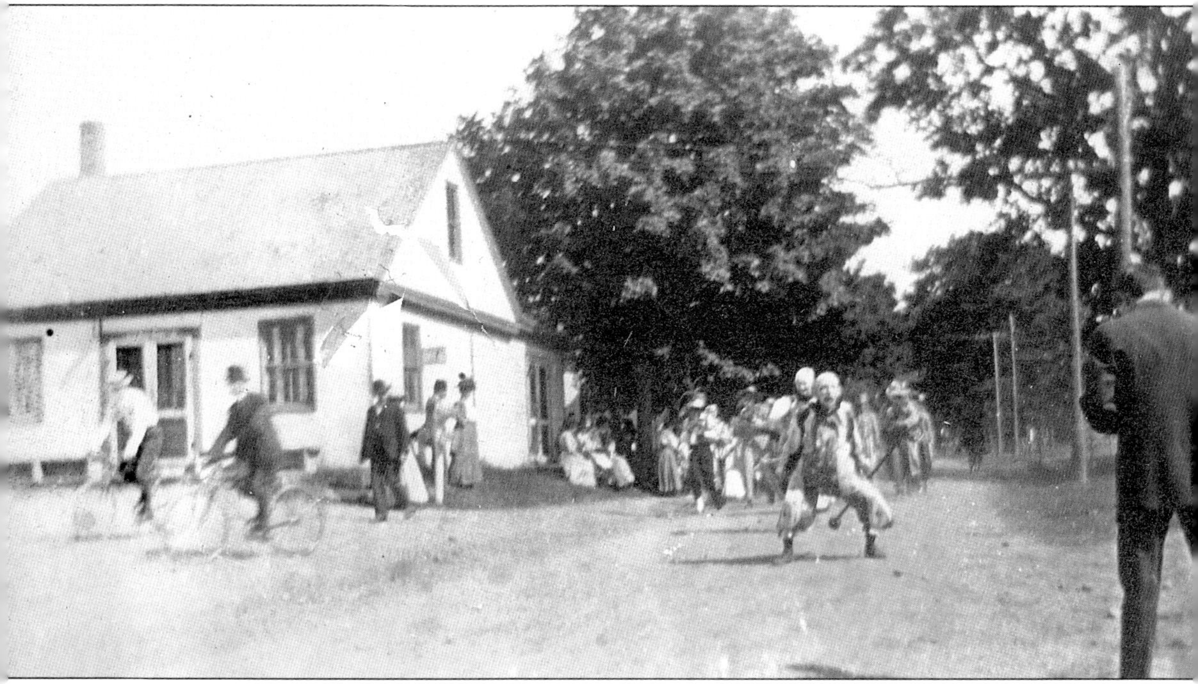

Perhaps a throwback to the carnivals of Early Modern Europe, the town's annual Horribles Parade gave residents the opportunity to dress and act outlandishly. In the street are masked marchers on parade putting on a show for a photographer, on the right. Contrary to an accompanying inscription, this *c.* 1890 photograph was not taken near the Pollard School. To cross-reference the building on the left with the actual Pollard School and its one-room predecessors, see the chapter entitled "Going to School" in this volume. (PHS.)

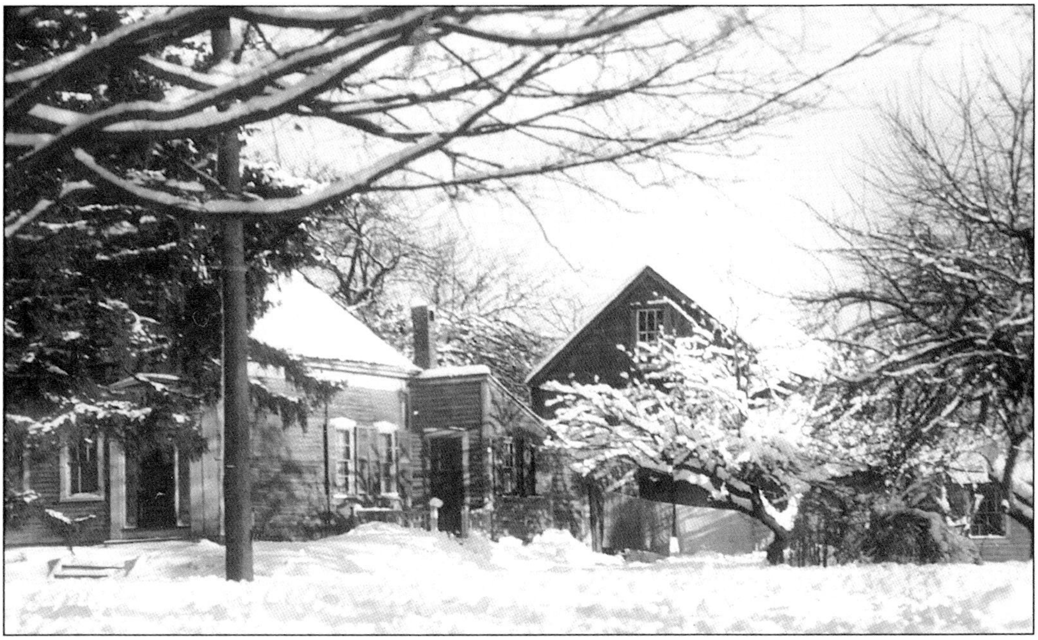

This is a December 1922 view of the Gates House, on Elm Street. (PH.)

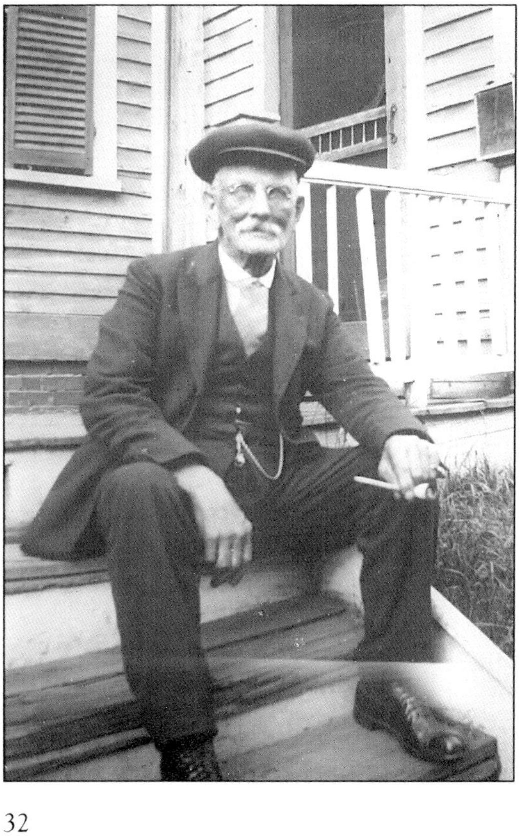

George Mason Gates, a Civil War veteran, pauses on his Elm Street porch. (PHS.)

Ella Furman Gates, mother of Reva Gates, is seen in front of the family's 11 Elm Street home in the late 1800s. (PH.)

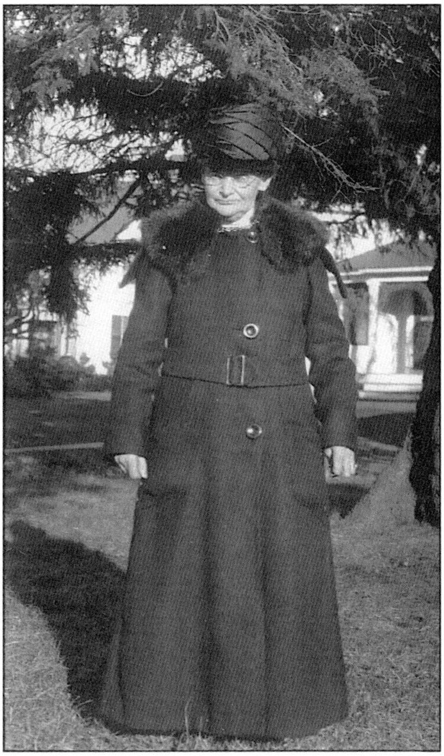

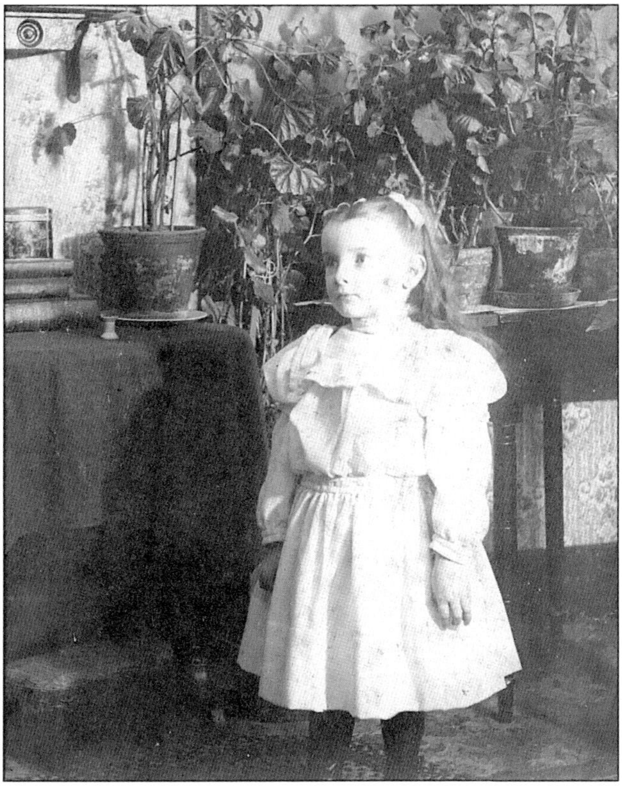

Reva Gates poses for a formal portrait c. 1900, presumably in her parents' Elm Street home. Her collection of images, now in the Plaistow Historical Society's archives, proved to be a valuable resource in the preparation of this volume. (PHS.)

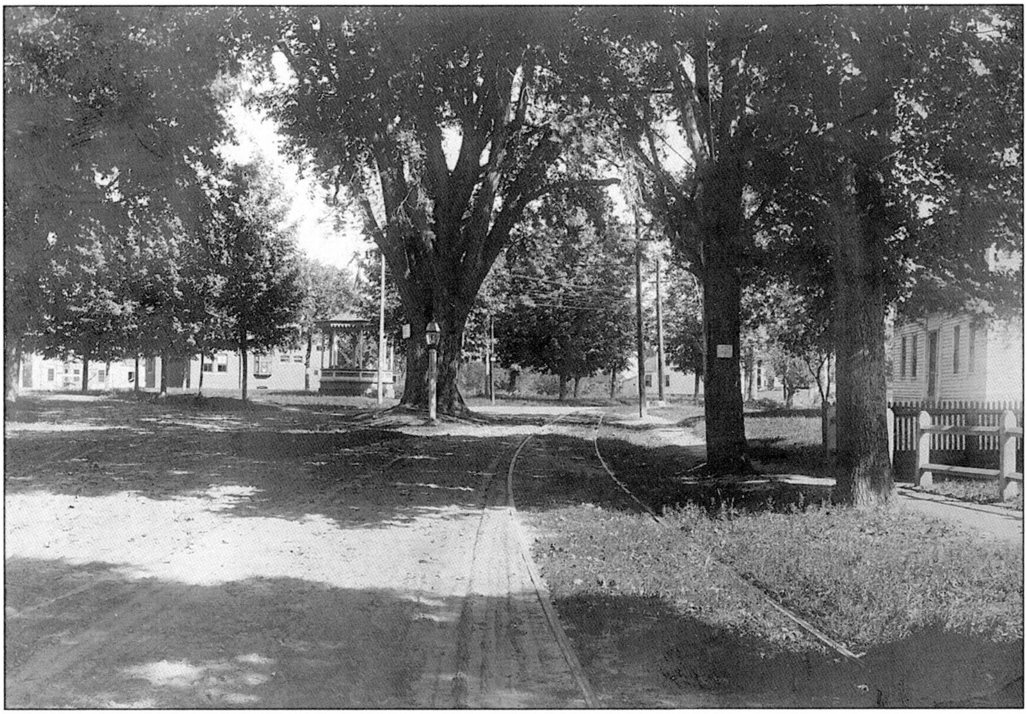

This view of Elm Street was taken looking east in the early 1900s. Through the trees to the left of the bandstand is the new town hall. Especially prominent is the building's memorial window, to the left of the bandstand. (PHS.)

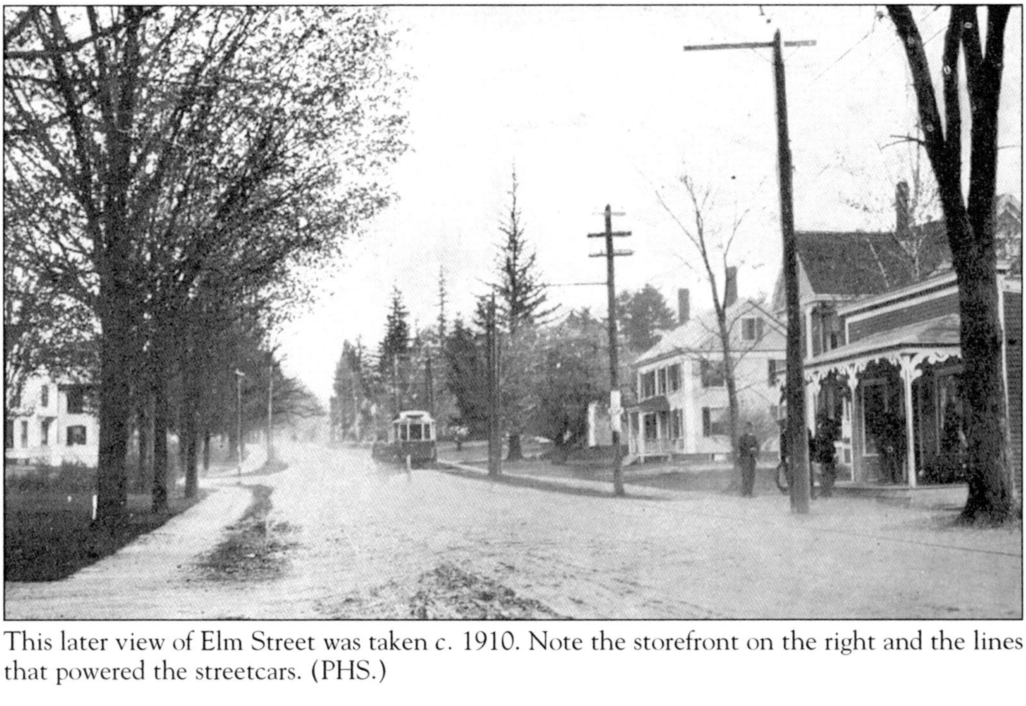

This later view of Elm Street was taken *c.* 1910. Note the storefront on the right and the lines that powered the streetcars. (PHS.)

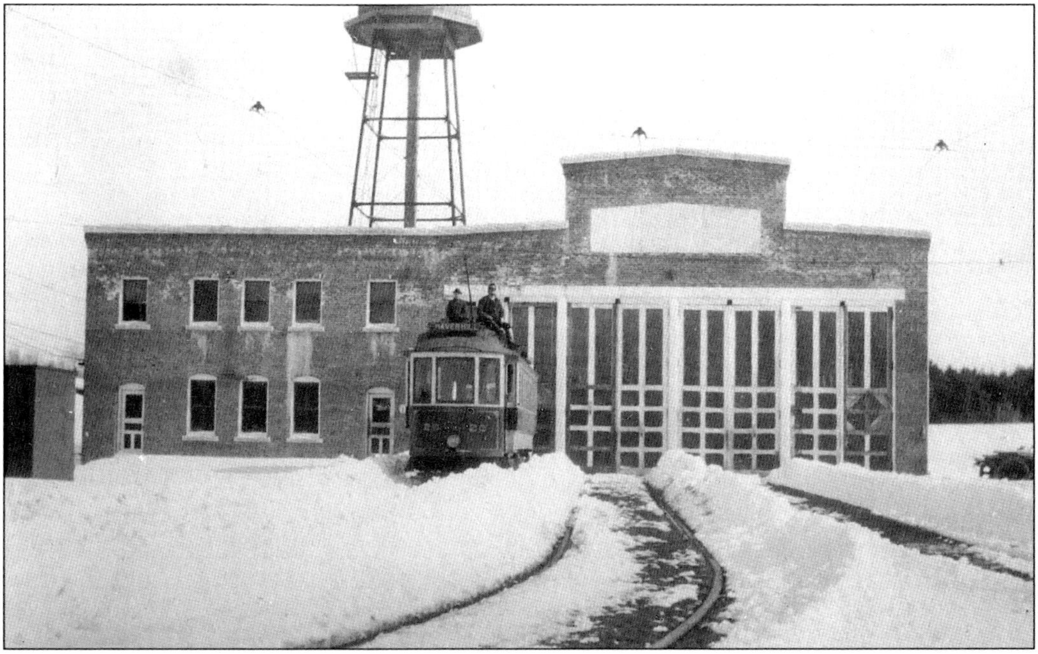

Once the hub of trolleys bound for Haverhill, Salem, and Hampton Beach, the old Plaistow carbarn was demolished to make room for the town's safety complex. Following the termination of trolley service in 1930, this structure housed a carnival equipment firm and an oil delivery company. Because of its importance as an artifact of the trolley age, the Plaistow carbarn was placed on the National Register of Historic Places. (PHS.)

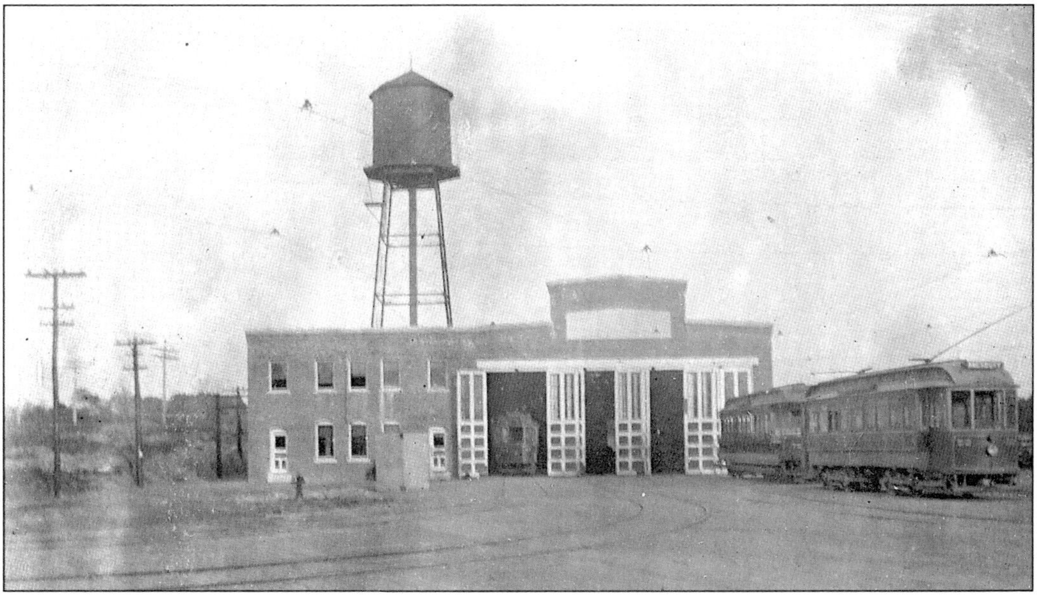

The Plaistow carbarn was used to store the trolleys of the Massachusetts Northeastern Street Railway. Trolleys were stored here in high bays and were cleaned and serviced. Paul Holmes recalls that children were not allowed in the building; however, employees of the railway used to give outdated posters and flyers to local youngsters, who used them to decorate their clubhouses. (PF.)

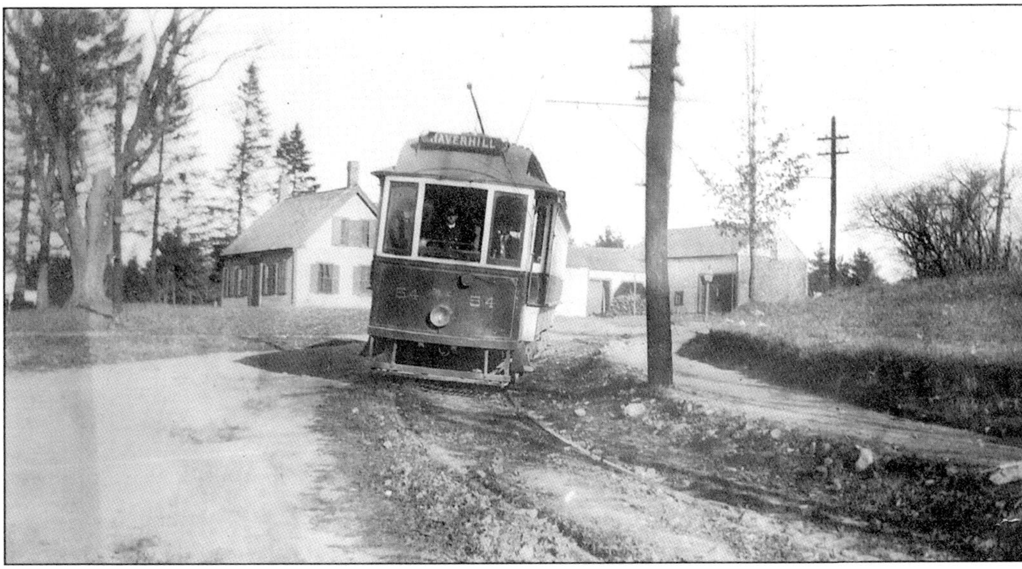

This early-1900s view shows the Haverhill-to-Plaistow trolley rounding the corner of Palmer Avenue onto Elm Street en route to Pollard Park from Highland Square. (PF.)

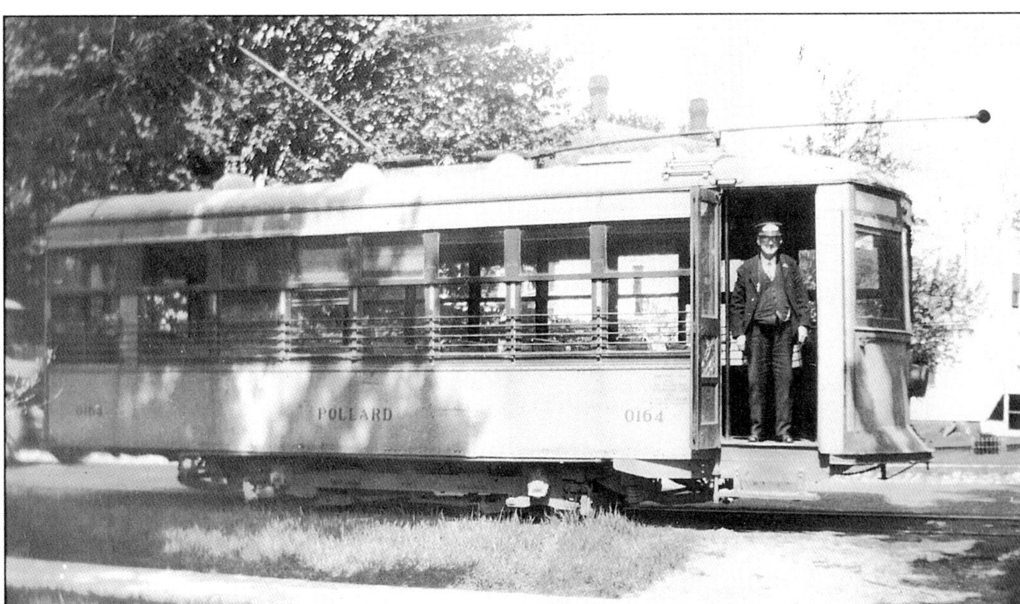

At 2:00 p.m. on September 3, 1930, the last trolley to run out of Haverhill to Plaistow arrives. This photograph was taken on Elm Street, opposite Harry Seaver's house. (PHS.)

Eugene Page Davis (1868–1931) is shown in a formal portrait. Davis achieved his livelihood by working for the railroad. Ironically, he was killed in a train accident. (PF.)

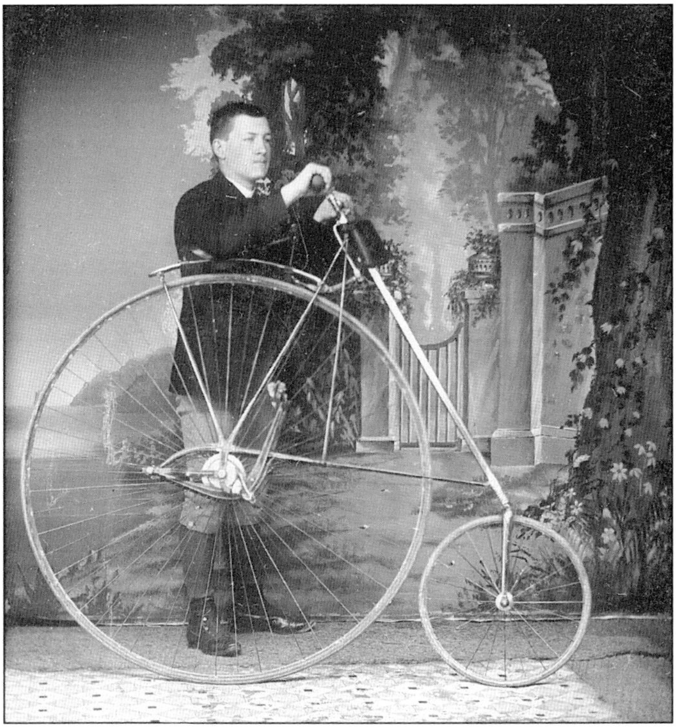

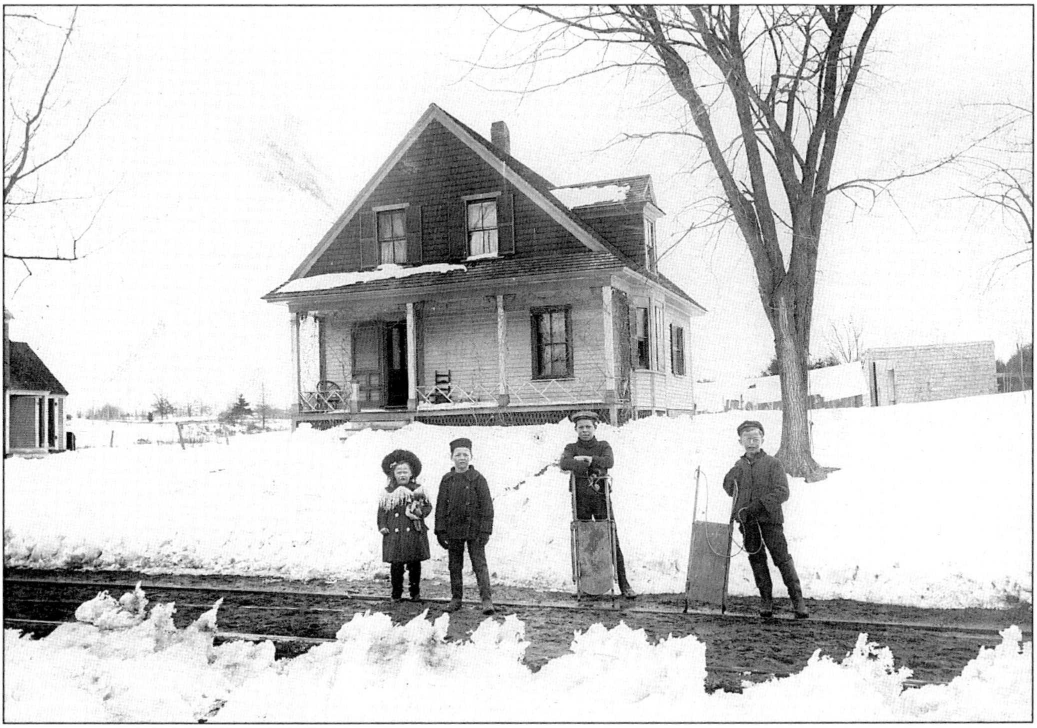

These are members of the Davis family of Elm Street. Photographed on March 26, 1906, the sons and daughters of Eugene and Abbie Davis are Christine, Albert, Phil, and Hayward Davis. Note the three-year-old trolley tracks in the foreground. (PF.)

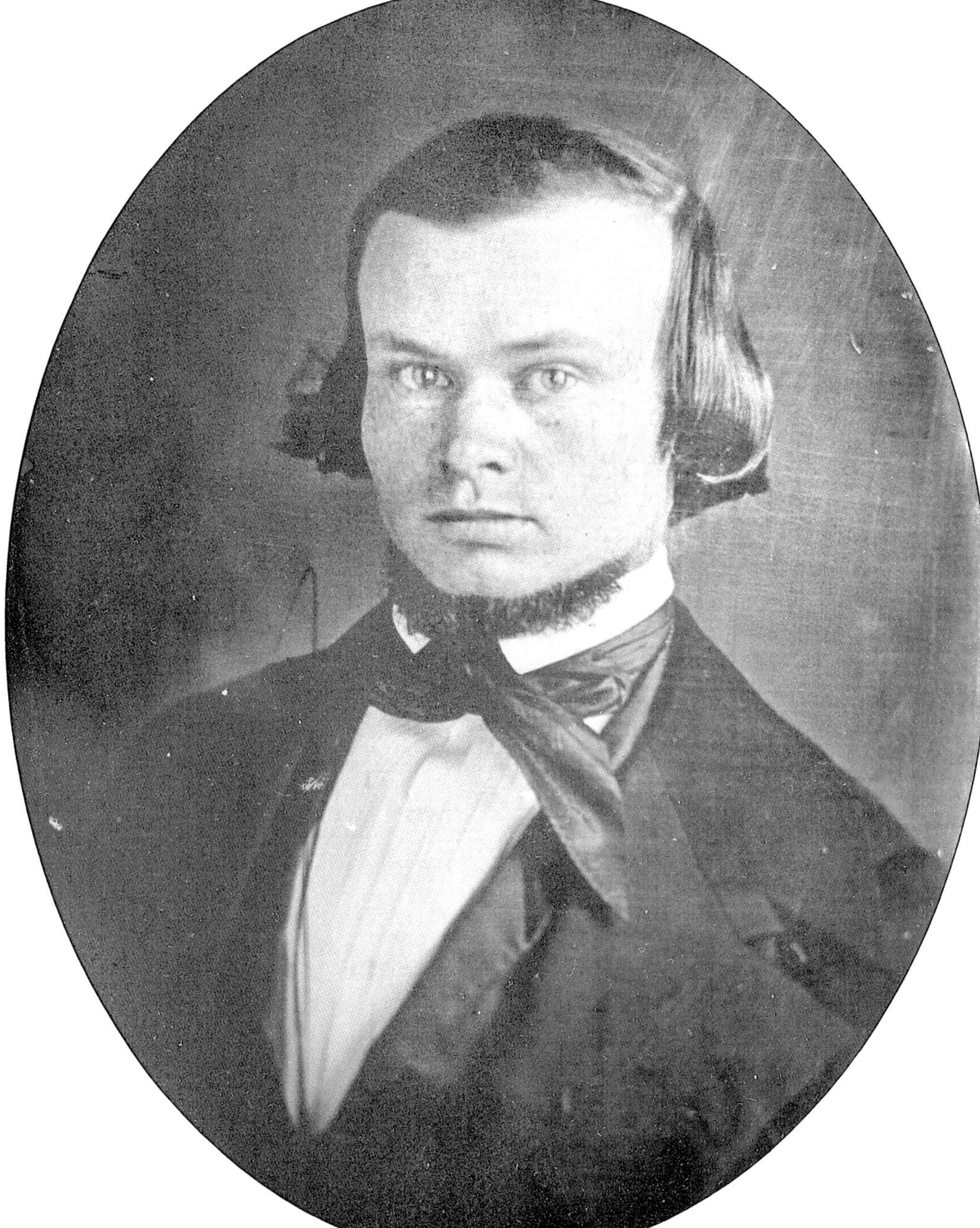

Charles Foss (1824–1856) lived a short and presumably troubled life. He is best remembered for his dramatic suicide, in which he "whipped all four [children] and then hanged himself on a rafter in the barn." Foss was the grandfather of Reva Gates. (PHS.)

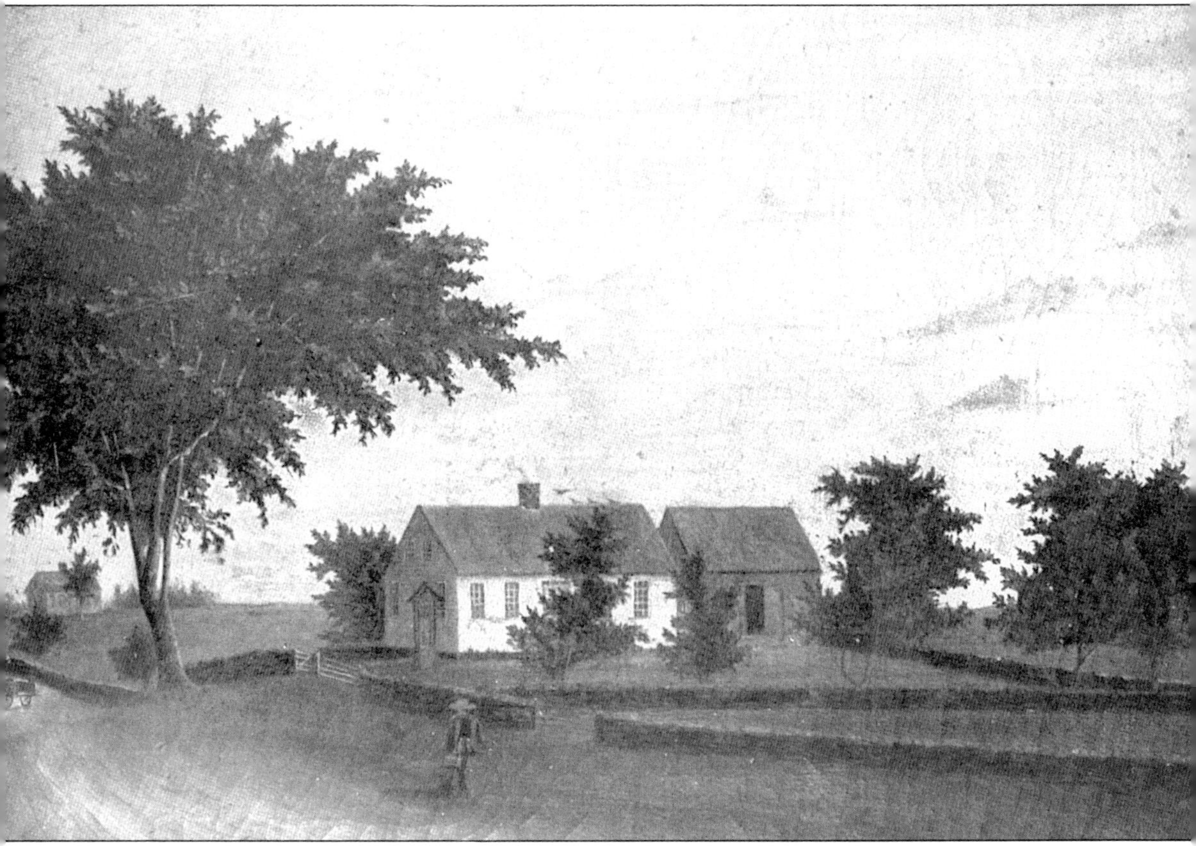

This oil painting of the *c.* 1776 Pollard-Sleeper House is said to have hung in this home from the time of its rendering until at least 1973. This Elm Street house, now greatly altered, was the boyhood home of Plaistow benefactor Arthur G. Pollard. It still stands east of the Plaistow Cemetery. (PHS.)

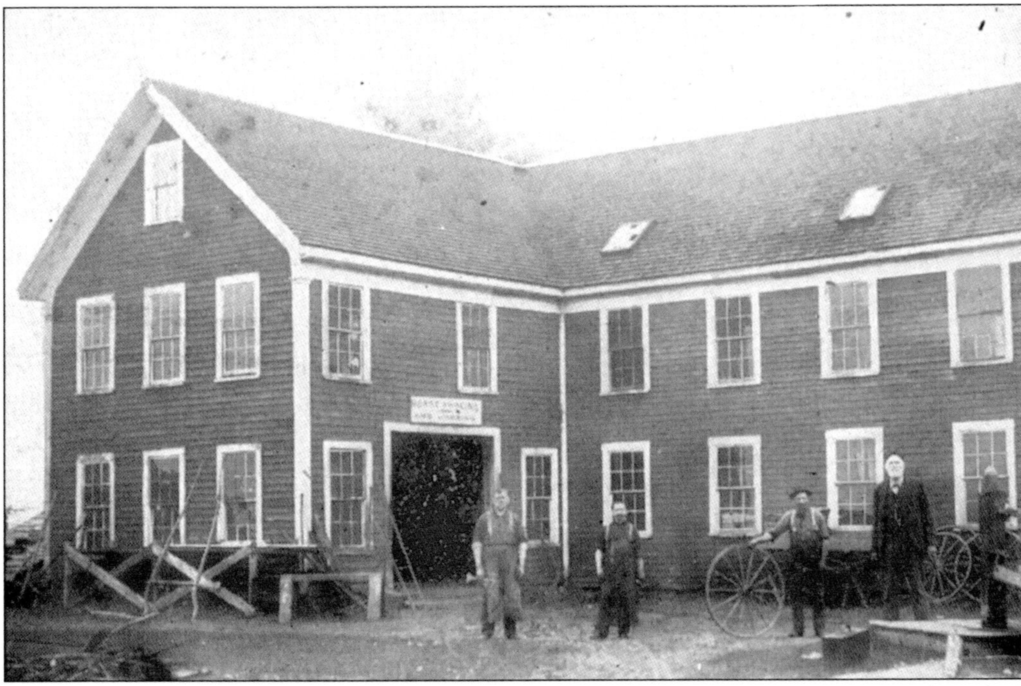

This is a pre-1899 view of Moses Dow's workshop, on Highland Square. Moses Dow built carriages, carts, coaches, sleighs, and sleds at a workshop connected to his home, which was also a stop for stagecoaches en route to Newburyport, Haverhill, Exeter, Concord, and beyond. Travelers used a well that was still in use in the mid-1900s. (PHS.)

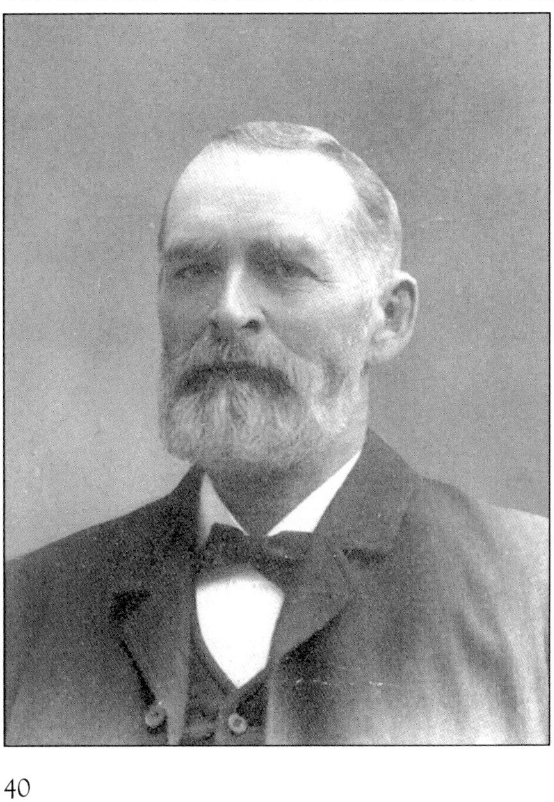

Moses B. Dow (1837–1909) lived his entire life in Plaistow and earned his livelihood as a carriage maker and blacksmith over a 40-year career, which ended upon his retirement in 1899. Dow served the people of New Hampshire as a town selectman, county commissioner, and state legislator. The son of Moses and Julia Bragdon Dow, he married Alice Emerson of Haverhill. (PF.)

Three

Town Hall and Pollard Park

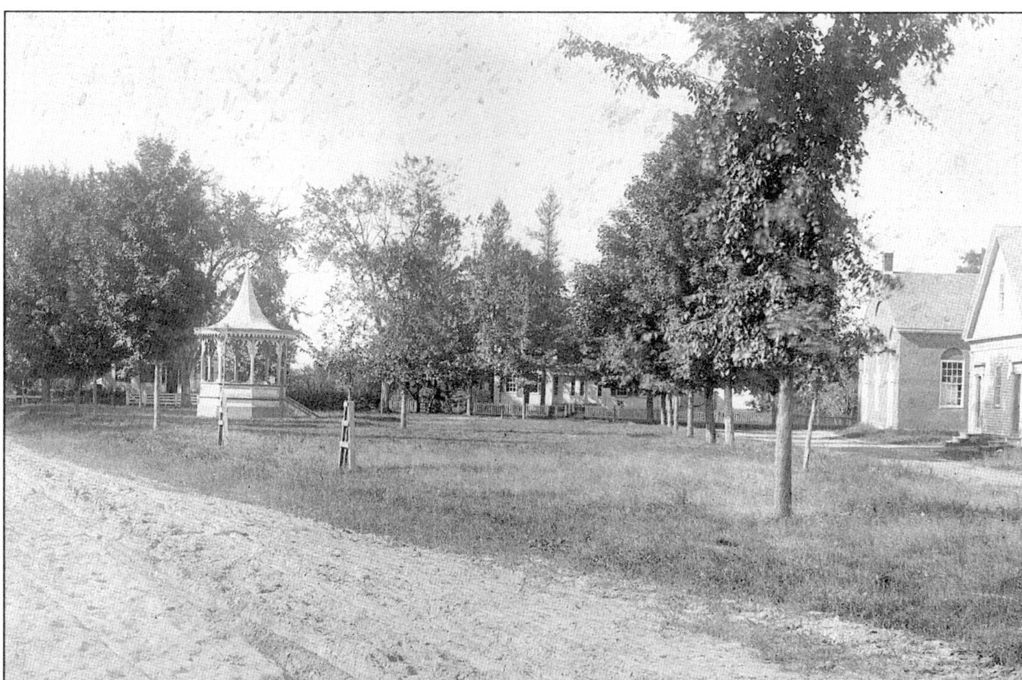

This *c.* 1890 view of the town common shows the following structures, from left to right: the old bandstand, the old town hall, and the District No. 1 Schoolhouse. The A-frame structures along the street were built to protect young saplings. (PHS.)

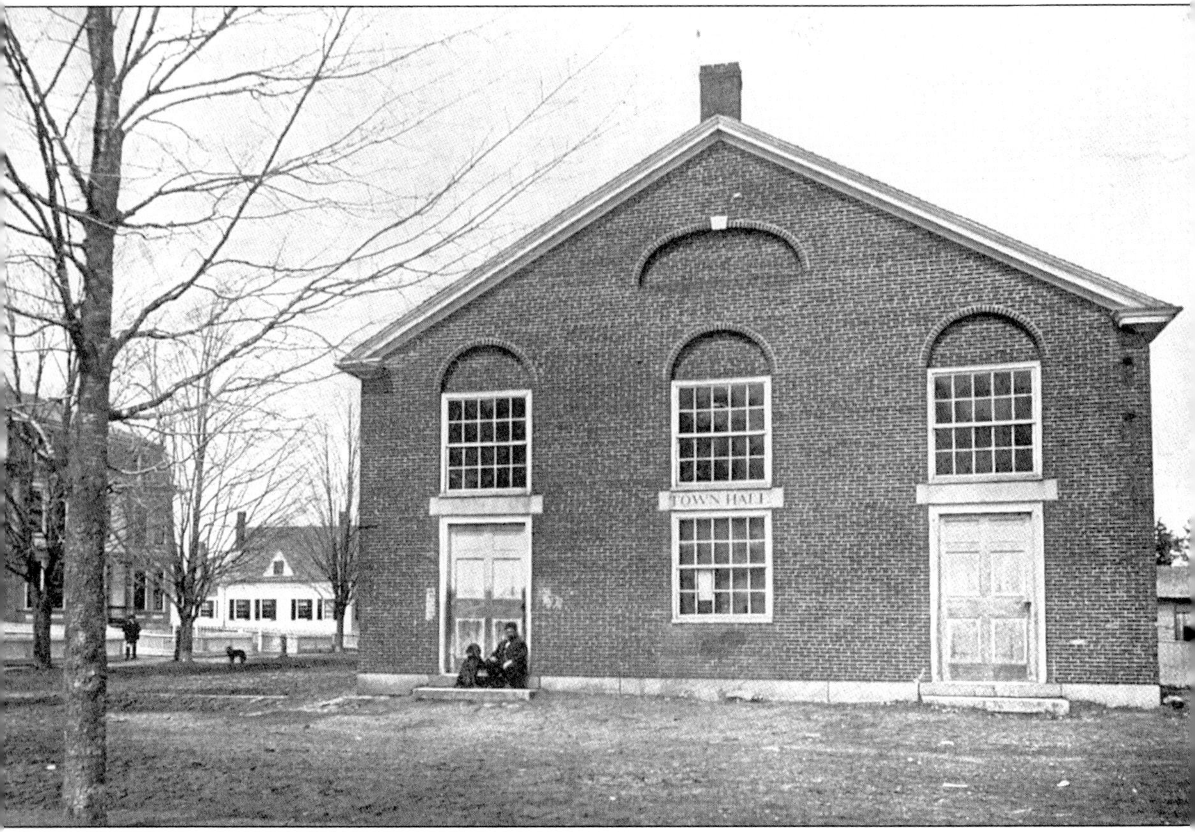

Built in 1831 with bricks produced by Jacob Davis, the old town hall—shown here c. 1890—represented a major change in the history of Plaistow. In contrast to the North Parish Meetinghouse, where town meetings were held from 1749 to 1830, this building was primarily a secular space, although it did occasionally serve as a meeting space for Baptists, Catholics, and Episcopalians. Unlike the present west-facing building, the original town hall faced south. The outbuildings on the right are perhaps a privy and a horse shed. (PF.)

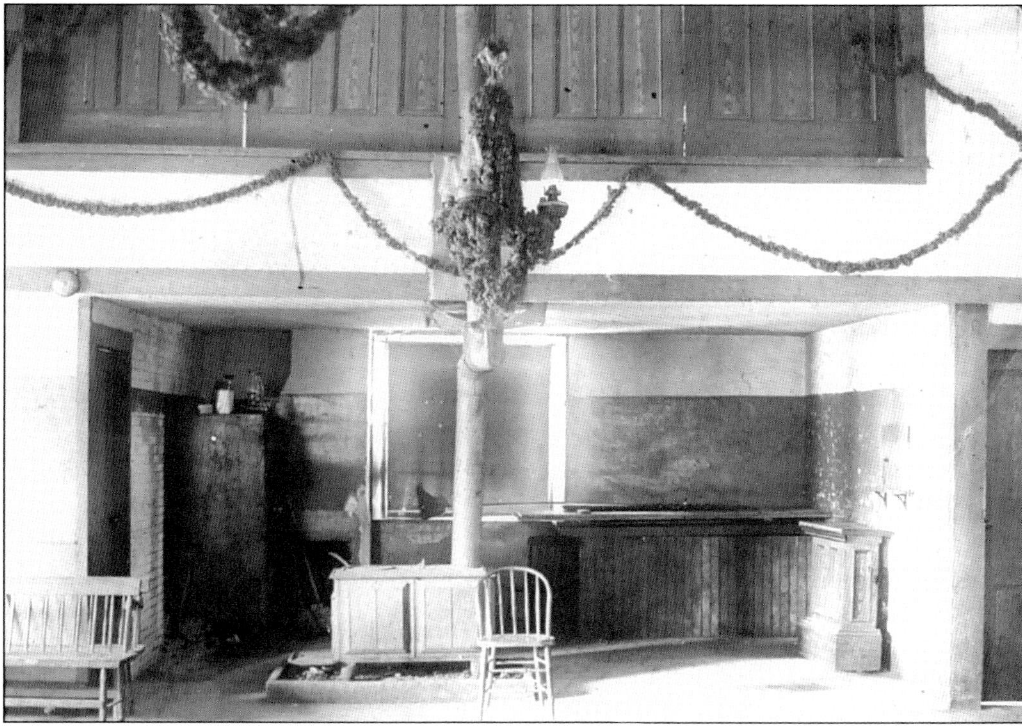

This interior view of the old town hall dates to the last quarter of the 19th century. Note the Christmas garlands, stove, and lamps. (PHS.)

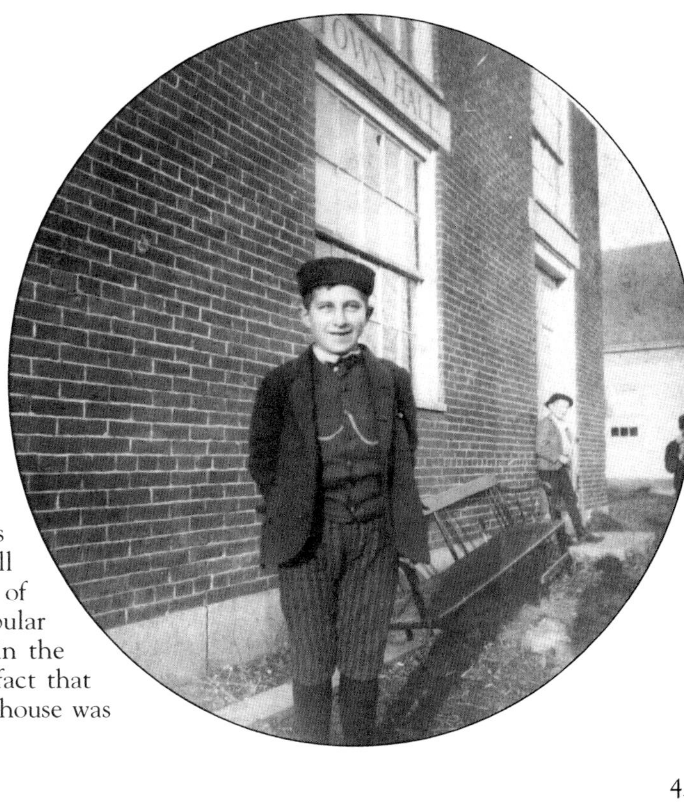

An unidentified boy poses in front of the old town hall c. the 1890s. The vicinity of the old town hall was a popular hangout for Plaistow youths in the 1800s, owing perhaps to the fact that the old District No. 1 Schoolhouse was located next door. (PHS.)

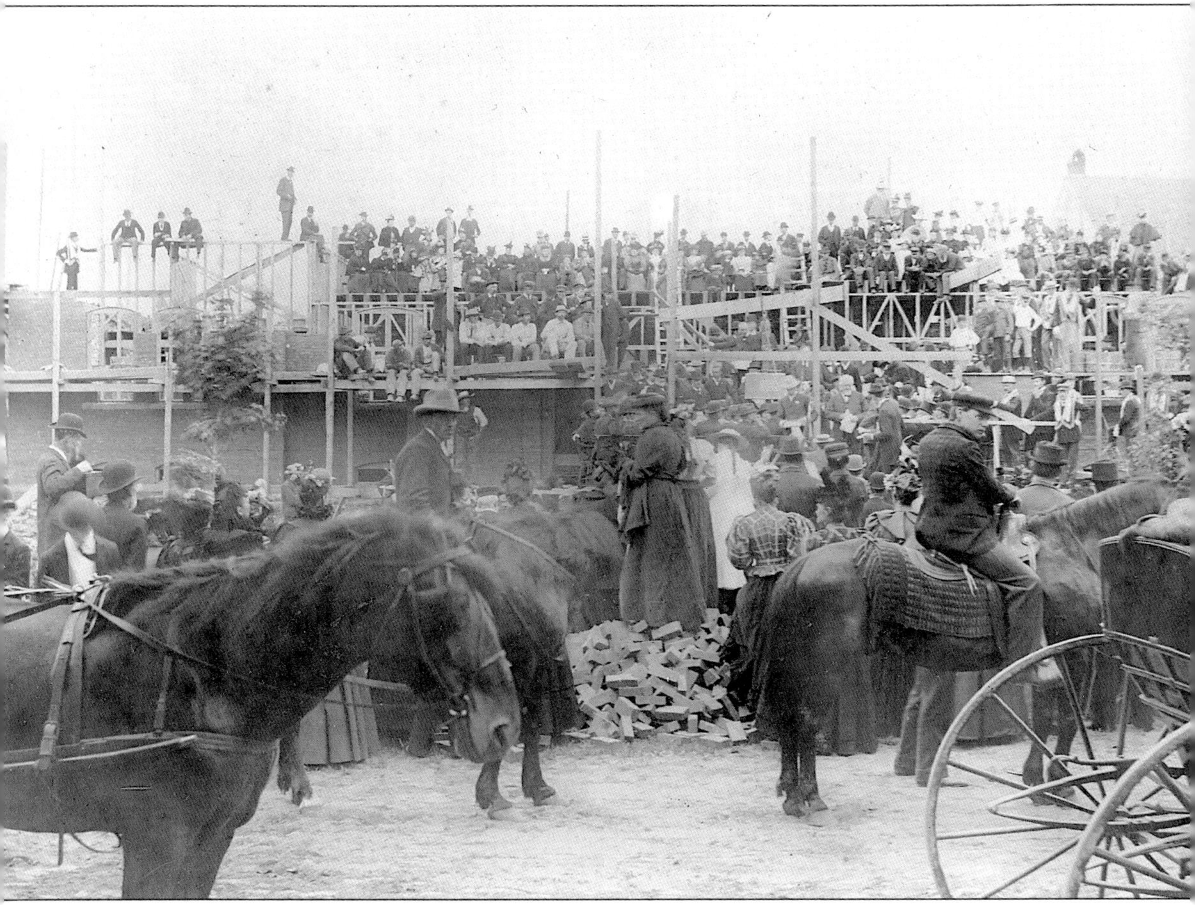

"Everywhere were the emblems of a glad day," read a *Haverhill Gazette* account of the June 4, 1895 dedication of the new town hall. Before and after the laying of the cornerstone, the "streets [were] filled with bands and plumed knights." Hundreds of townsfolk turned out to observe the festivities from rafters erected upon the building's scaffolding. Representatives of the Gideon Lodge of Masons, Kingston, oversaw the cornerstone-laying ceremony. The cornerstone housed a time capsule, which was opened a century later. (PHS.)

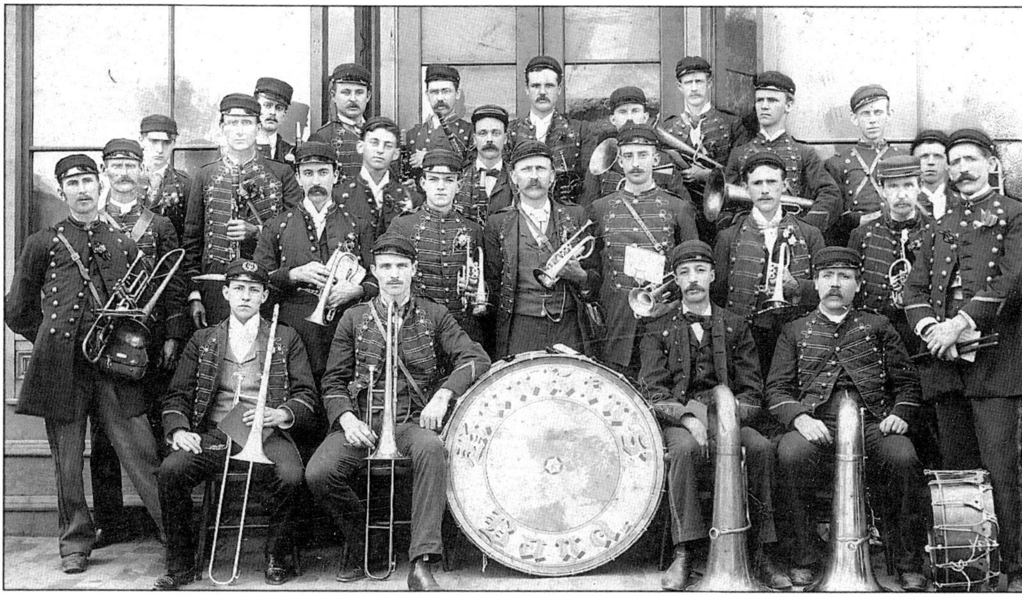

Hunkins's Band, which performed at the cornerstone-laying ceremony, is shown here *c.* 1890 to 1900. Robert Hunkins, who played the trumpet, organized this brass band in 1884. Shown, from left to right, are the following: (first row) Elmer York, Otis Currier, Eben Bailey, and Andrew Nelson; (second row) Frank Currier, Charles Johnson, Frank Battles, George Clay, Robert Hunkins, Harry Noyes, Sidney Knight, John Harvey, Frank Davis (head above Harvey's shoulders), and Barry Allison; (third row) "Tiner" Knight, Alden Caldwell, Carl Lloyd, Ross Eaton, Herold Hudson, and Sumner Hoyt; (fourth row) Herbert Eaton, Frank Emery, George Eaton, Tom Walton, and Ben Wood. (PHS.)

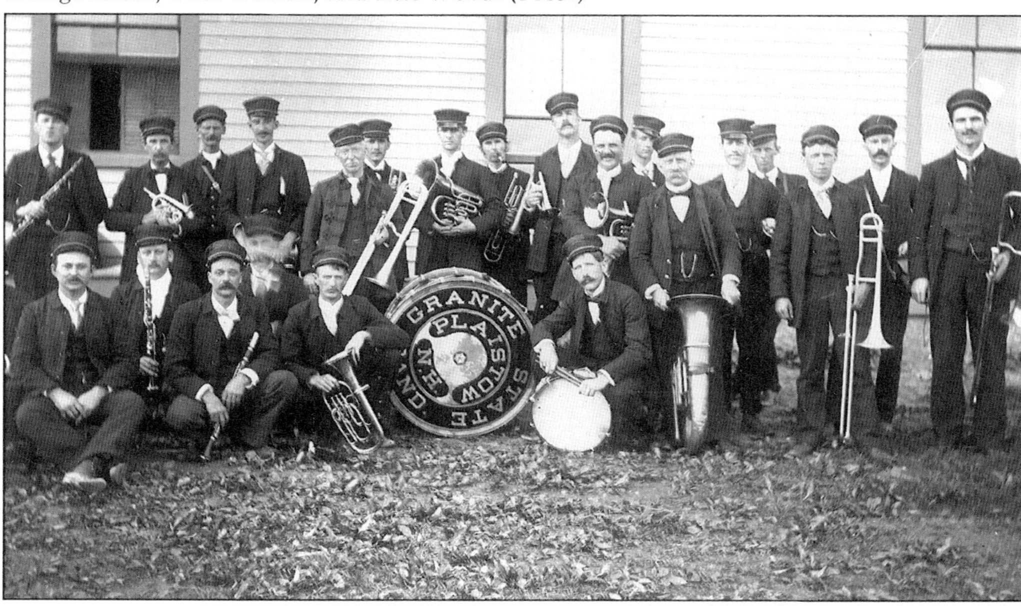

Hunkins's Band renamed itself the Granite State Band *c.* 1900. Like its predecessor, this band drew its membership from Plaistow and surrounding towns, such as Newton, Haverhill, Kingston, and Hampstead. By this point, John Harvey of Newton had replaced Robert Hunkins as leader. (PHS.)

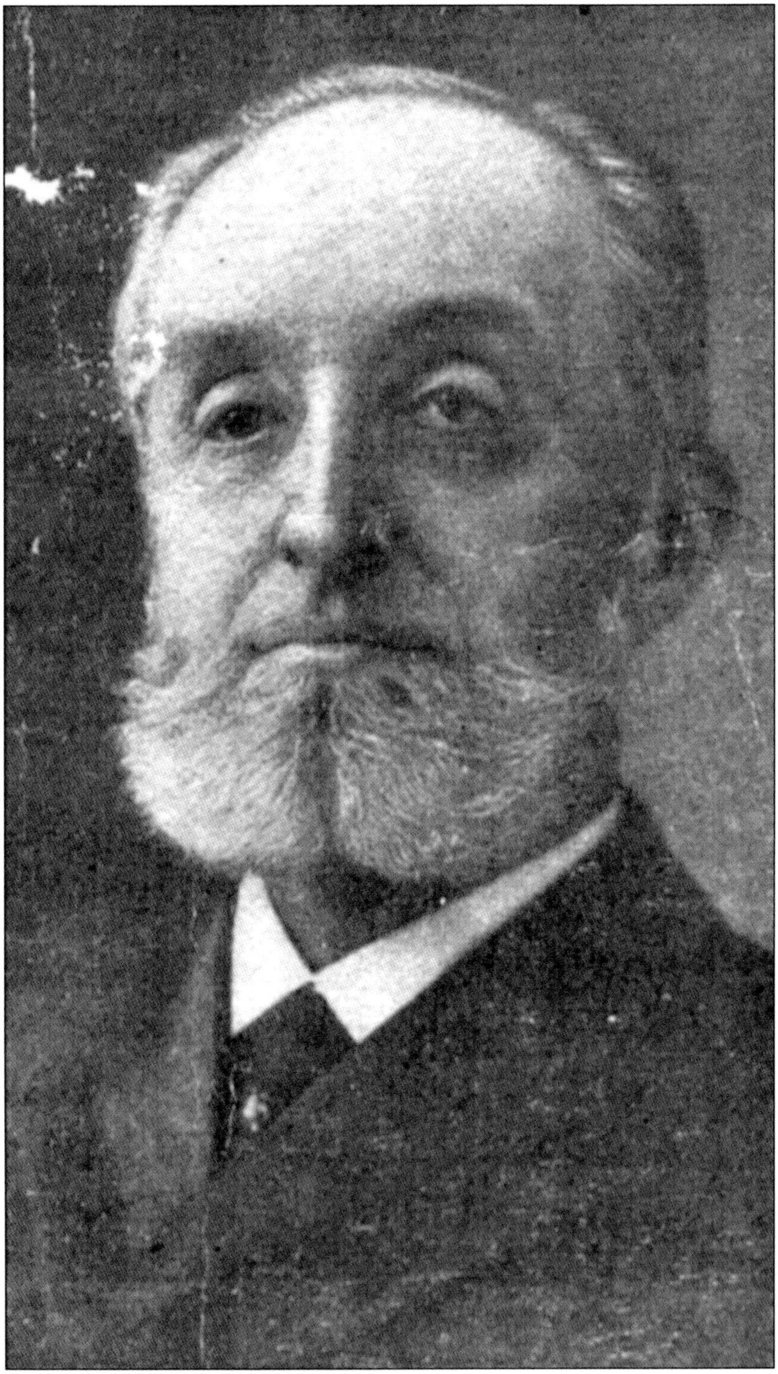

Because of his dedication to beautifying his native town, Arthur G. Pollard was known as the Father of Plaistow. Born in his family's Elm Street home in 1843, Pollard was the founder of a major department store in Lowell. His generosity made possible the town's flagpole, the Civil War monument, the improvement of the commons, and the erection of two schools that were named in his honor. His wife, Cora Pollard, was president of the Village Improvement Society. (PHS.)

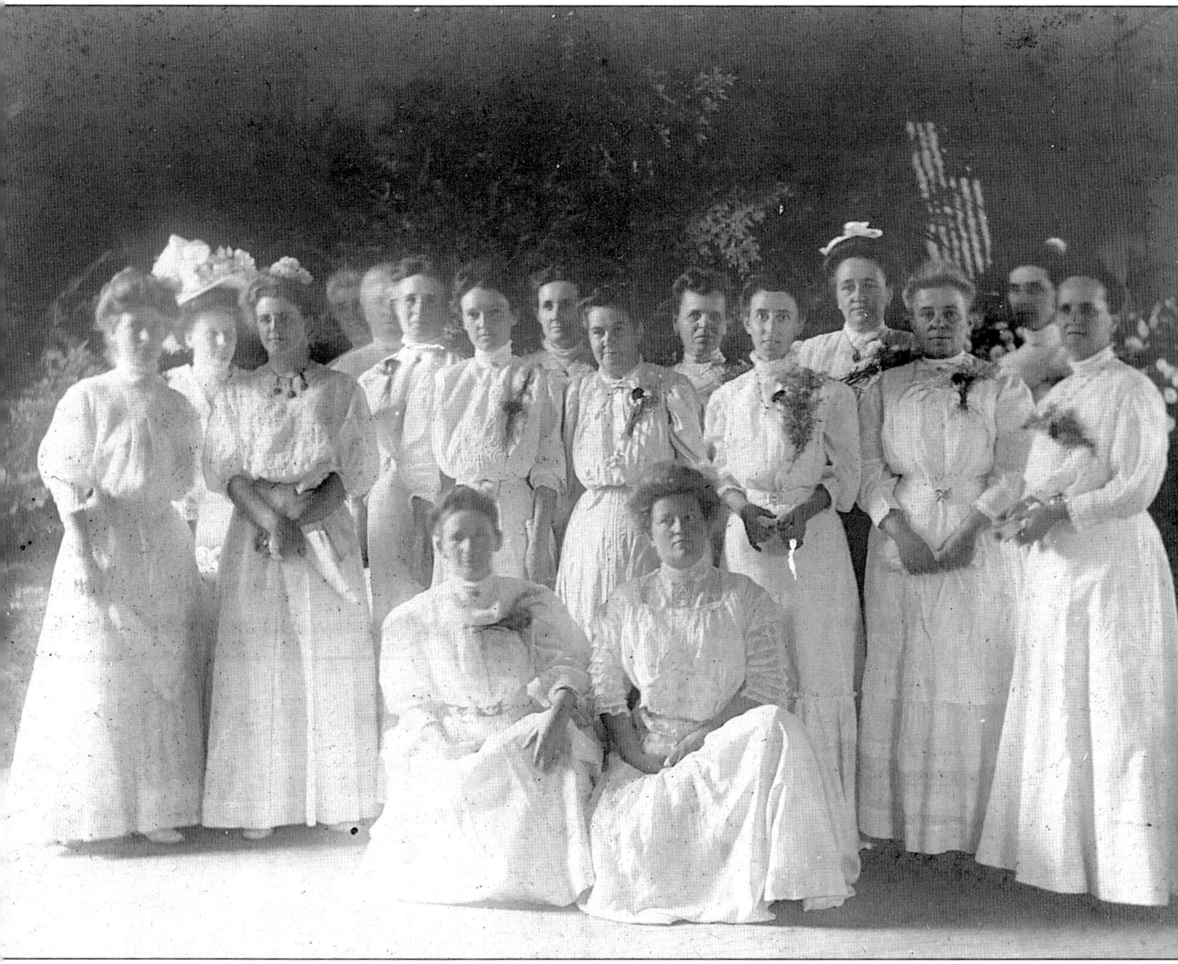

Twenty-two women of the village founded the Village Improvement Society in April 1890. Shown here *c.* 1890 to 1900, this organization sought to enhance the beauty of Plaistow's center. Much of their focus was placed on the commons, which was swampy and unadorned at the time of the group's founding. By 1892, the society's membership had swelled to 133. With the financial support of Arthur G. Pollard, this group oversaw the landscaping of Pollard Park. The women's crowning achievements were the erection of the park's flagpole in 1905 and the dedication of the Soldiers' Monument in 1908. (PHS.)

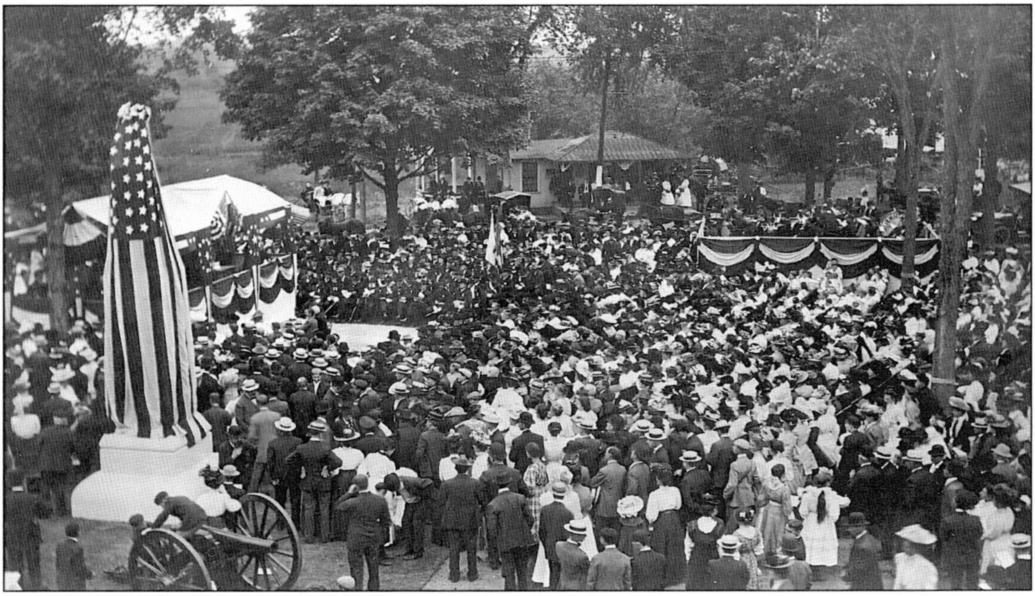

This picture was taken just prior to the unveiling of the Soldier's Monument, on September 12, 1908. Before television and other household-based forms of entertainment, dedications such as this one provided lively distractions for the people of Plaistow. The ceremony featured multiple orations and band performances that spanned the course of the afternoon. (PHS.)

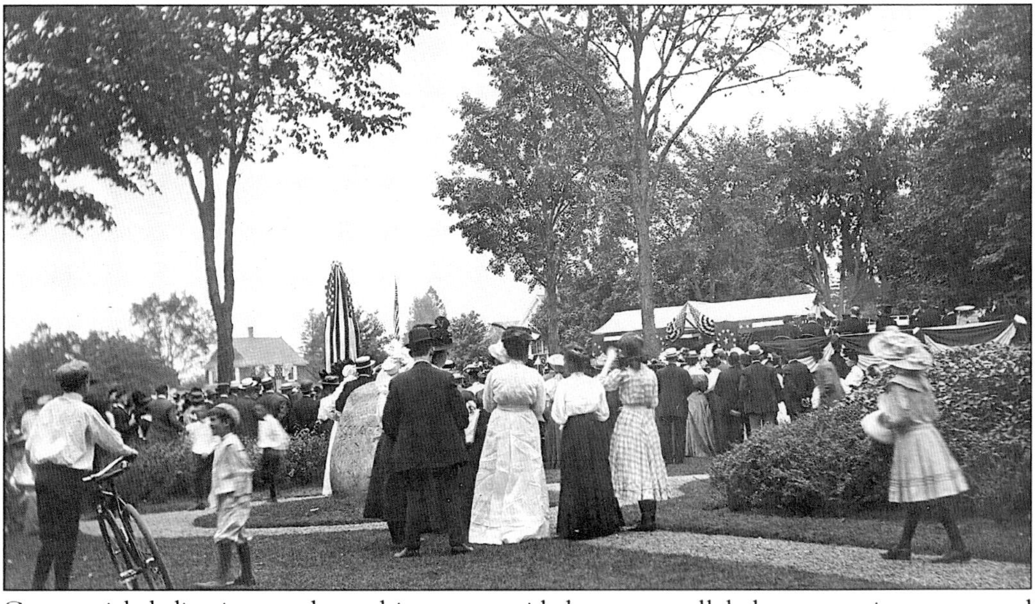

Ceremonial dedications such as this one provided an unparalleled opportunity to see and be seen by fellow townspeople. Note the elegant hats worn by the women surrounding the monument. Veterans of the service could also demonstrate their patriotism by wearing their uniforms to these kinds of events. (PHS.)

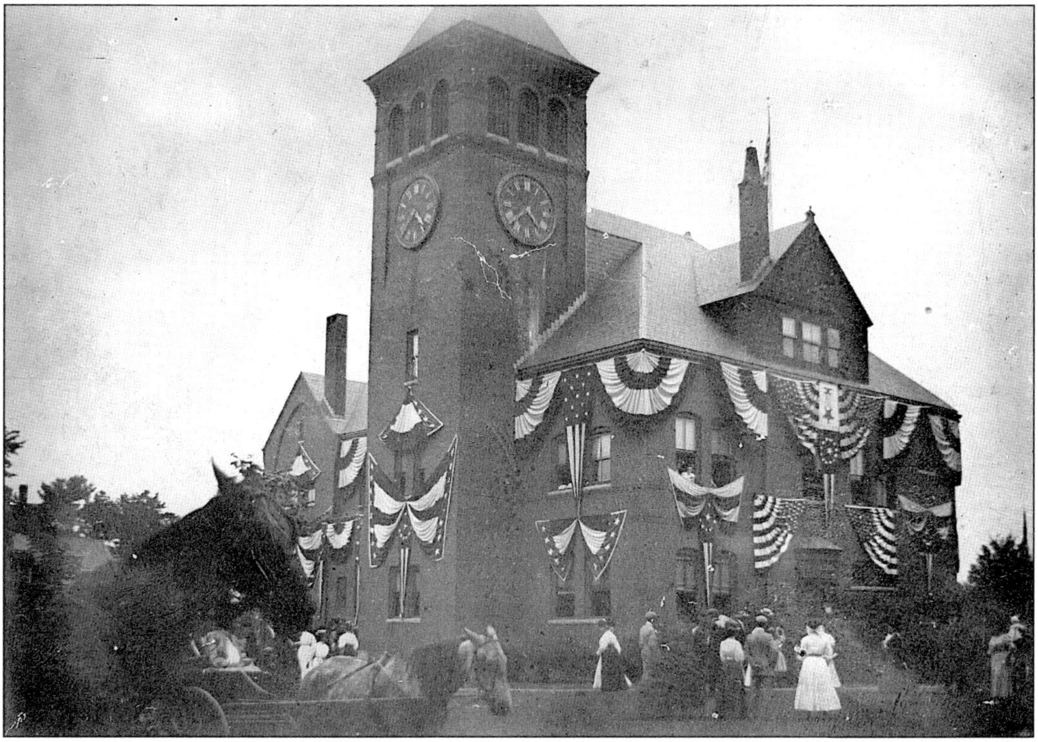

The town hall is decked out in bunting in the early 1900s. (PF.)

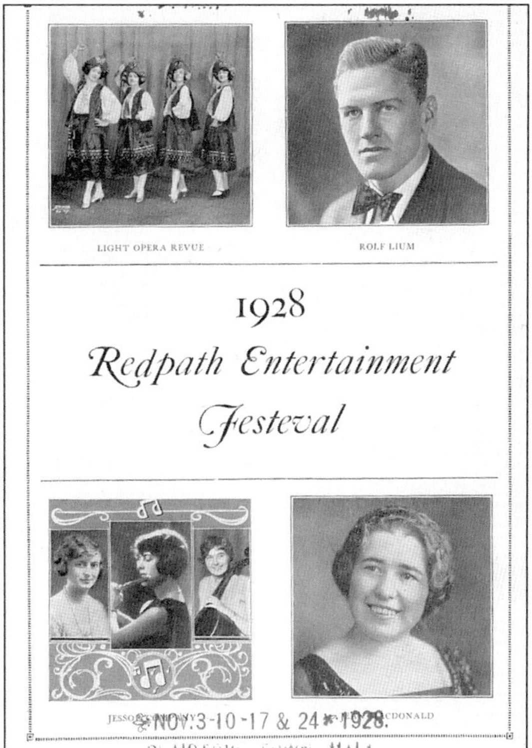

In addition to local and regional talent, the new town hall attracted performers and speakers of national note. Among them was Rolf Lium, who spoke on the "Spirit of Modern Youth." Pastor to President Coolidge, Lium rivaled Charles Lindbergh in the publicity that he garnered nationwide. Interested in ameliorating the "youth problem" of the Roaring Twenties, Lium was an exemplar of "American youth at its very best." (PF.)

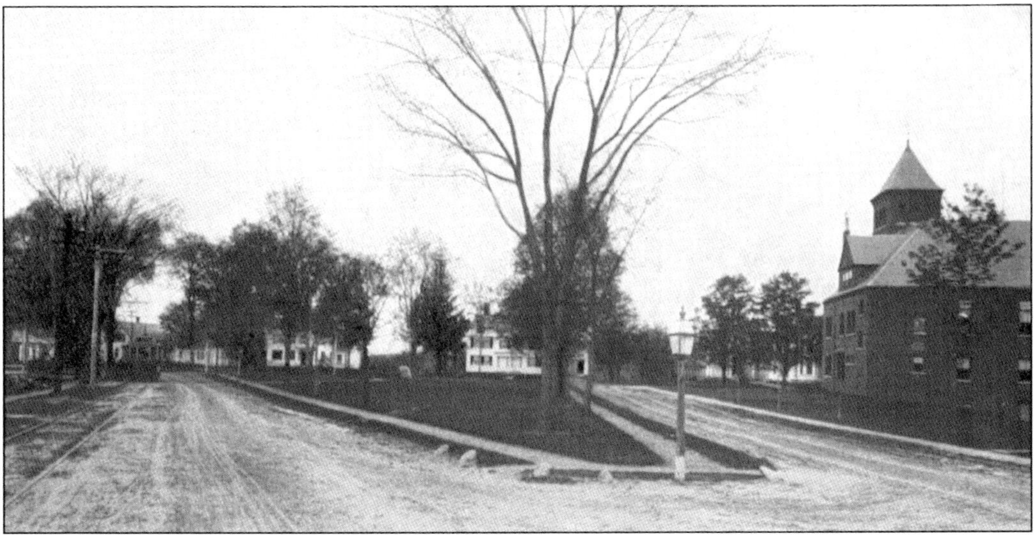

These two views are of the town hall environs. The top image shows Pollard Park prior to the 1908 erection of the Soldiers' Monument. The fanciful lower image presents a conjectural Plaistow of the future, which would feature air travel by dirigible and mass subway transit to points beyond, such as Chester and the Big Apple. (PHS & PF.)

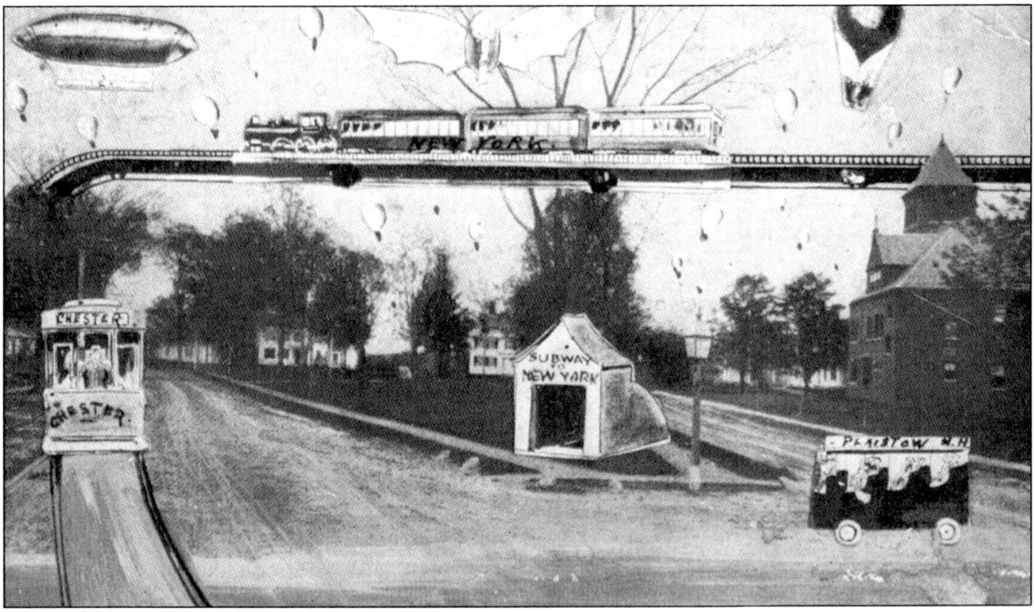

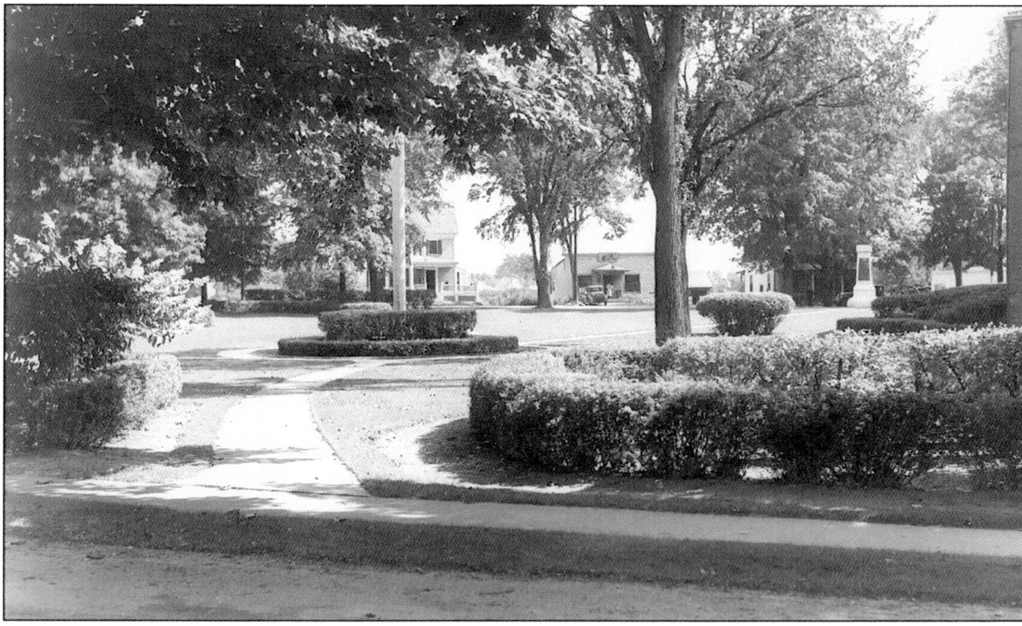

This pre-1938 view shows a well-manicured Pollard Park. Out of a feeling of devotion to his native town, A.G. Pollard of Lowell footed the bill for the landscaping of the once-swampy town common. His generosity also paid for the flagpole (left of center) and the Soldiers' Monument (background, at right). (PHS.)

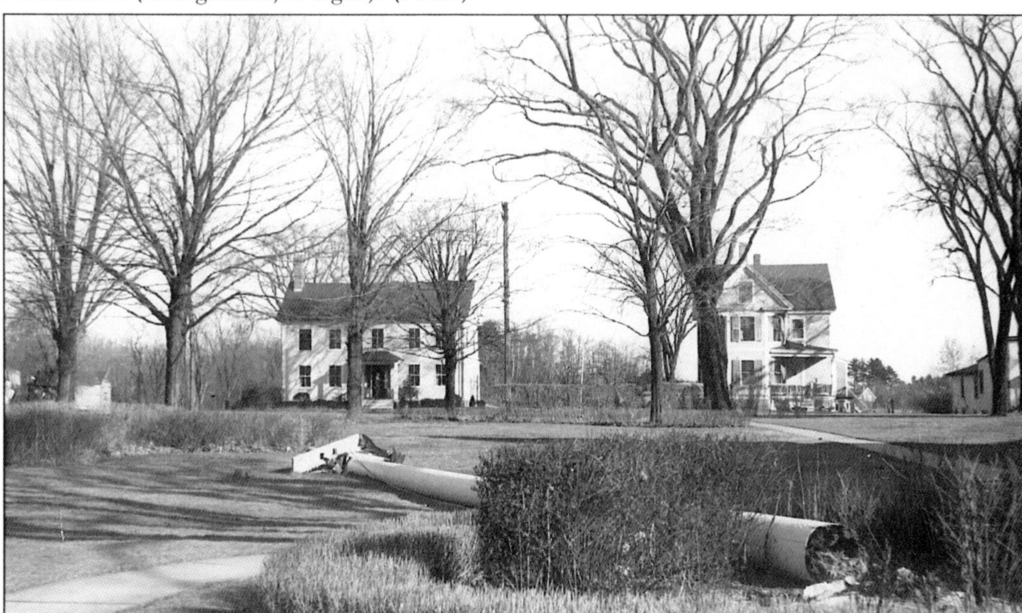

Pollard Park is pictured following a windstorm in April 1947. Erected on what was formerly known as Plaistow Common, this 80-foot flagpole was the gift of Arthur G. Pollard and the Village Improvement Society. Shipped from Oregon by freight car to Boston and hauled from the Hub by a team of 14 oxen, this formidable pine pole was raised in place on July 3, 1905. The flagpole was visible from three New Hampshire towns and from across the Massachusetts border. (PHS.)

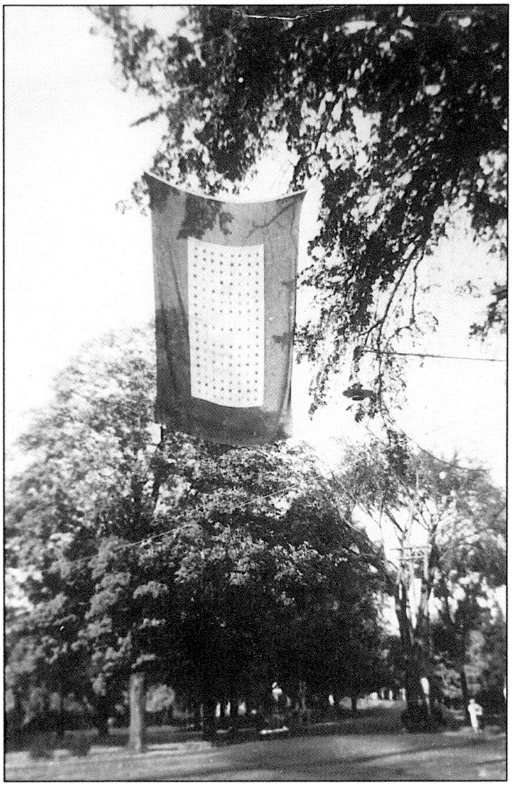

During World War II, this banner was hung from the Great Elm to honor Plaistow's participants in World War II. Each star represented one soldier; one count put the number at 125 stars. This image, looking up Elm Street, was captured on October 1, 1943. (PH.)

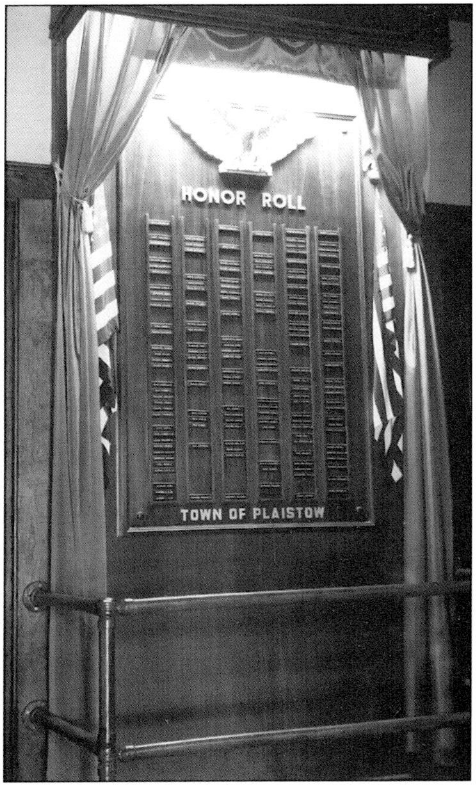

Shortly after VJ Day, the town erected this monument, which lists the names of Plaistow's World War II veterans. The monument is located in the ground-floor lobby of the town hall. (PHS.)

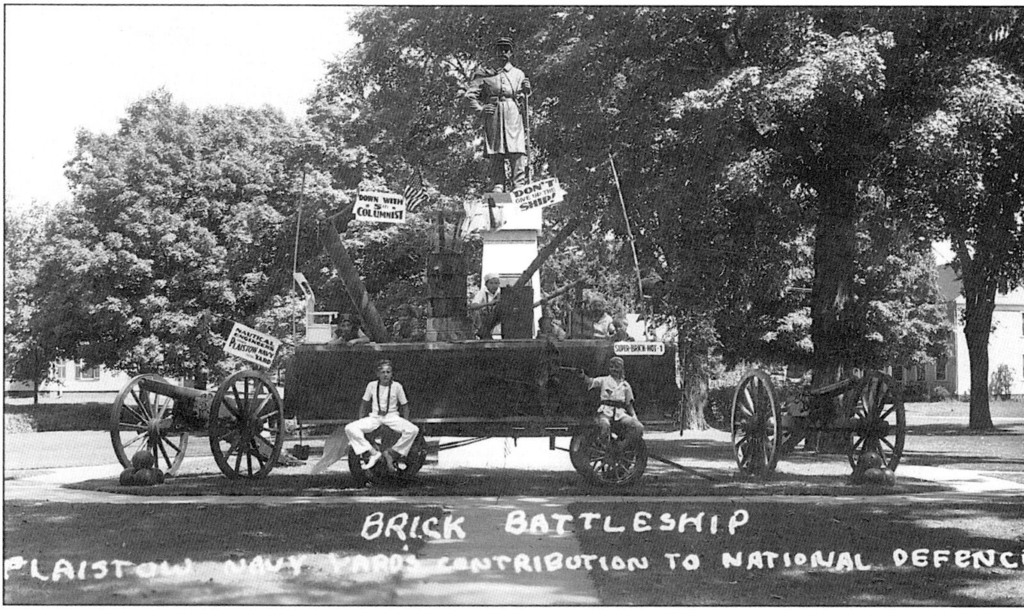

This brick-shaped float was built in 1944, nearly a half-century after Plaistow's brickyards closed for want of clay. Machinery from abandoned brickyards had been donated as scrap as part of the home-front war effort during World War I. The spirit exhibited here reflects the same sentiment. Posters read, from left to right, "Nautical Engineers Plaistow Navy Yard," "Down with 5th Columnist," "Don't Give up the Ship," and "Super Brick No. 1." (PHS.)

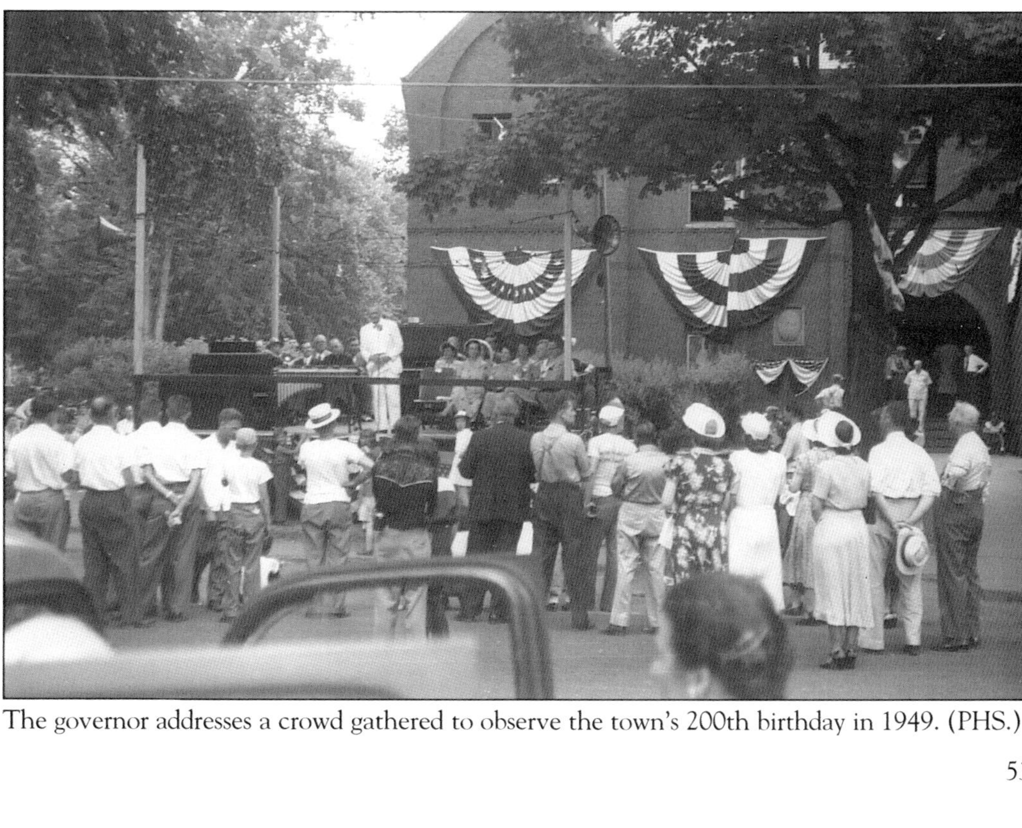

The governor addresses a crowd gathered to observe the town's 200th birthday in 1949. (PHS.)

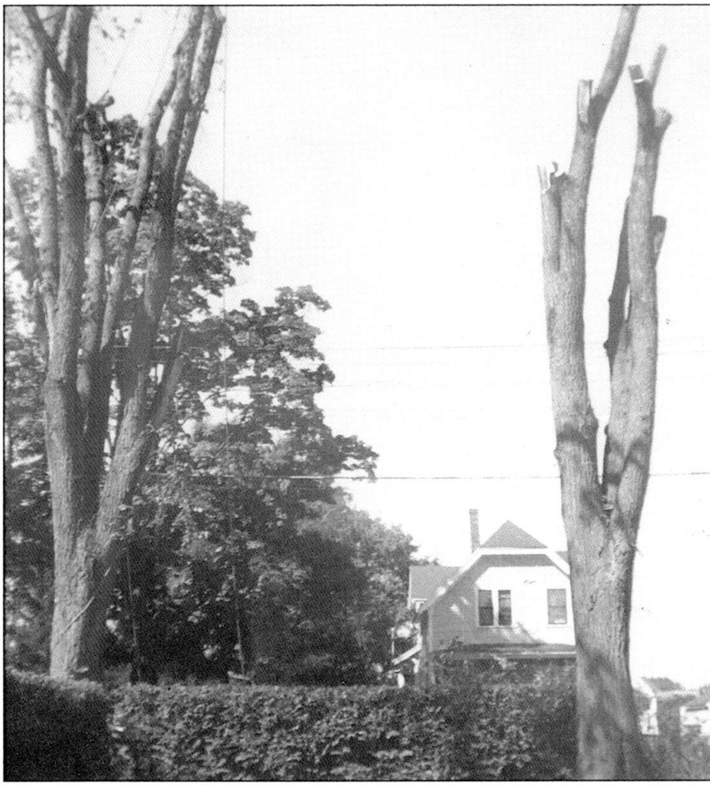

Like many New England towns, Plaistow was once the home of dozens of stately elms. Over the course of the first half of the 1900s, these grand trees succumbed to the dreaded Dutch elm disease. This 1955 photograph shows two elms abutting Pollard Park shortly before being felled. (PHS.)

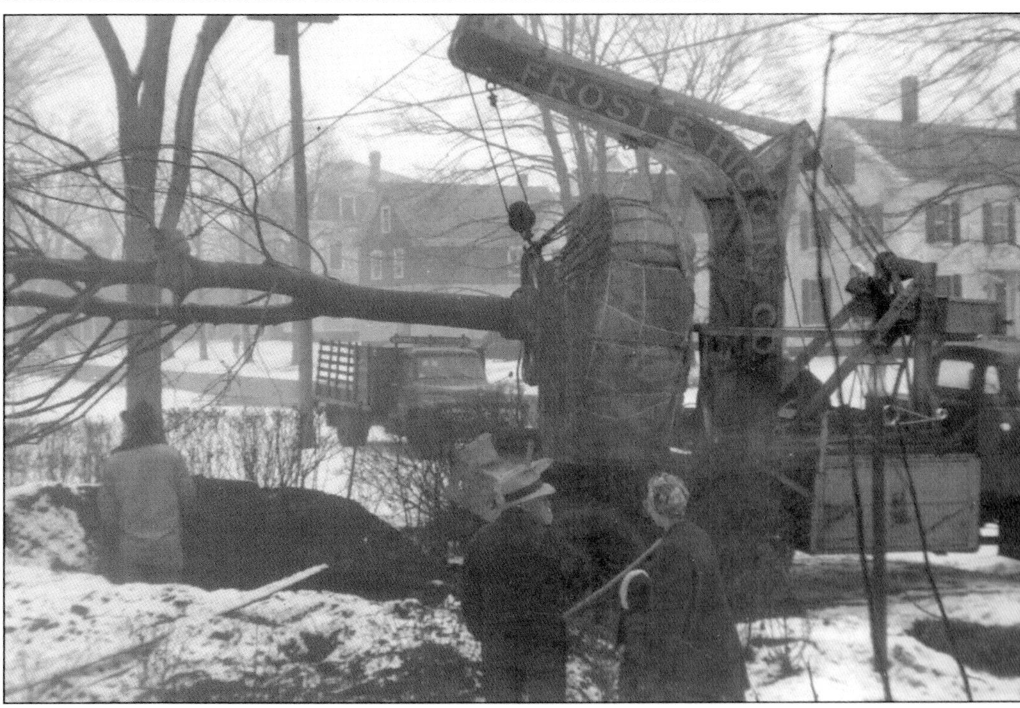

In the stead of the elms, disease-resistant maples were planted. Witnessing this 1955 "changing of the guard" are John, Ruthie, and Kathy Barring. (PHS.)

Four

From Seaver Brook Southward

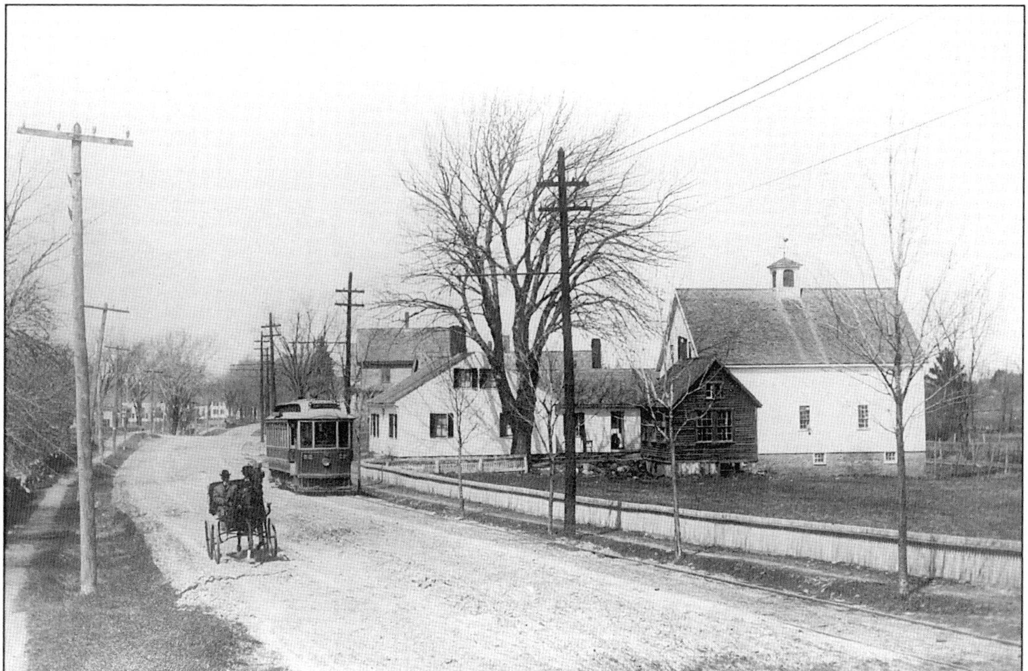

Looking south from the Westville Road intersection, this c. 1905 glimpse of Main Street literally shows the machine age gaining ground on the days of horse-drawn vehicles. (PHS.)

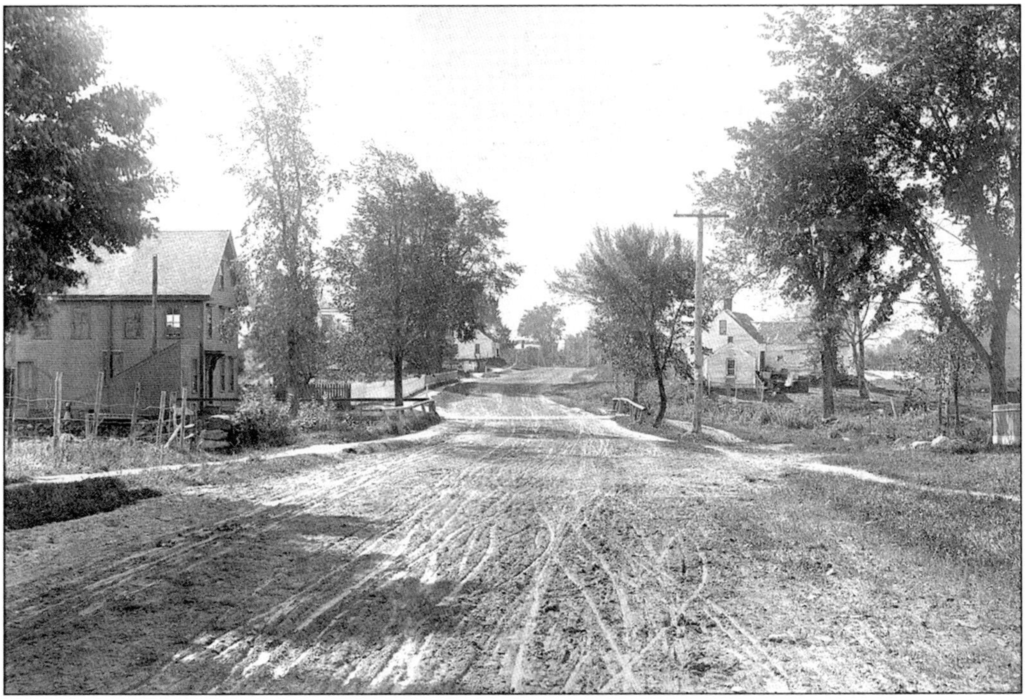

This view was taken looking south along Main Street *c.* the late 1800s. Note the bridge over Seaver Brook, which aided in the identification of this scene. A map created by Ed McKenzie in 1974 identifies the building on the left as a shoe shop. (PHS.)

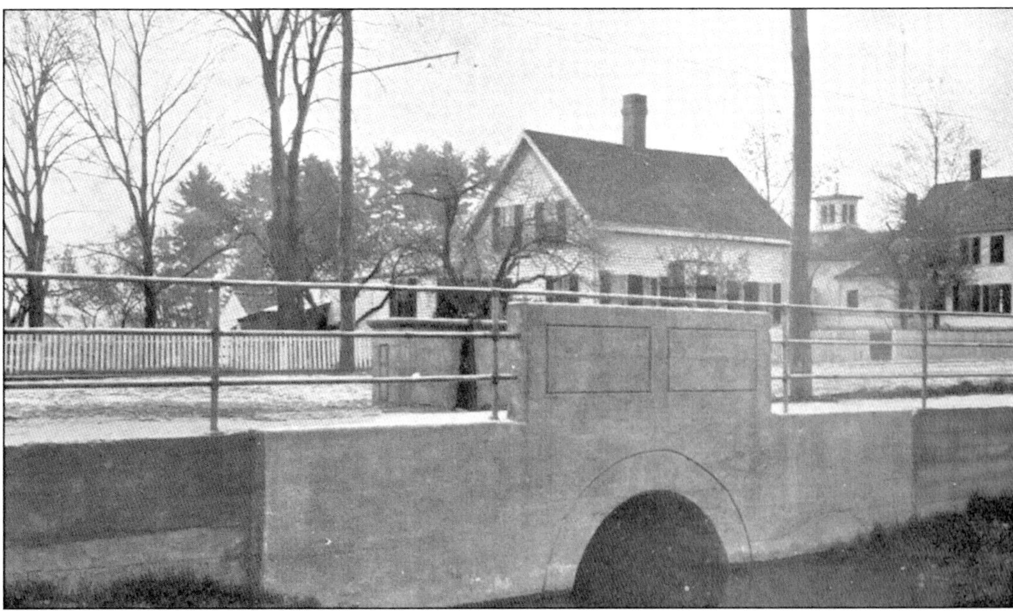

Shown here in the 1930s or the 1940s is the Seaver Bridge, built in 1912 by John Germundson of Newton. (AC.)

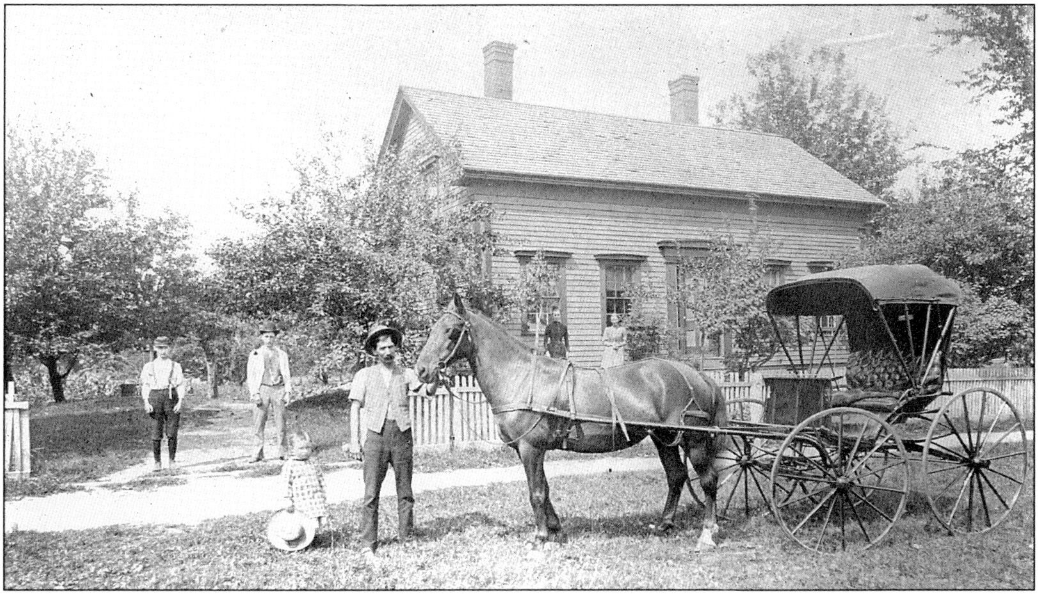

Here is Duffill Farm, on Main Street, around the period from 1875 to 1885. John Duffill was born in 1838 in Sussex and settled in Plaistow, where he died in 1907. (PHS.)

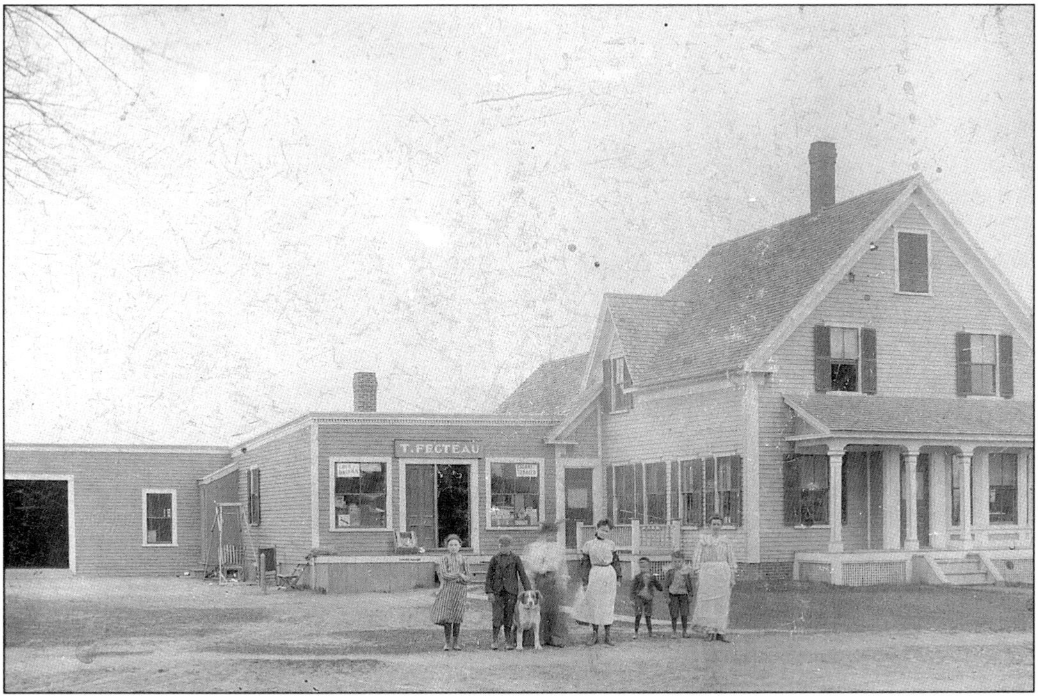

This July 1910 scene shows Fecteau's Store, located at 114 Main Street, across from the Duffill Farm. The fuzzy figure (third from left) is Lilly, the oldest child of Aurore Fecteau (far right); the dog's name was Daisy. Also pictured are Nelson, Oscar, and Sadie Fecteau. (PHS.)

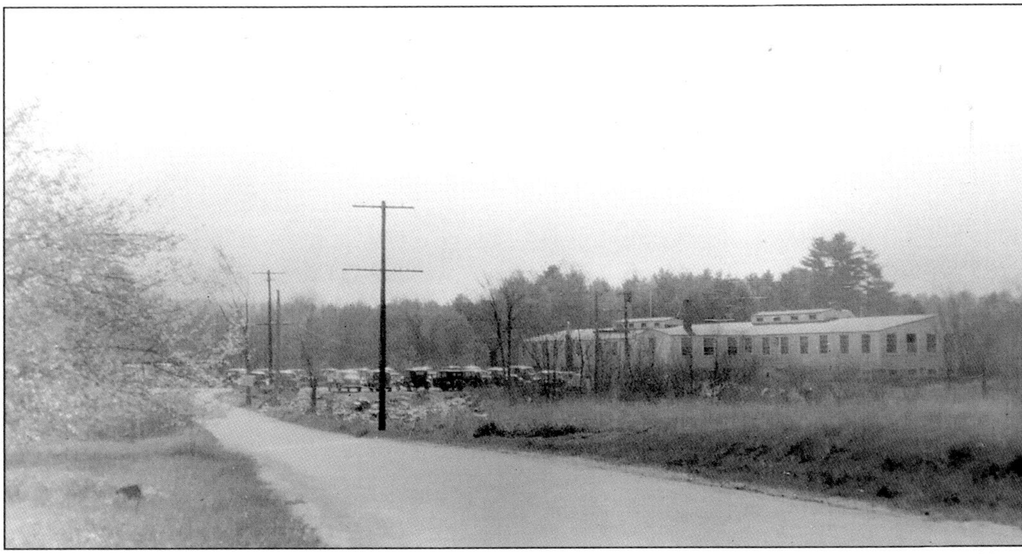

This c. 1930s view of Lasknit Avenue (later Chadwick Avenue) shows the Colcord & Dobbins Shoe Factory. Later, this was the site of a chicken-processing plant before C.D. Keezer moved his Feltcrafter's factory here in 1948. Keezer renamed Lasknit Avenue after Stanley Chadwick, the first Plaistow soldier killed in World War II. (PHS.)

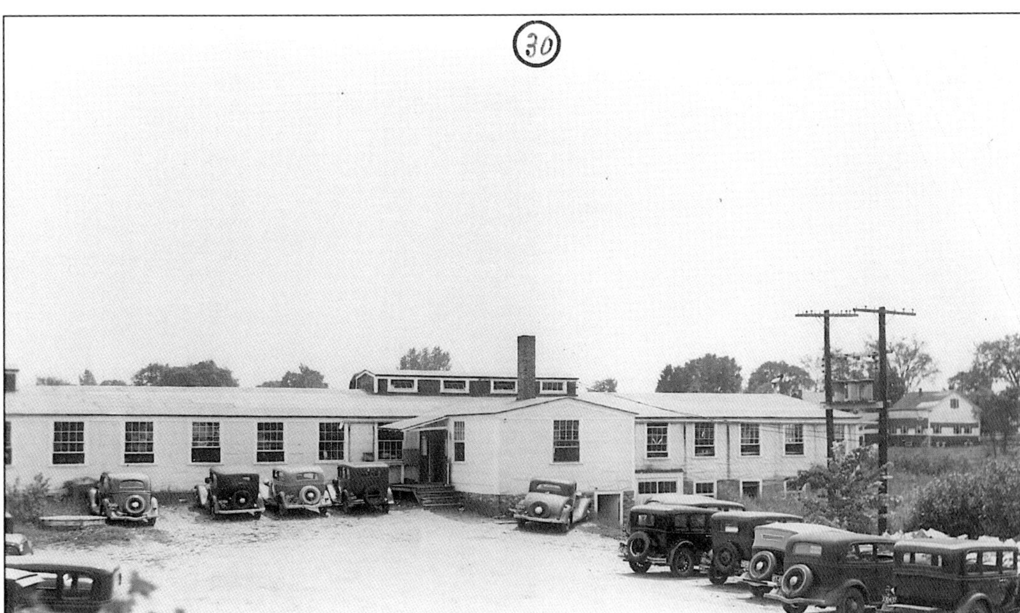

Started in 1928 by Carter Dimond Keezer while a college student, the Keezer Manufacturing Company first operated out of the Massoit and Spinney buildings on South Main Street and moved into the former Dolbins-Colcord shoe shop in 1948. Keezer specialized in logos that were used for team and product identification. (PHS.)

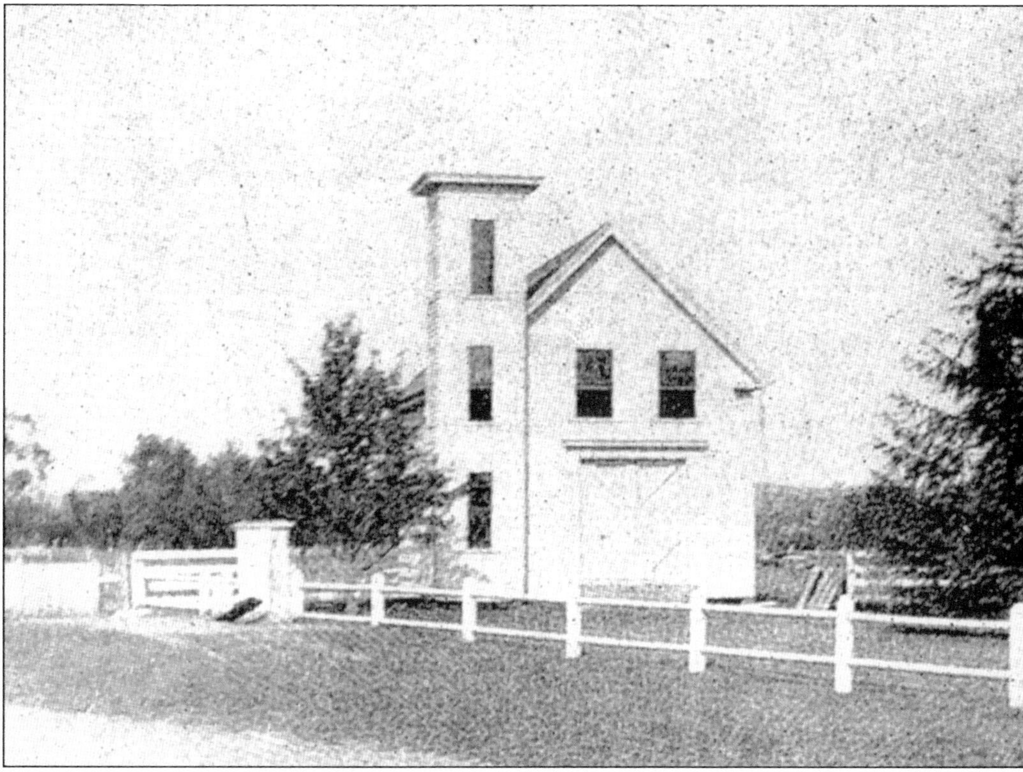

This is a view of the old firehouse. Note the tower in which hoses were hung to dry. (PHS.)

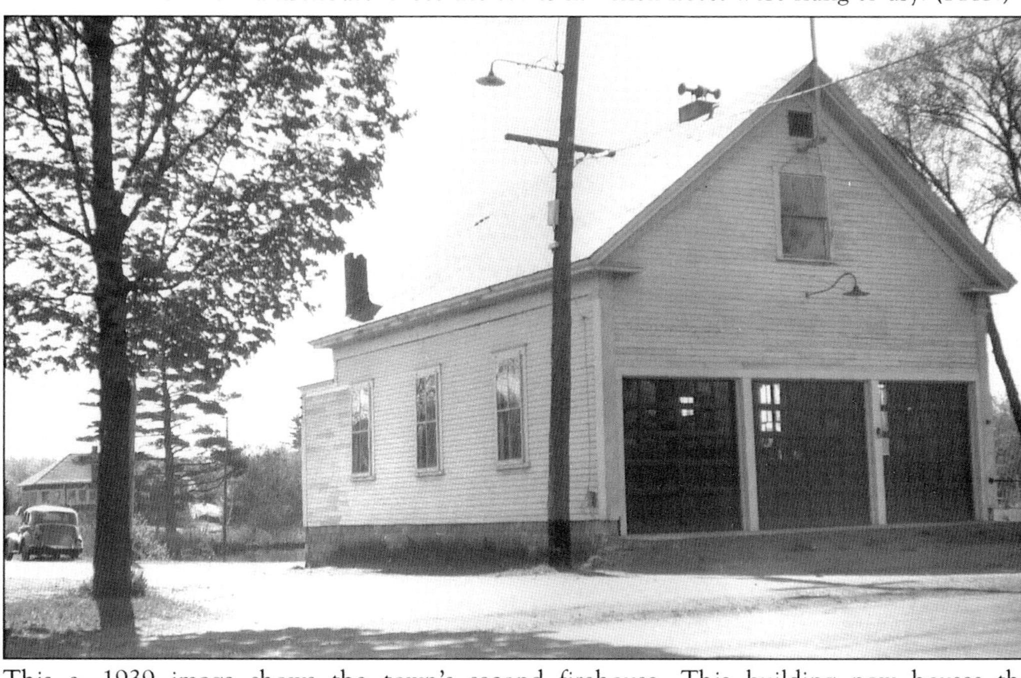

This c. 1939 image shows the town's second firehouse. This building now houses the Plaistow Historical Society. In 1940, the fire department made the transition from being a volunteer-based service to a professional one. (PHS.)

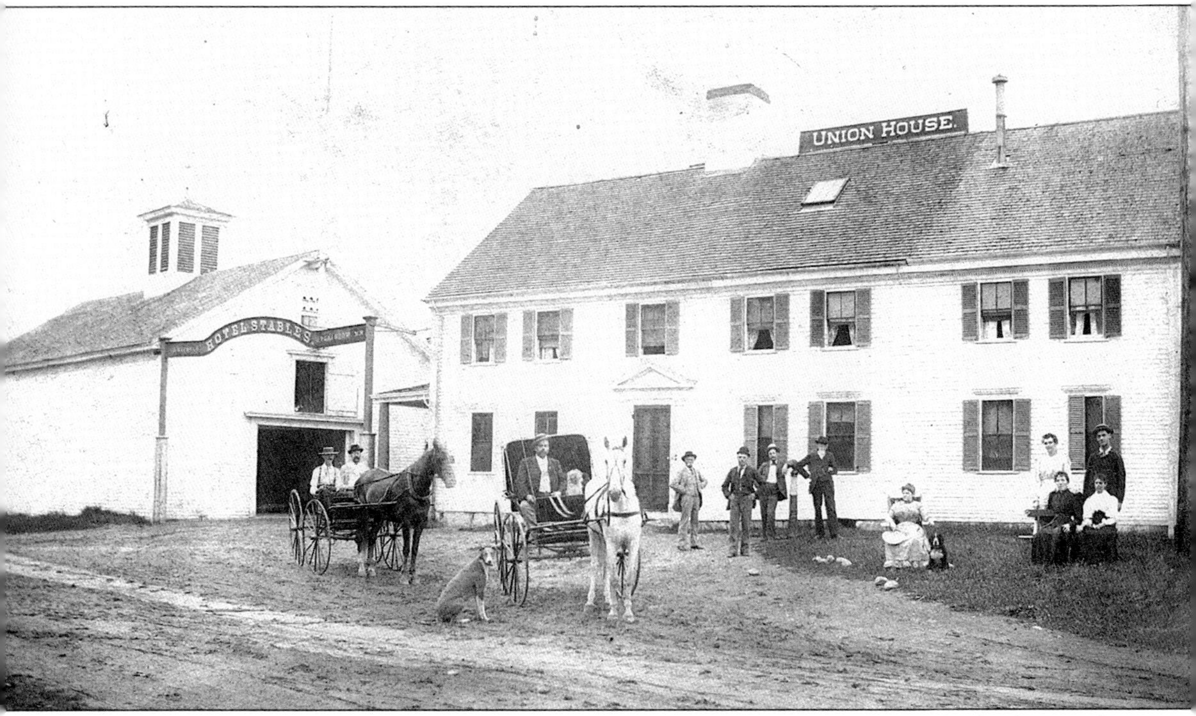

The Union House Tavern is shown *c.* the late 1800s. The tavern was built during the mid-1700s. Part of the structure (the section from the chimney to the left edge) survives and was moved from its original location to its present site, across from Timberlane Plate Glass. The Union House enjoyed a national reputation for the excellence of its meals, its card room, and the size of its livery stable. George Washington is said to have stopped here in 1796 to water his horses while en route from Exeter to Haverhill. (PHS.)

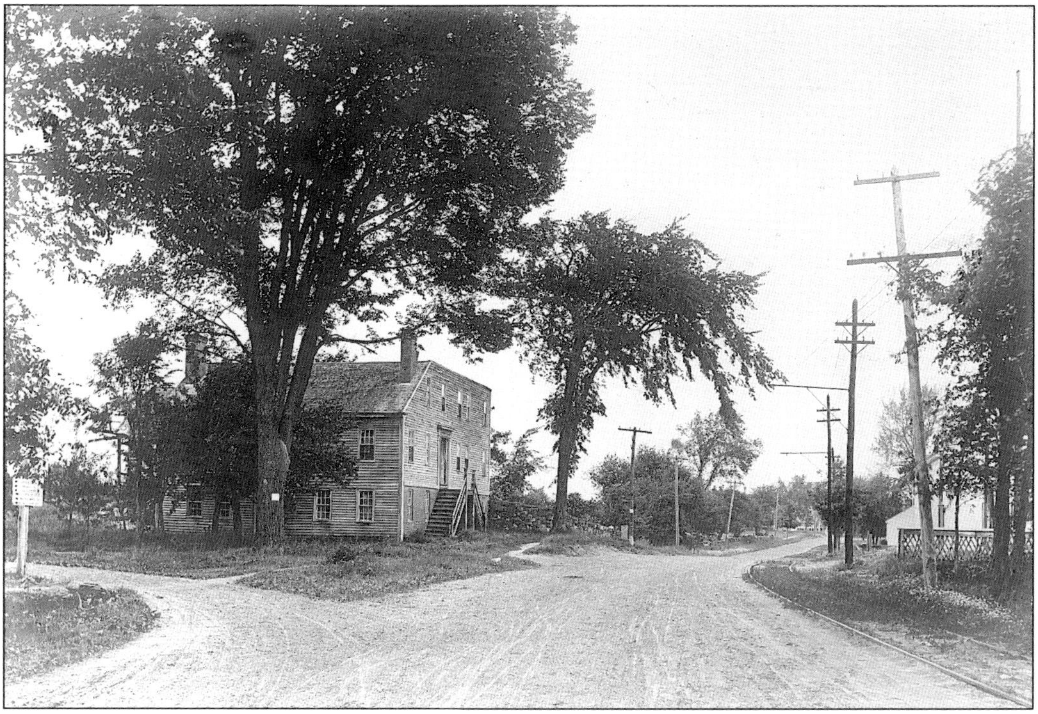

This view shows the intersection of Main Street and Westville Road. The trolley tracks, laid in 1903, suggest that this photograph was taken *c.* 1905 to 1910. At the left center is Tucker Tavern; there is evidence of fire damage on the left side of the structure. The sign on the far left points the direction to Sandown, Danville, and Chester in one direction, and Rocks Bridge, Merrimac, and Newburyport in the other. (PHS.)

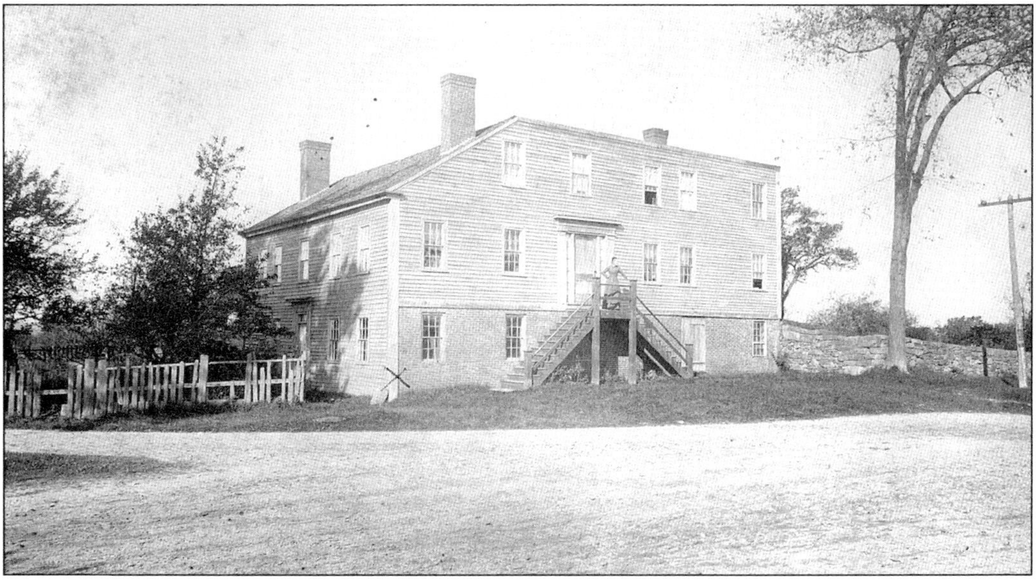

This is Tucker Tavern in the late 1800s. On the left is the road to Westville. (PHS.)

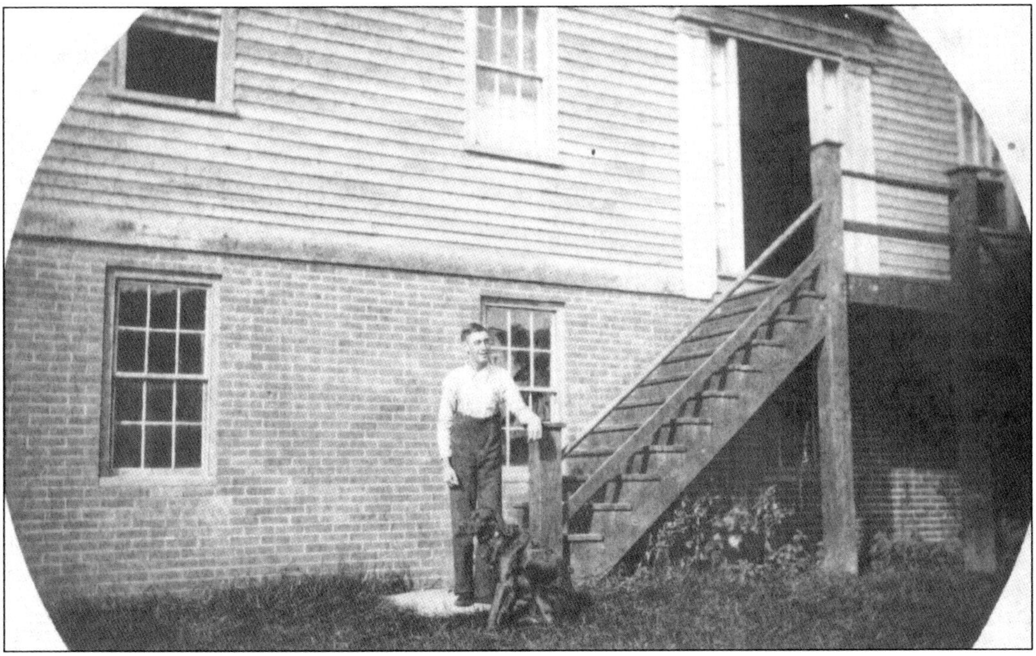

In the late 1800s, Tucker Tavern was the home of the George family. Shown here before the building's eastern elevation is Ashley George. Prior to the Tuckers and the Georges, this was the home of Isaac Pollard. (PHS.)

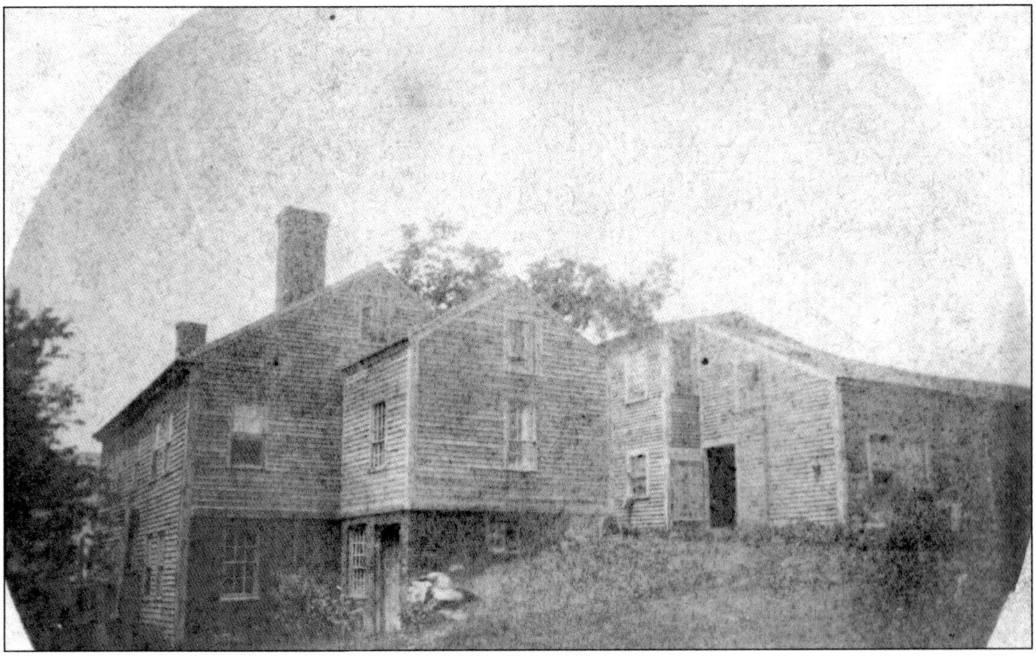

Tucker Tavern, built *c.* 1770, is shown here *c.* 1880. Like many Colonial-era houses, the tavern was built facing south to maximize exposure to the sun; this orientation was extremely important in an age before electric light and central heating. The presence of additions, destroyed by the early 1900s, and the size of surrounding trees help establish this imprecise date. (PHS.)

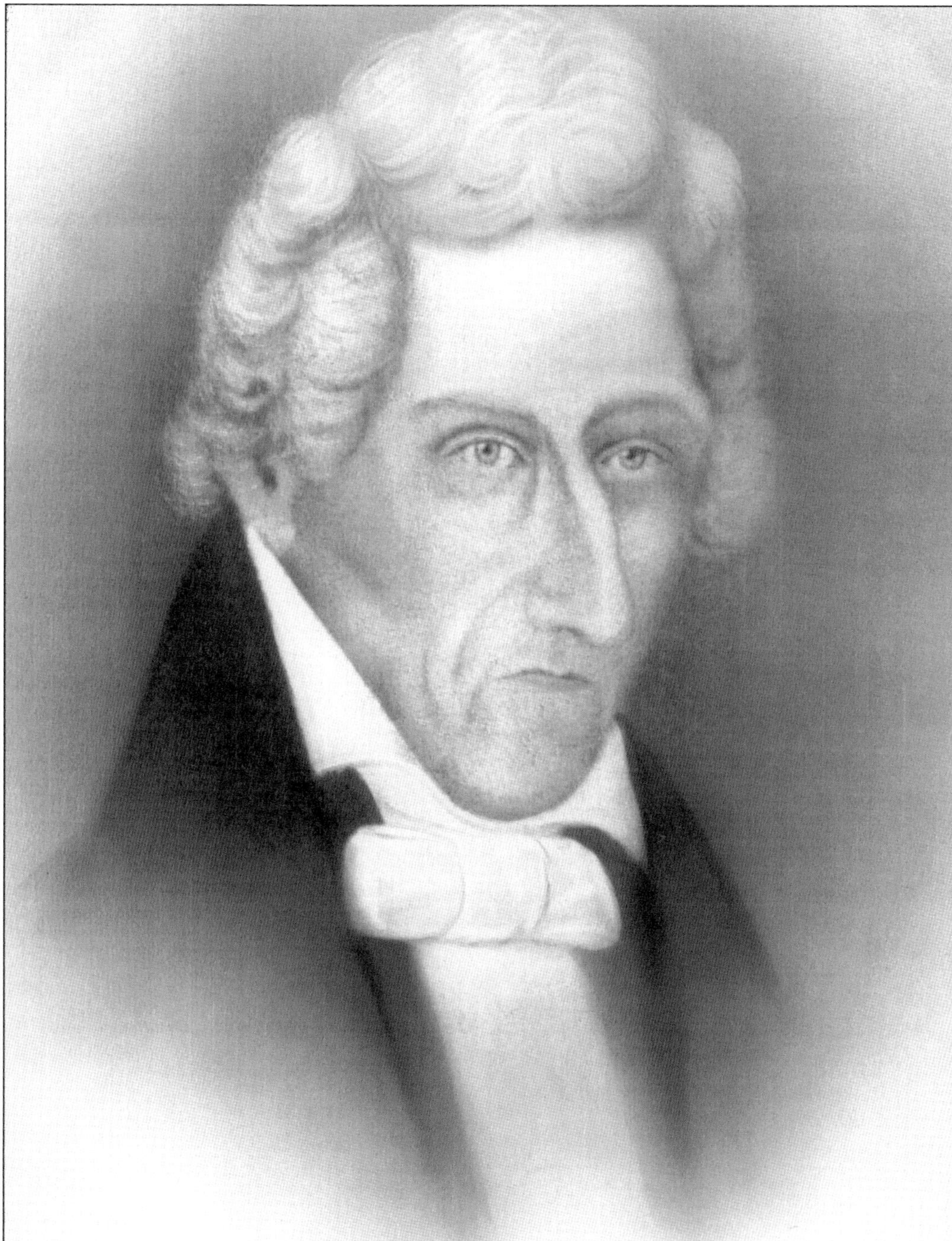

Deacon Isaac Pollard (1758–1836) was the son of Sarah and Francis Pollard of Kingston and the grandfather of Arthur G. Pollard. Isaac Pollard was a major landowner in Plaistow, a tavern keeper, and a "loan shark" according to family historian Maurice Pollard. He was the owner of the tavern on the corner on Westville Road and Main Street before it was taken over by his relatives, the Tuckers. The Pollards were among the leading families of Plaistow's nascent Baptist congregation that established a church in the 1830s. (PHS.)

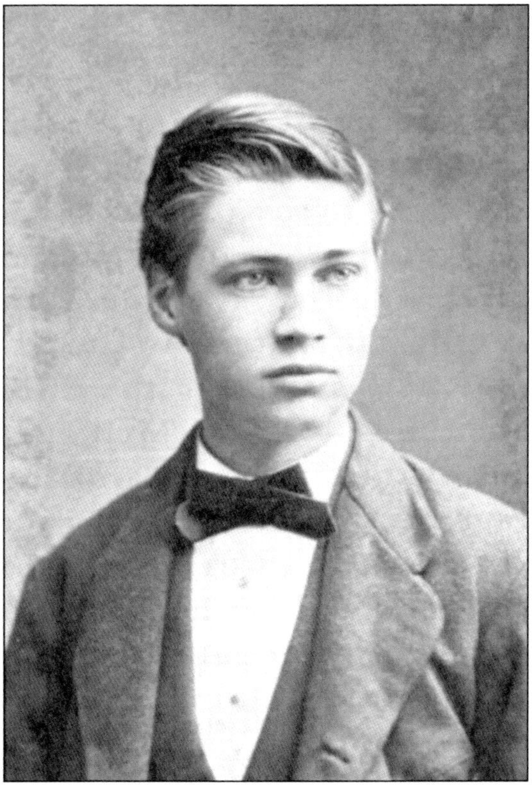

At 14, Frank E. Pollard (1856–1943) was among the youngest pupils to graduate from Philips Andover Academy. During his adolescence, he displayed a proficiency for invention. Among his creations was a machine for turning out baseball bats. Prior to the perfection of photography, he invented a camera whose prints he developed with his own chemicals. As an adult, the prospect of creating a perpetual motion machine served as an outlet for his creative energies. Although not successful in his attempt to defy the laws of physics, his blueprints and models did garner the attention of MIT faculty. (NHHS.)

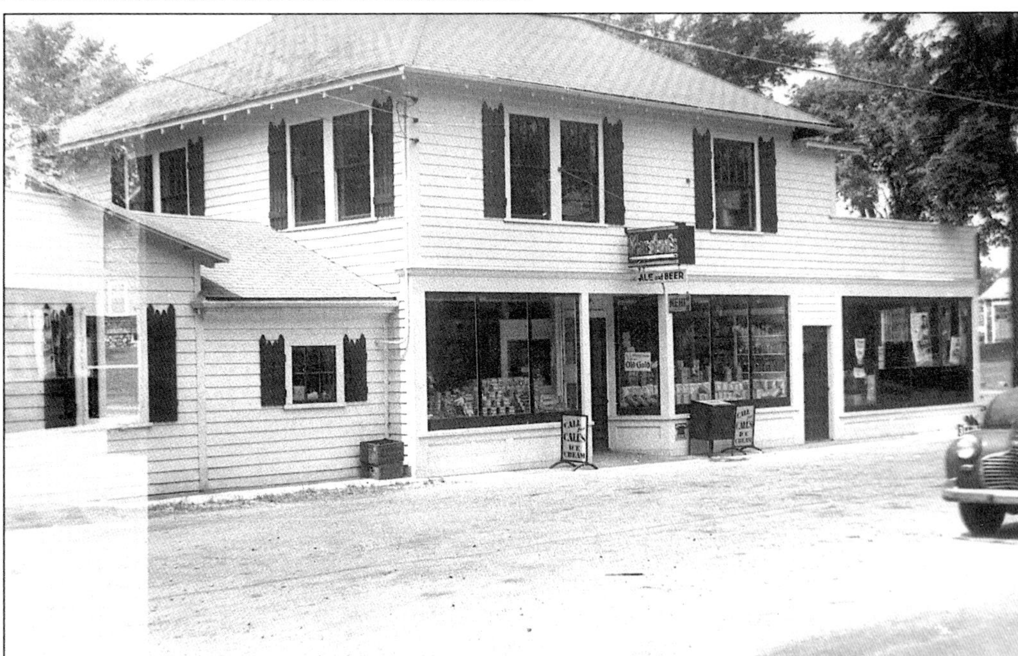

This view of Marston's Store dates to the late 1940s. Since that time the store, which is located at the corner of Main Street and Westville Road, has changed hands many times. Recently it was Common Cents Variety. (PHS.)

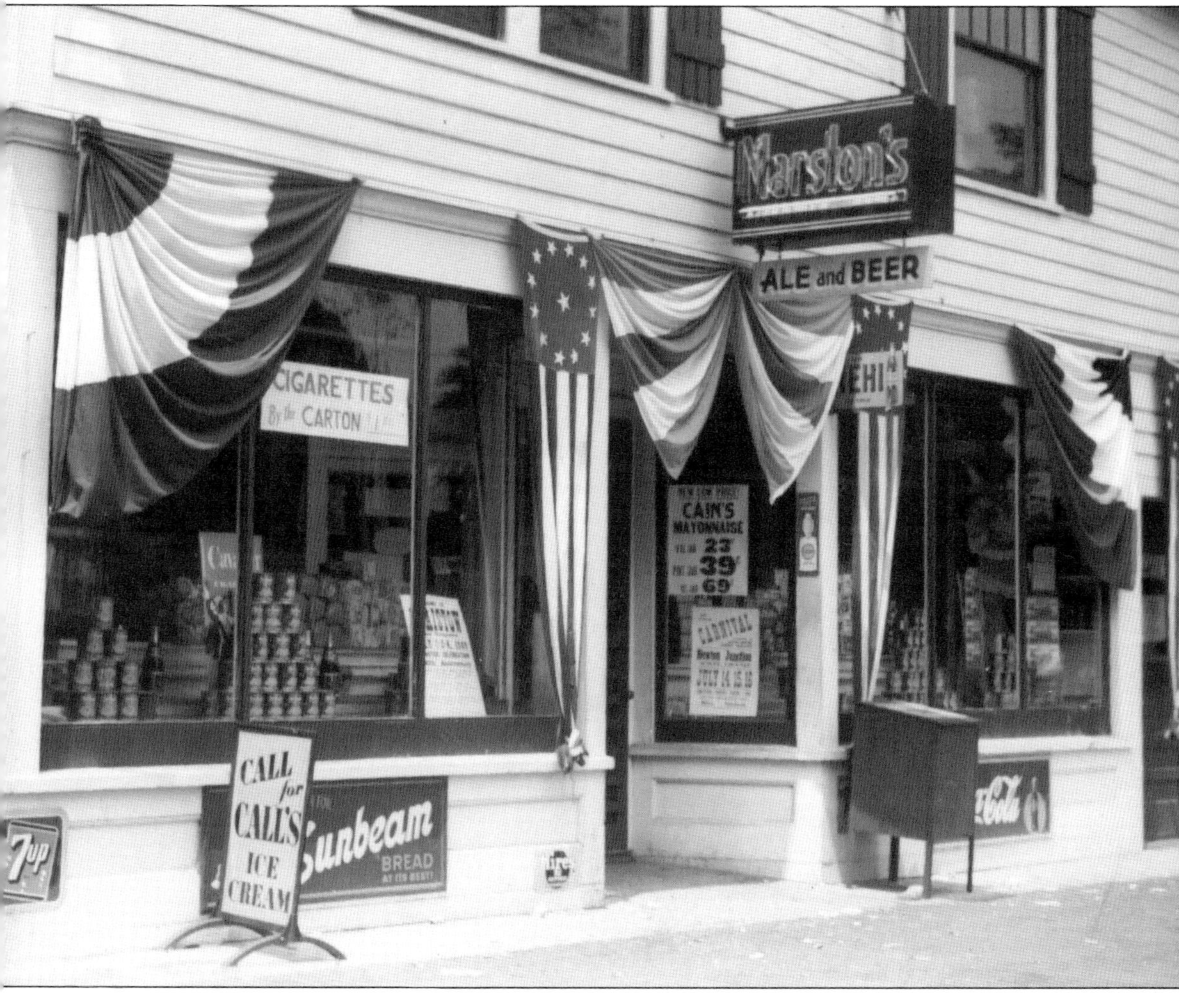

Marston's Store is shown in another view from the late 1940s. (PHS.)

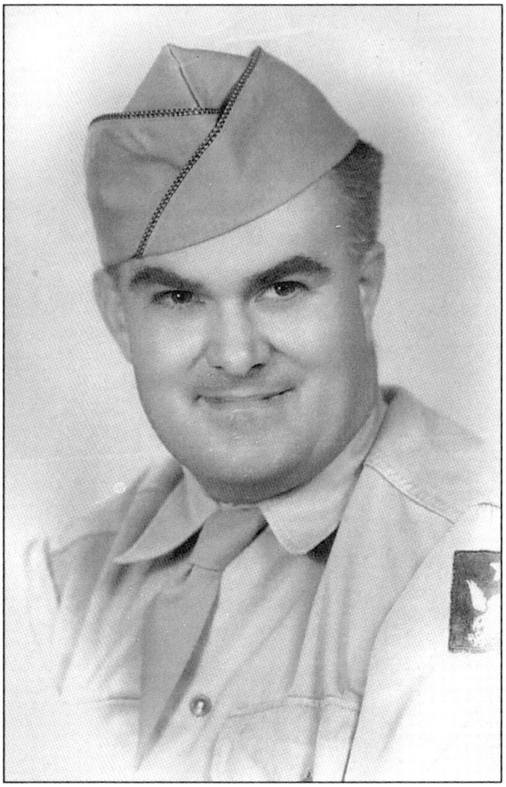

Willard M. Tozier was born in Plaistow in 1915. The grandson of the last superintendent of the Plaistow Brick Yard, Tozier enlisted in the air force in 1940. A direct descendant of Pres. William Howard Taft, Tozier died in Plaistow in 1953. (PHS.)

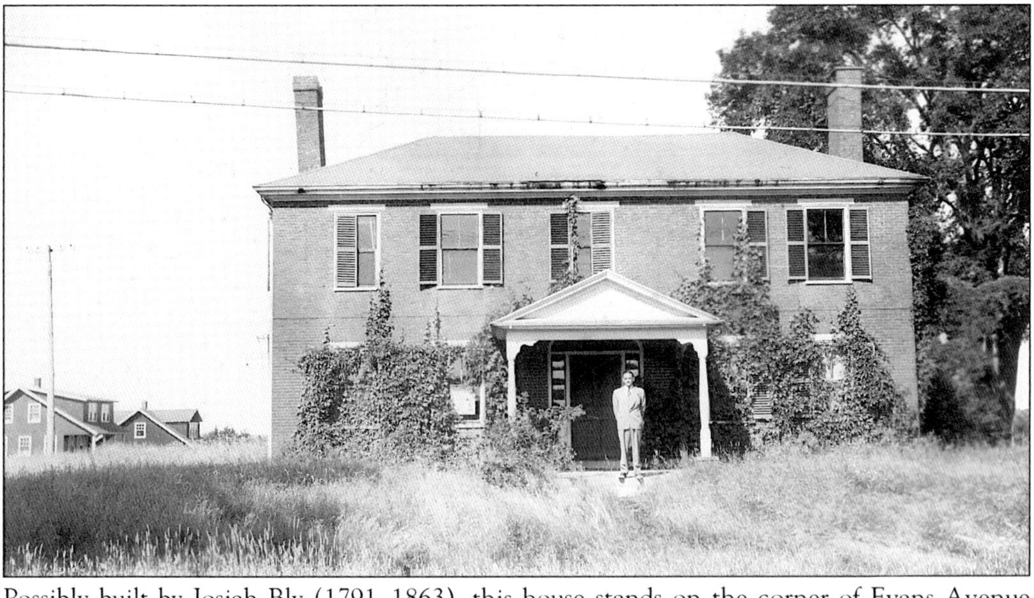

Possibly built by Josiah Bly (1791–1863), this house stands on the corner of Evans Avenue and South Main Street. Bly came from a brick-making family who owned woodlots throughout town, suggesting that he required a steady supply of charcoal to fire brick kilns. Bly, who married Fanny Ordway in 1821, was called one of the richest men in Plaistow by the North Parish diarist Isaac Merrill. (PHS.)

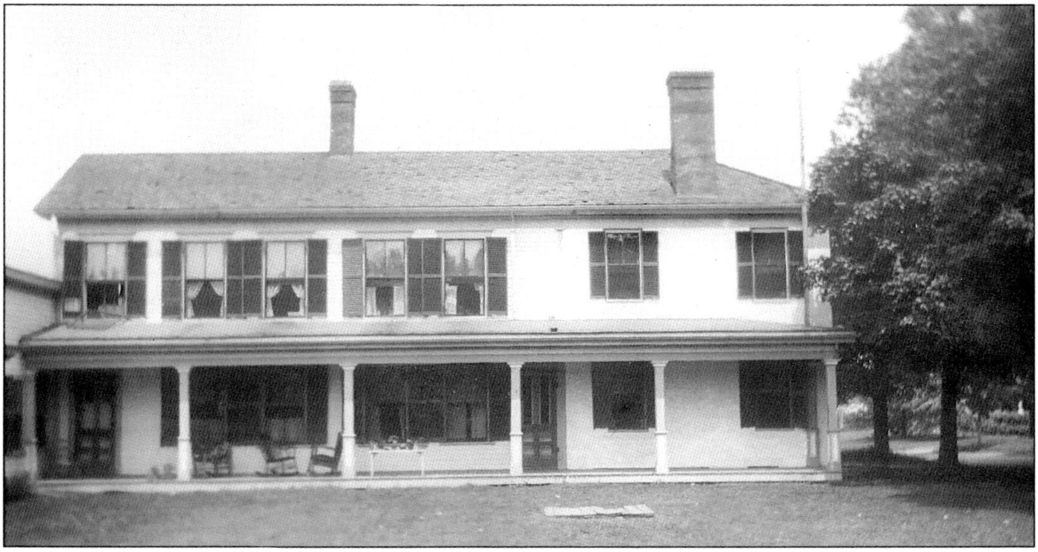

The *c.* 1855 Peaslee-Osgood House was built with locally manufactured brick and is now the home of the Community Bank & Trust Company. Known as the Homestead Inn in the late 1800s and Maple Leaf Farms in the early 1900s, the house's hip roof and central entry recall the style of the Federal period. (PHS.)

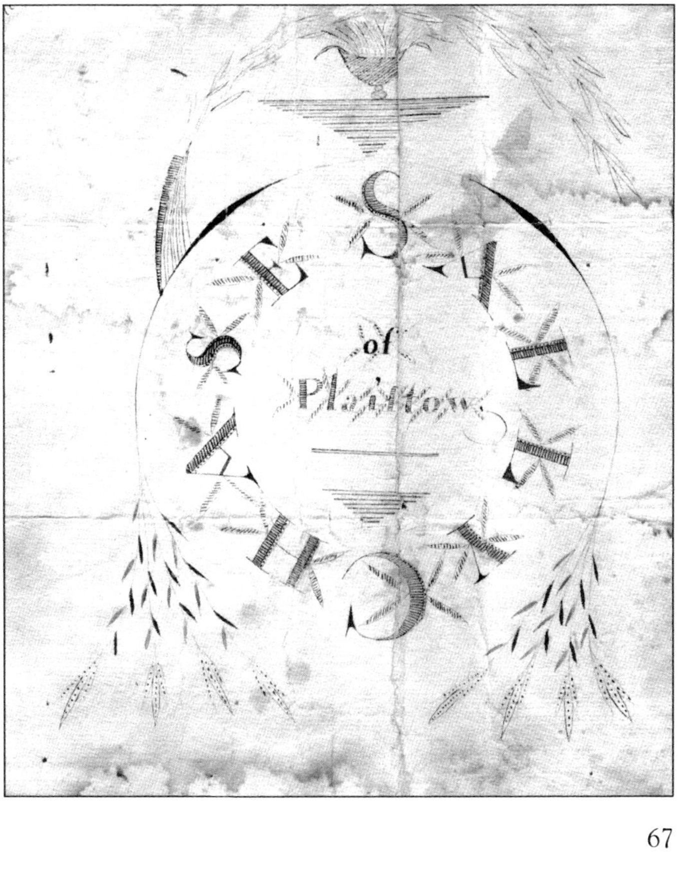

From a Peaslee family scrapbook, this mid-1800s memorial illustration is accompanied by the following verse: "Know that our days and months and years / Are all made up of smiles and tears, / Of wedded joy and sorrow; / and the form that seemed so light and gay, / the eyes that shone so bright to day, / May close in death to morrow." (PHS.)

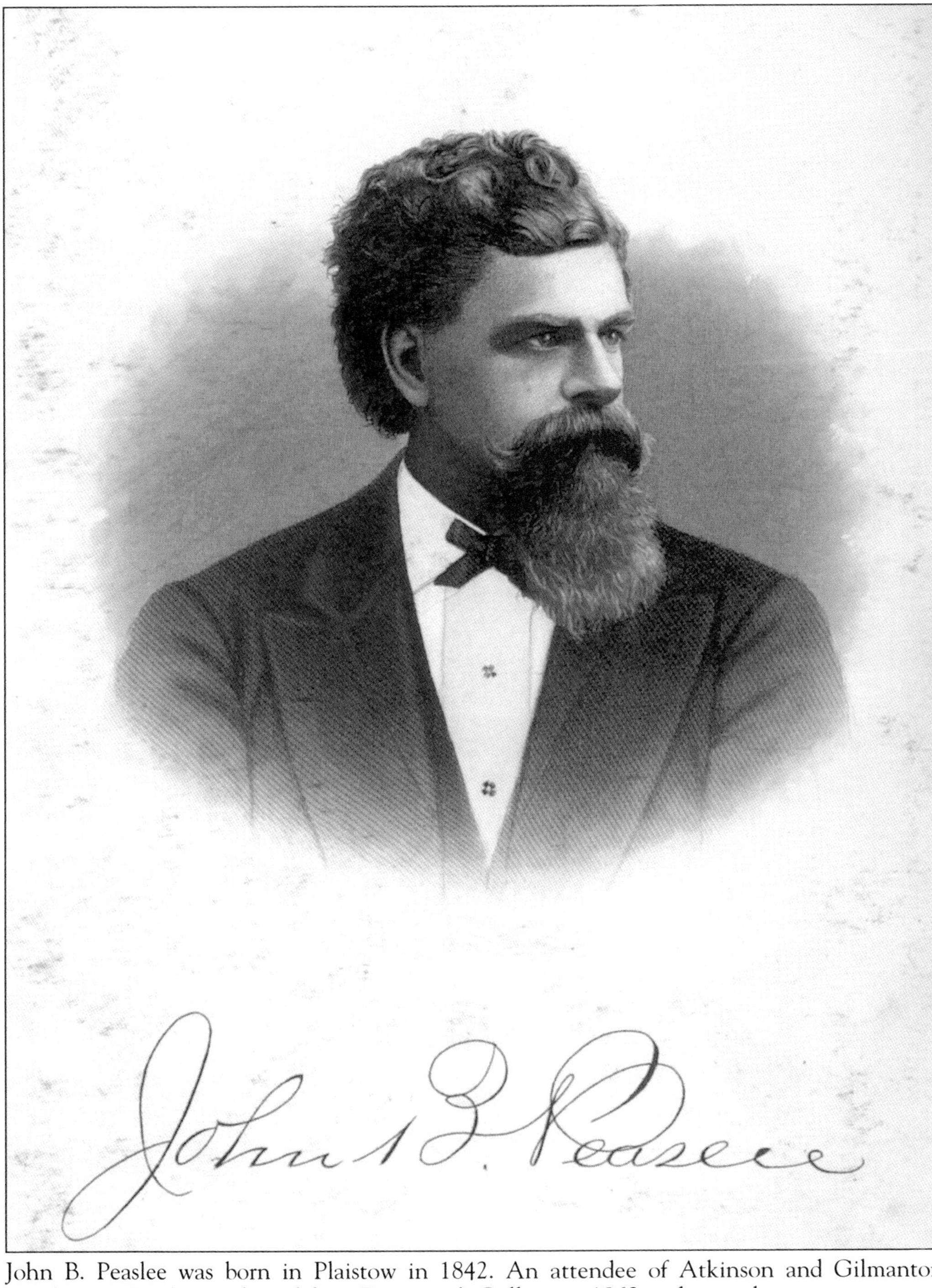

John B. Peaslee was born in Plaistow in 1842. An attendee of Atkinson and Gilmanton Academies, Peaslee graduated from Dartmouth College in 1863 and gave the commencement address. Ralph Waldo Emerson, who was in attendance, is believed to have personally praised Peaslee for his oratory. By his early thirties, Peaslee had become the youngest superintendent of the Cincinnati school district. His career peaked when he was named Ohio's candidate for lieutenant governor. (PHS.)

Five

Plaistow Depot and North to Pollard Brook

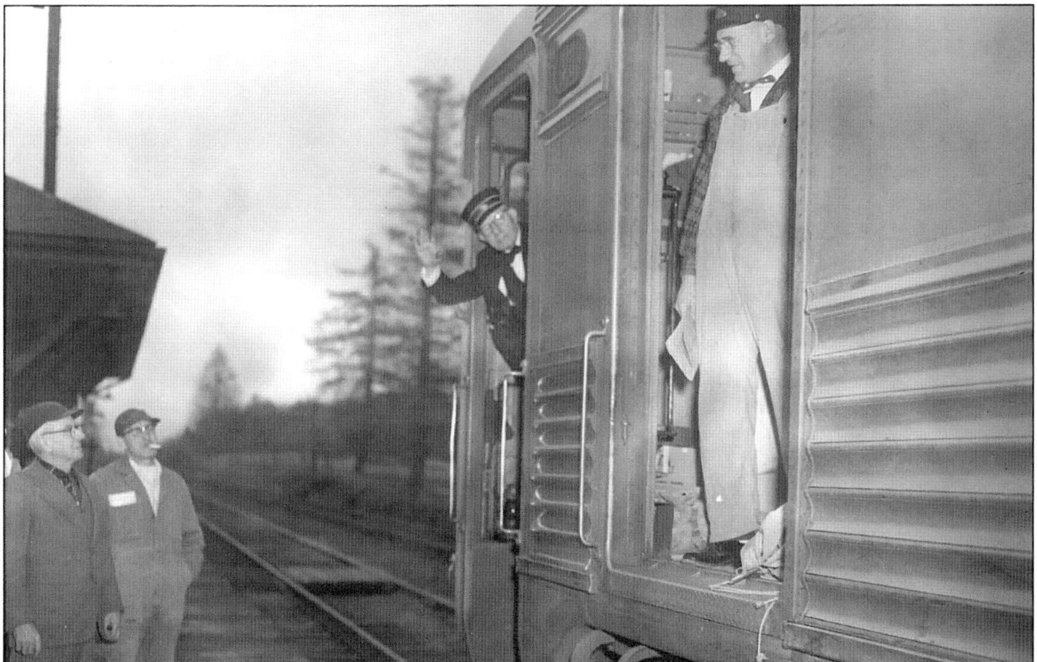

This December 1956 view of Plaistow Depot shows Joseph B. Dupras (left), the station agent, and Ken Senter (right), who brought mail to the depot. (PHS.)

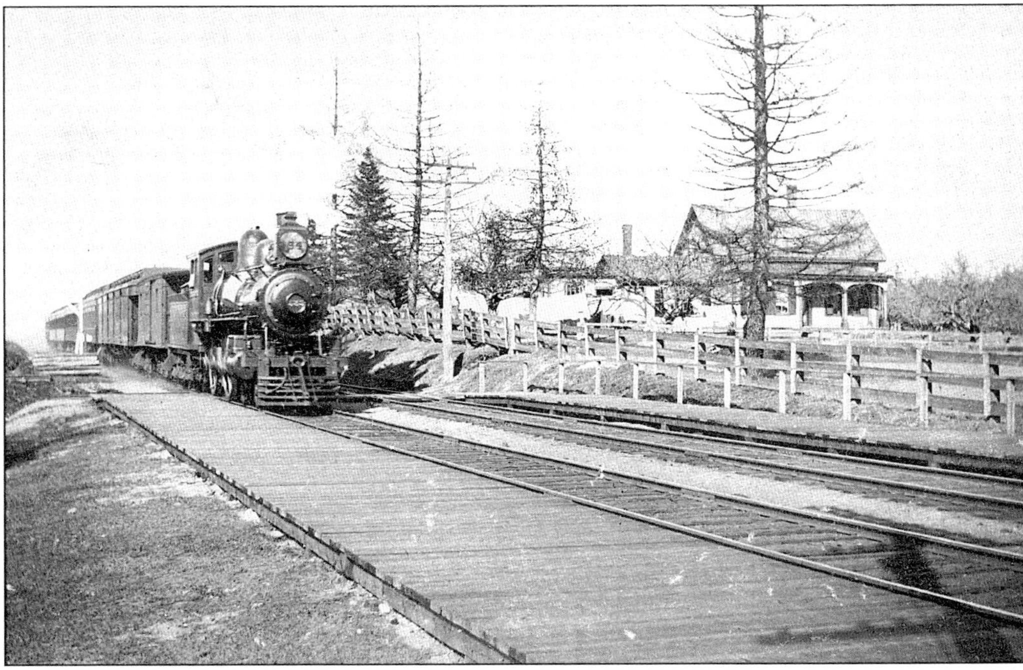

The Portland Express heads southbound through the village in April 1895. The trees at right are larches, a deciduous conifer that the Hills family sowed throughout town. (PF.)

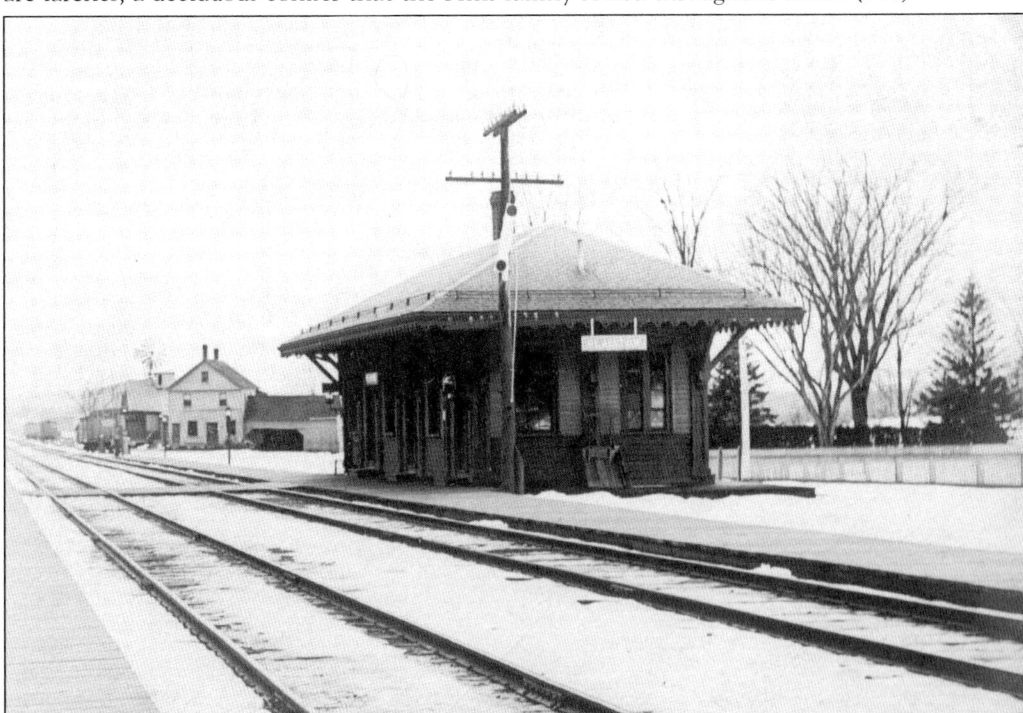

This view was taken looking west at the Plaistow railroad station and landing. The building was later used as a meeting place for the town's Boy Scouts and is currently the property of J. Alden Palmer. In the background are John Sleeper's store and stable. (PHS.)

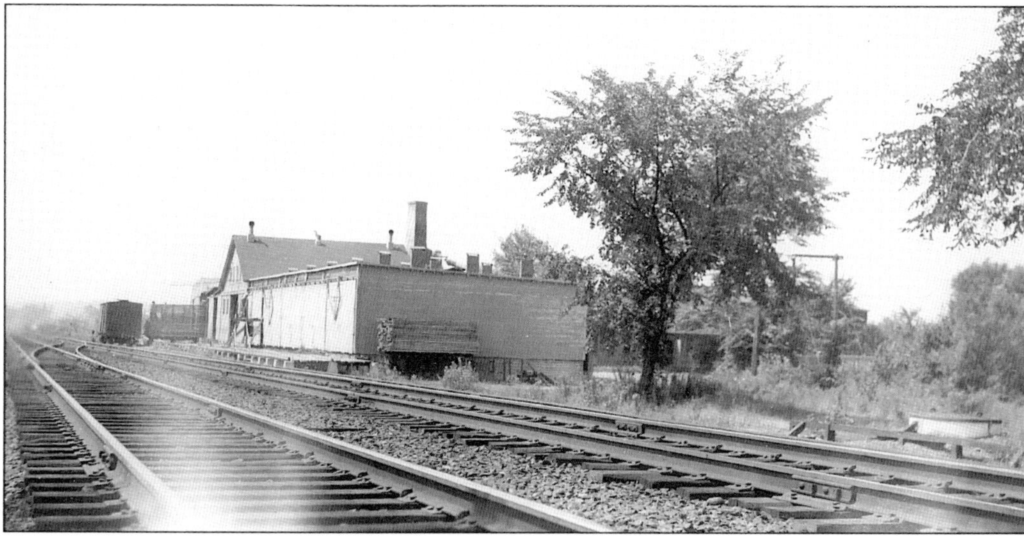

The Russell Wood Heel Company, located near the present Process Engineering plant, is shown c. 1936. Originally known as Goldbaum's Wood Heel, the company had a whistle that was used as a fire alarm. The building was later the site of the PA Box Company, before being abandoned. The structure was demolished near the end of the 20th century. (PHS.)

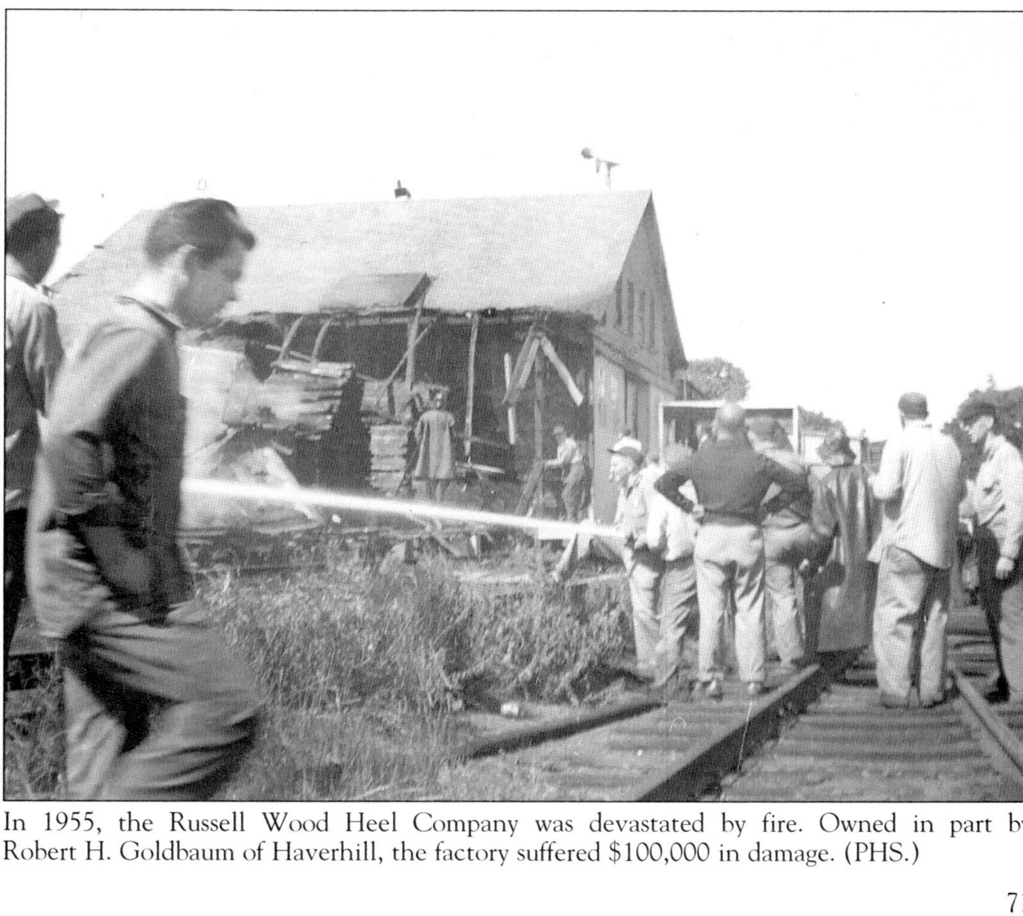

In 1955, the Russell Wood Heel Company was devastated by fire. Owned in part by Robert H. Goldbaum of Haverhill, the factory suffered $100,000 in damage. (PHS.)

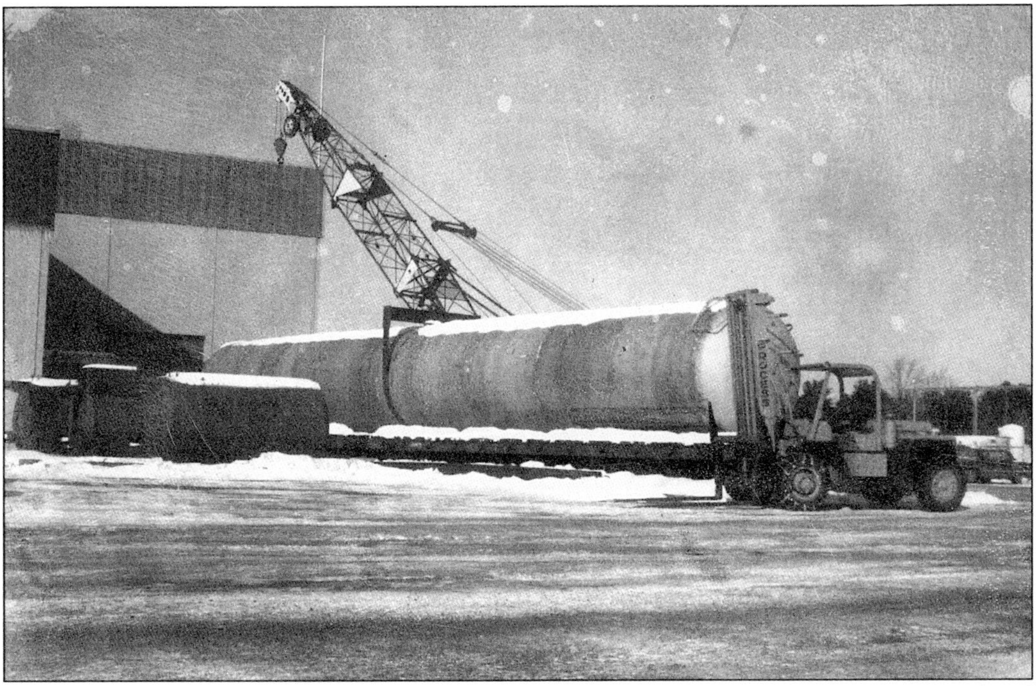

A milestone in Plaistow's industrial history came in 1968 with shipment of the first completed tank produced at Process Engineering. (PHS.)

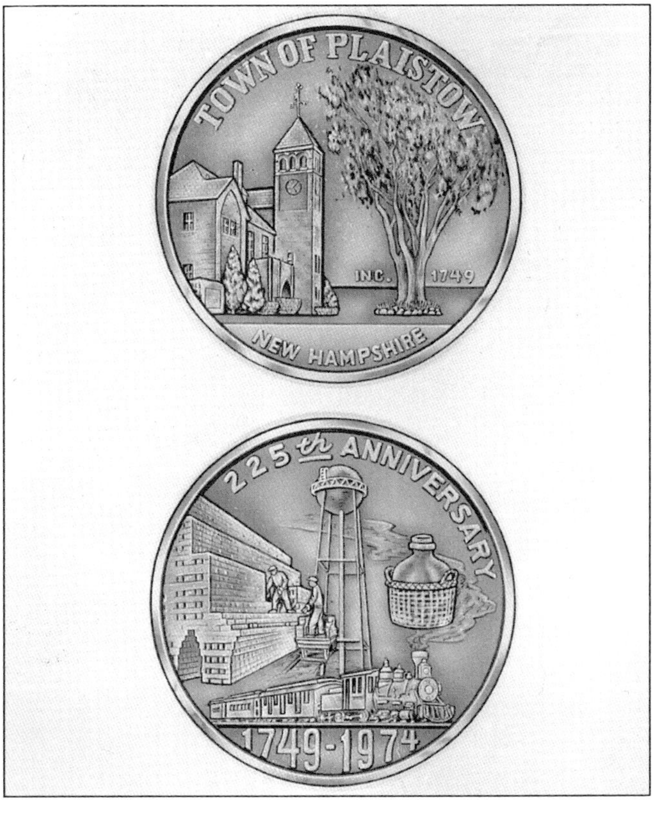

To celebrate the town's 225th anniversary, the town created this design to commemorate Plaistow's industrial heritage. The design was minted as a limited-edition coin. On the reverse side, it pays homage to the community's notoriety as a 19th-century brick-making center, recognizes the importance of the railroad in the development of the town, and celebrates the arrival of Process Engineering. The bottle signifies the contributions of the Wentworth bottling company of Atkinson Depot, which marketed the Hi-Brow line of soft drinks. (PHS.)

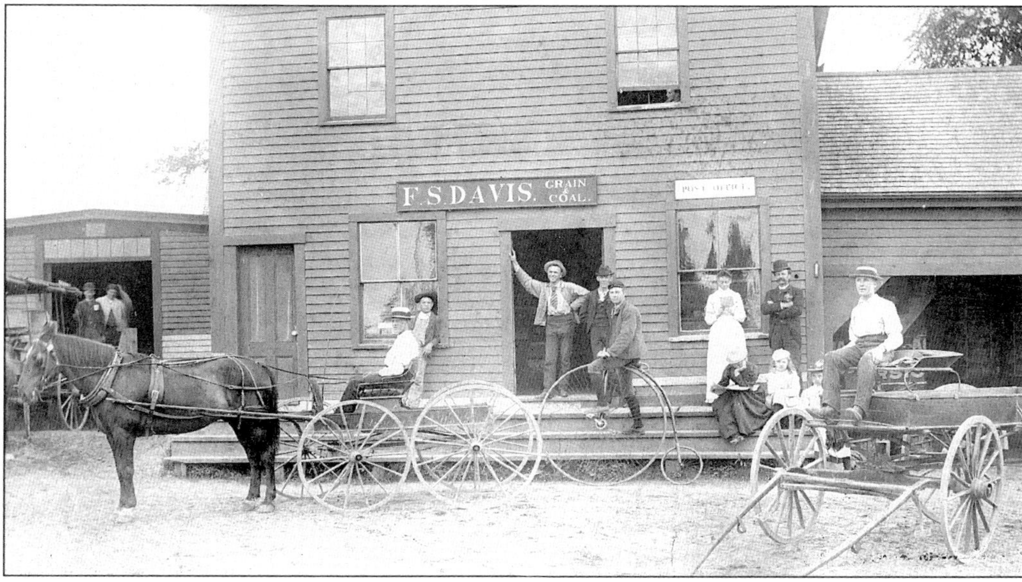

Forrest S. Davis stands in the doorway of the Forrest S. Davis Grain & Coal store and post office in late 1800s. The shop, later owned by John W. Sleeper, was located on the north side of the tracks near the present entrance to Process Engineering. (PHS.)

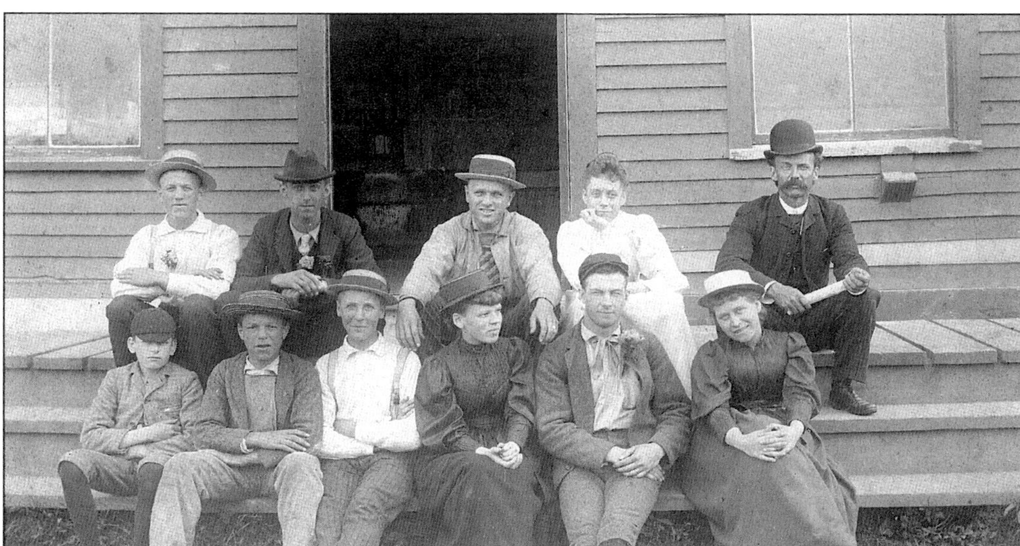

In front of Forrest Davis's store in the 1890s are Maude Sleeper (front row, center) and Forrest Davis (second row, center). Davis, born in 1867, got his first job in a Haverhill shoe shop. He prospered as a financier and as a raiser of Rhode Island Red chickens in Plaistow. He was appointed constable in 1893 and made chief of police in 1903. (PHS.)

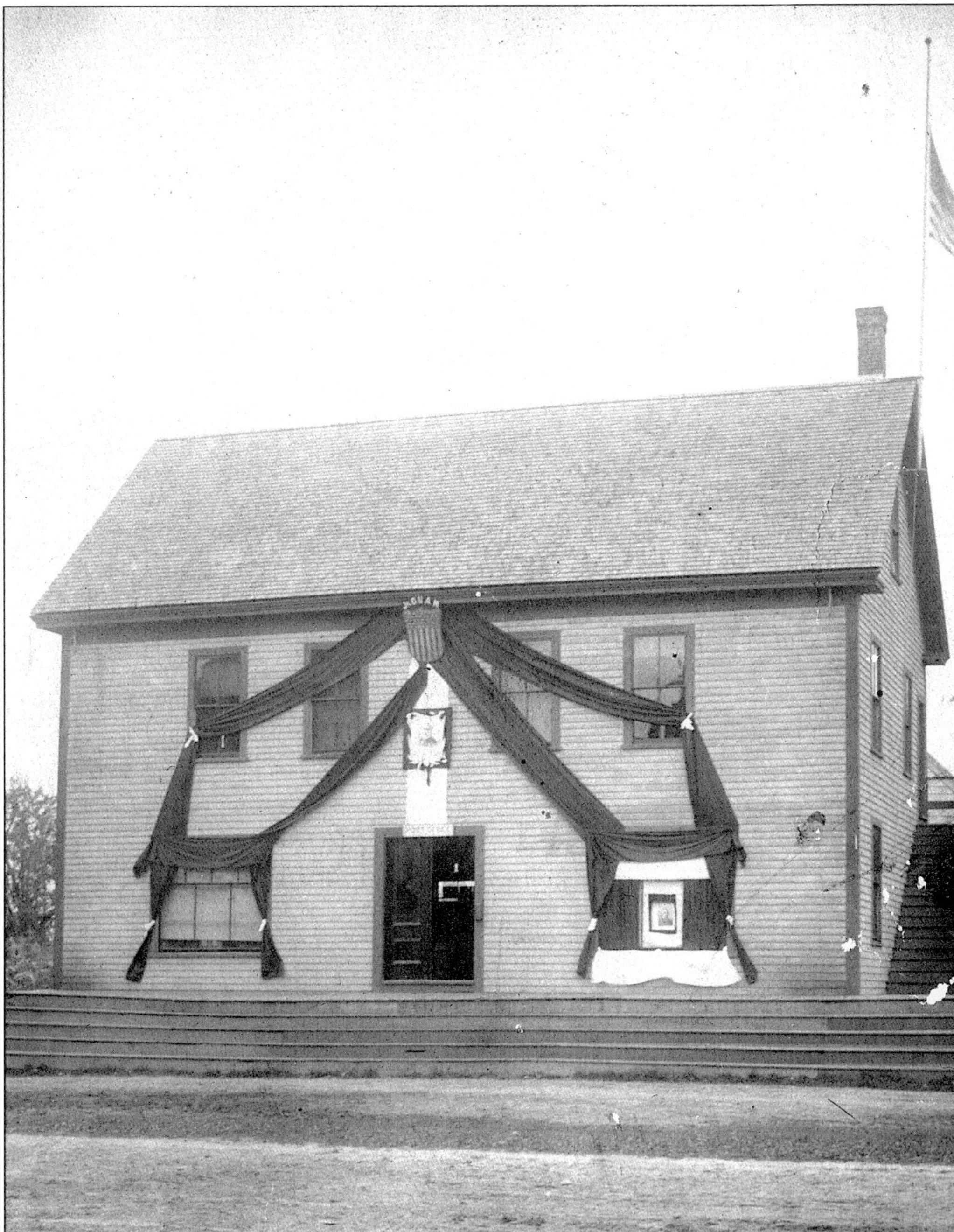

Sleeper's store and post office was draped in flags of mourning following the assassination of Pres. William McKinley in September 1901. Note the flag at half-staff. At this time, the location of post offices was determined by the political party in power, because postmasters were politically appointed employees. This was, therefore, the location of just one of many post offices in Plaistow prior to the 1940s. The grandeur of this display of mourning might betray the political loyalties of the store's proprietor. The shield shown here bears the logo of the Junior Order of United American Mechanics. (PHS.)

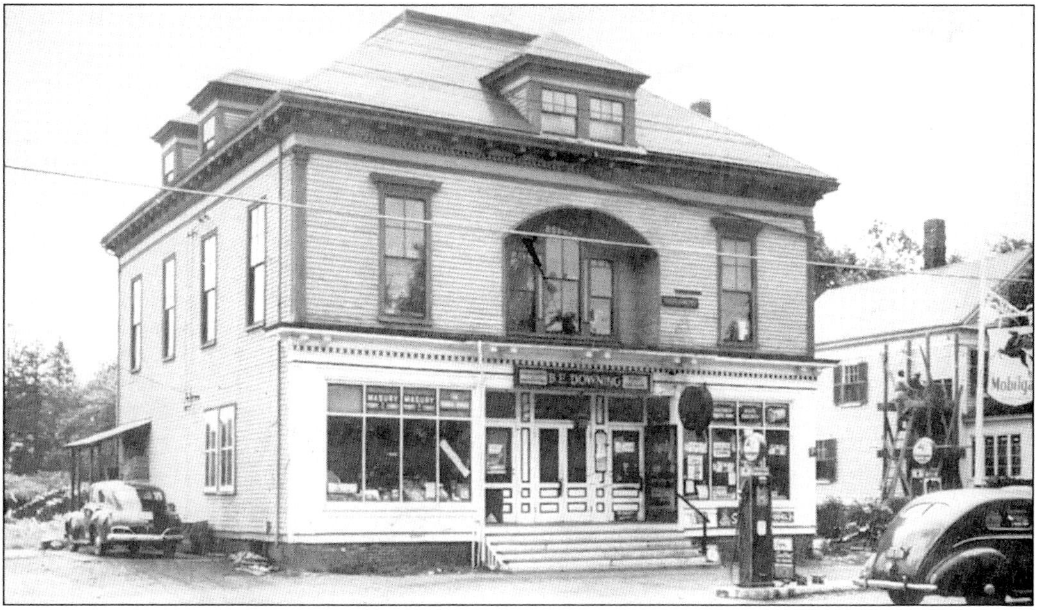

Downing's Store was located in the old Knights of Pythias building, built in 1898; this image dates from *c.* 1945 to 1950. (PHS.)

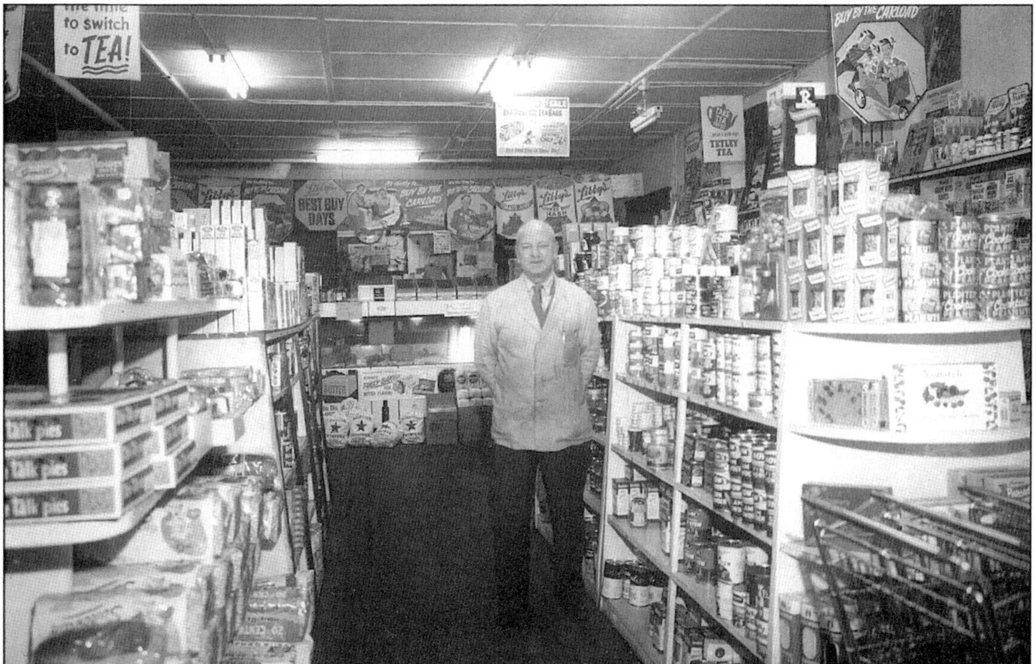

Byron E. Downing Sr., proprietor of Downing's Store, is shown here *c.* 1941. (PHS.)

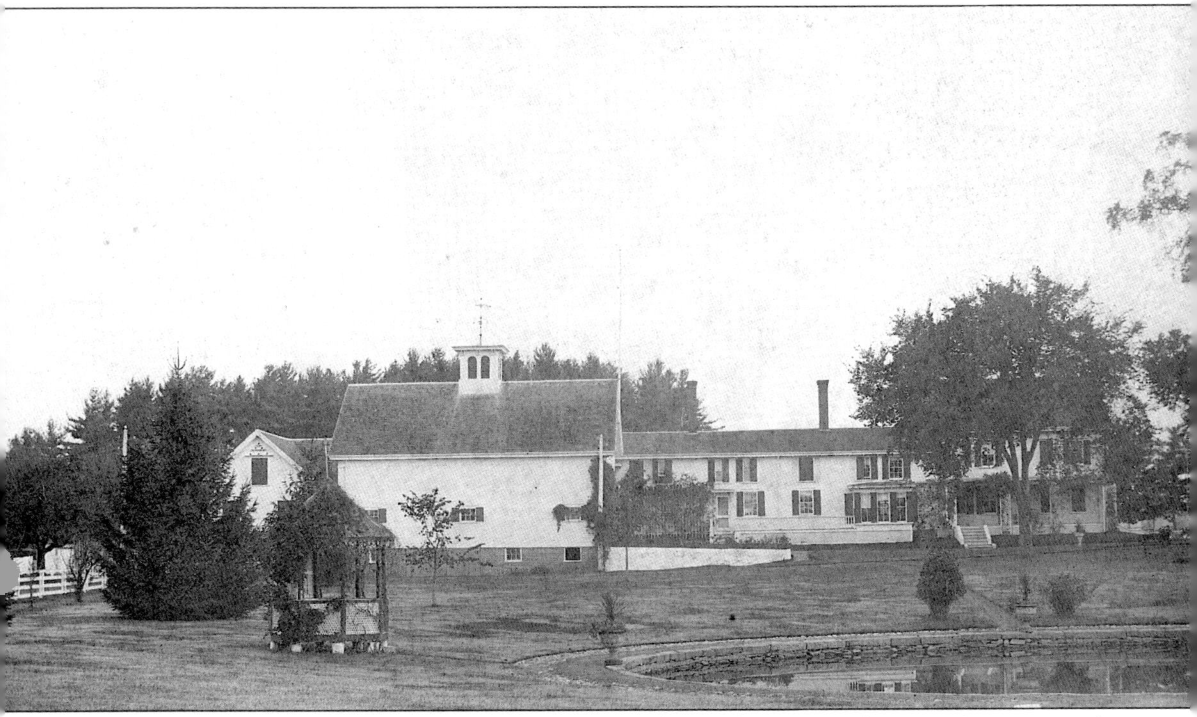

This classic "connected house," located just over the tracks on North Main Street, was the home of railroad executive James Newall George. After authorizing the construction of a depot in the town's western village, George coined the name Westville. The fire department later used George's reflecting pond to fill its hand pump. This was later the home of Dr. Elbert A. Landman. (PHS.)

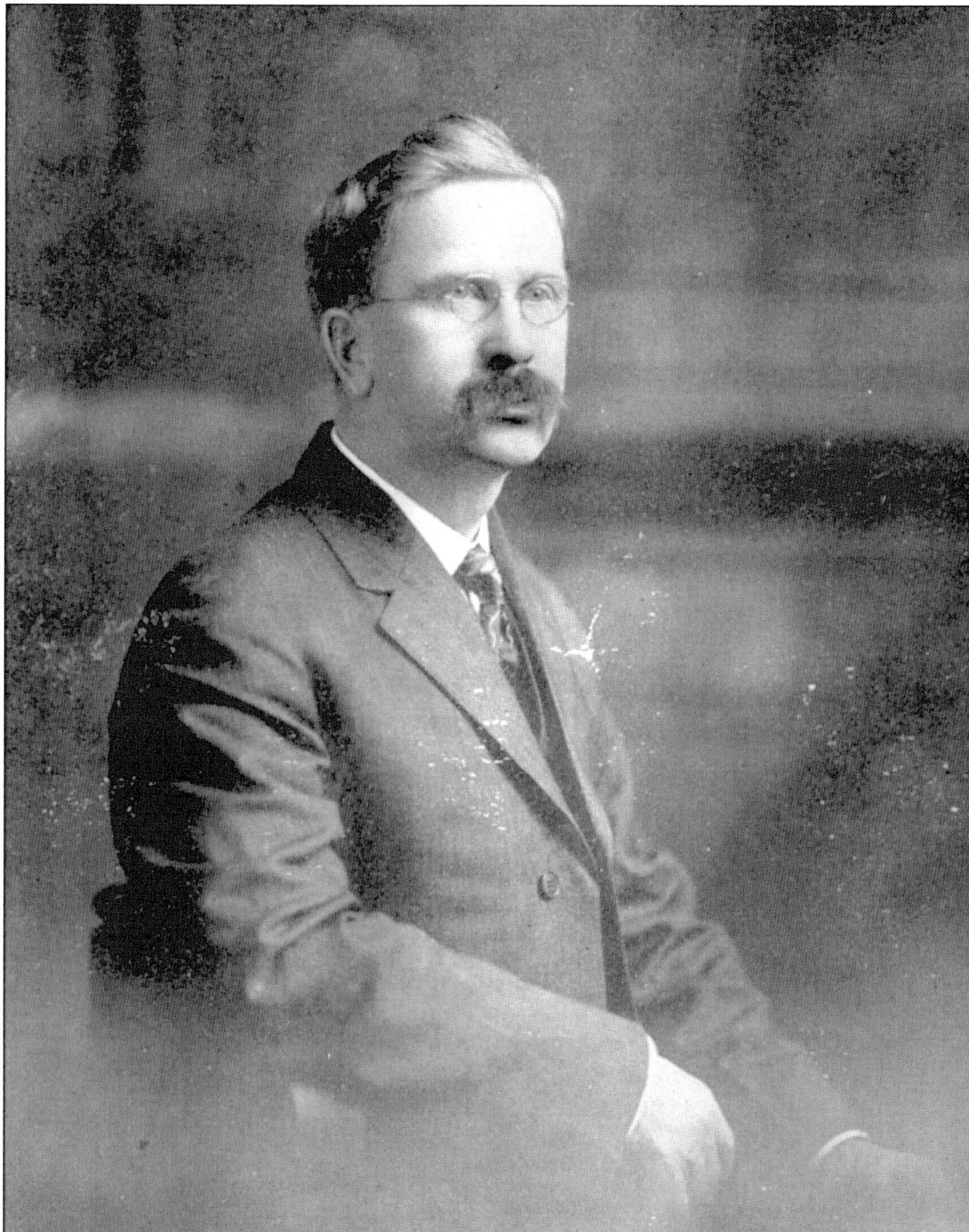

Elbert A. Landman, M.D., was born in Londonderry, Vermont, in 1867. After graduating from Dartmouth in 1899, he practiced medicine for five years in Danville before coming to Plaistow in 1904. Landman cofounded the Plaistow Electric Company in 1911 and served as its president. He made emergency house calls—medical and electrical—in a "snowcat" that allowed him to fulfill his duties even in the worst winter weather. (NHHS.)

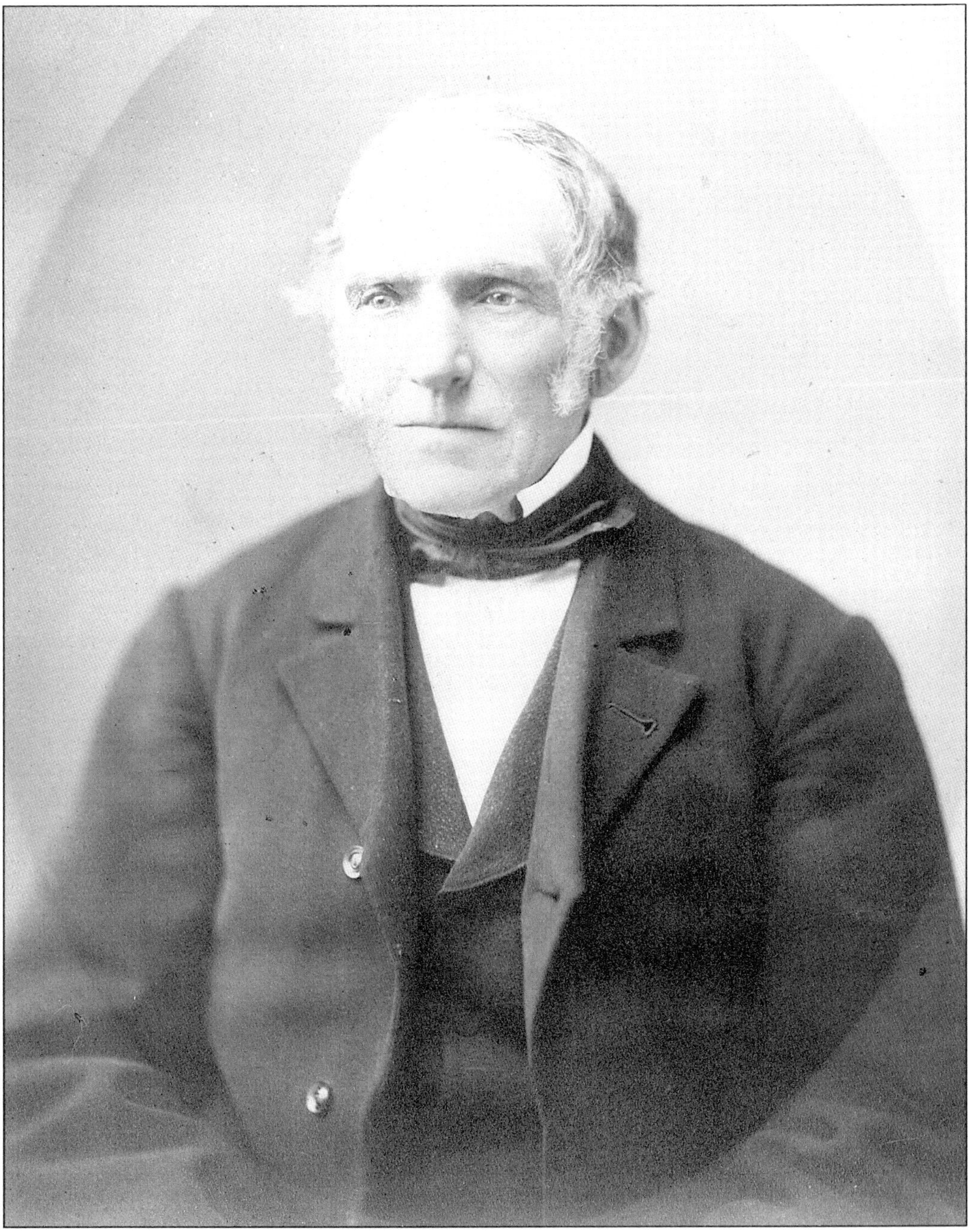

John Greenough George (1798–1871) was born in Kingston. He set up housekeeping with his wife, Rebecca P. George, in the George-Thompson House, next door to the old Palmer place, on North Main Street. George at one time lived on Crane Crossing Road on land that was originally part of Kingston but was later annexed by Plaistow. He also owned property in Vermont. He was the father of James Newall George, who in the mid-1800s lived across the way from his parents. (HPL.)

Rebecca P. George (1804–1879) was the wife of James Greenough George and the mother of James Newall George. (HPL.)

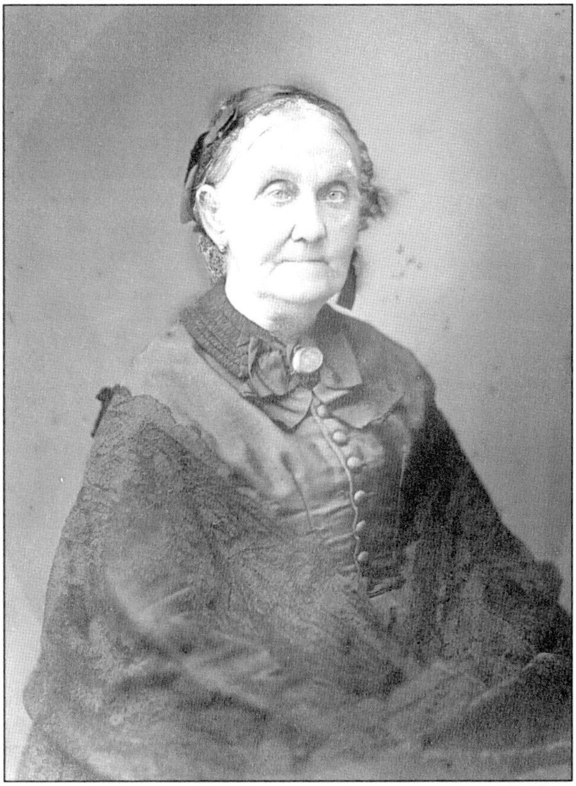

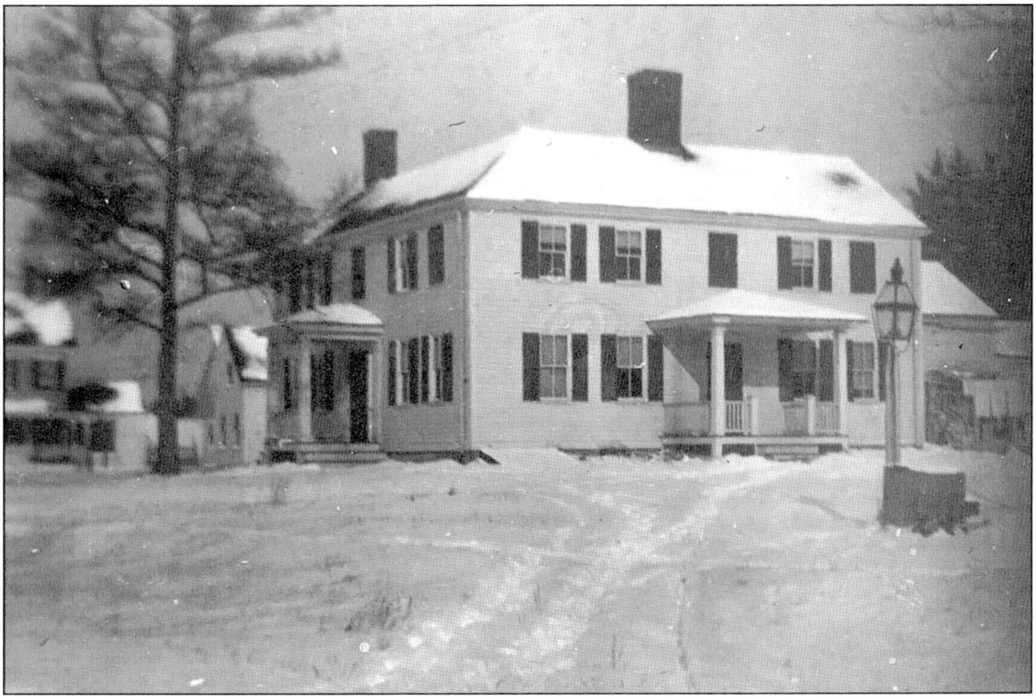

The George-Thompson House, on North Main Street, was the boyhood home of James Newall George and the birthplace of Stella M.G. Thompson. (HPL.)

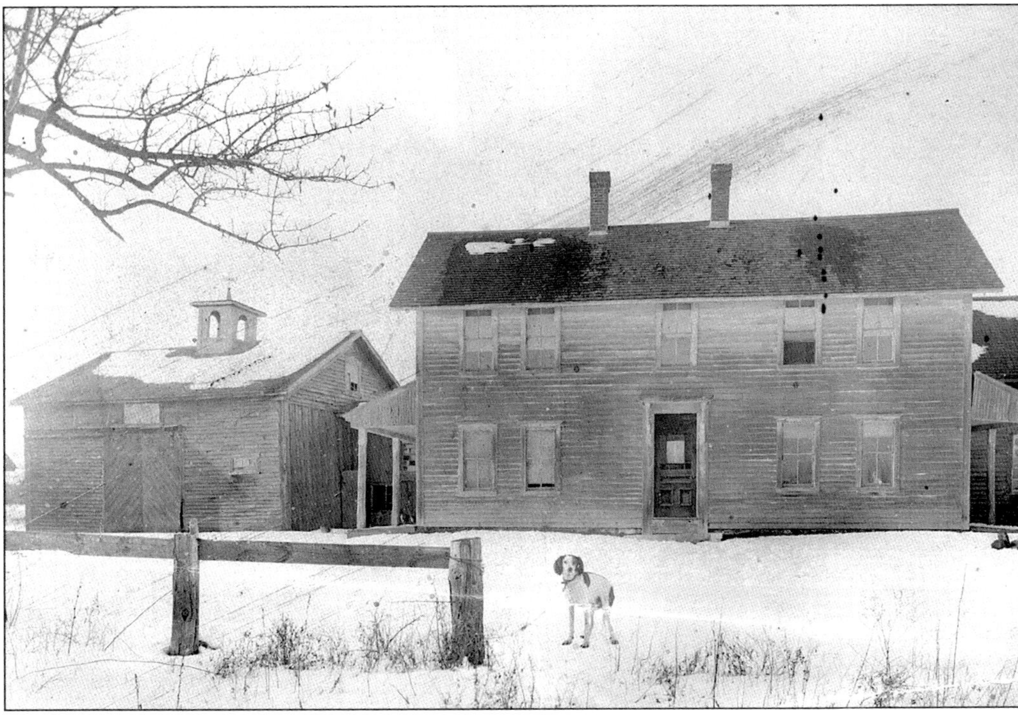

The oldest part of this house, located at the corner of Jesse George Road and Main Street, was built *c*. 1725 by Reuben Peaslee and Bartholemew Heath. In the 1800s, it was the home of Jesse George, Plaistow's best-known Civil War veteran. Now demolished, the house is said to have been a stop on the Underground Railroad. (PHS.)

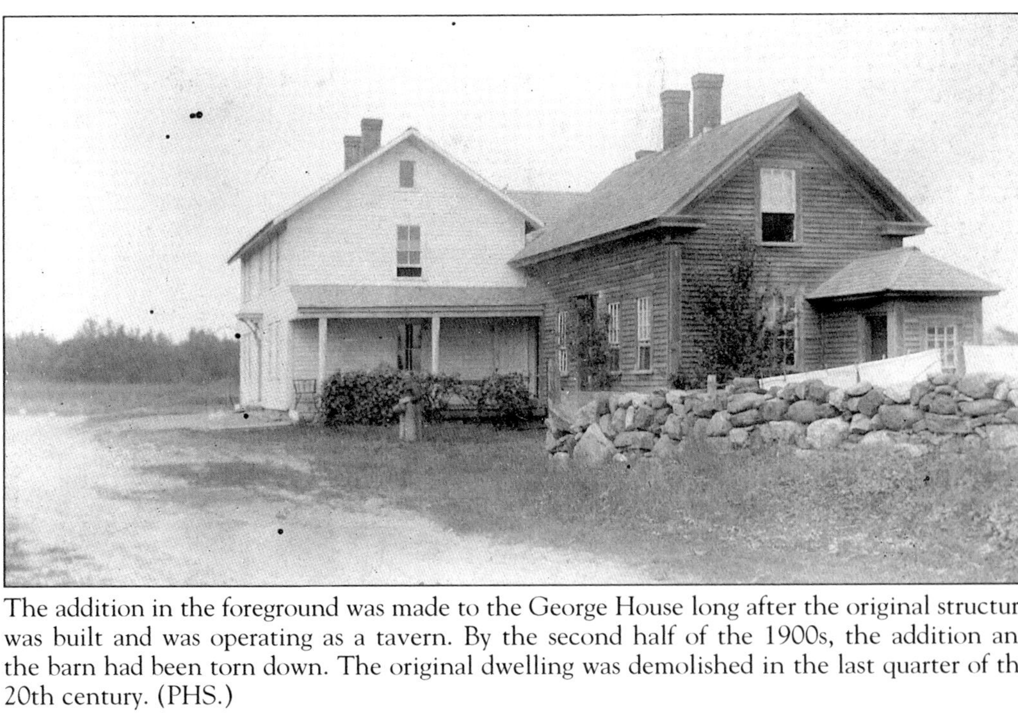

The addition in the foreground was made to the George House long after the original structure was built and was operating as a tavern. By the second half of the 1900s, the addition and the barn had been torn down. The original dwelling was demolished in the last quarter of the 20th century. (PHS.)

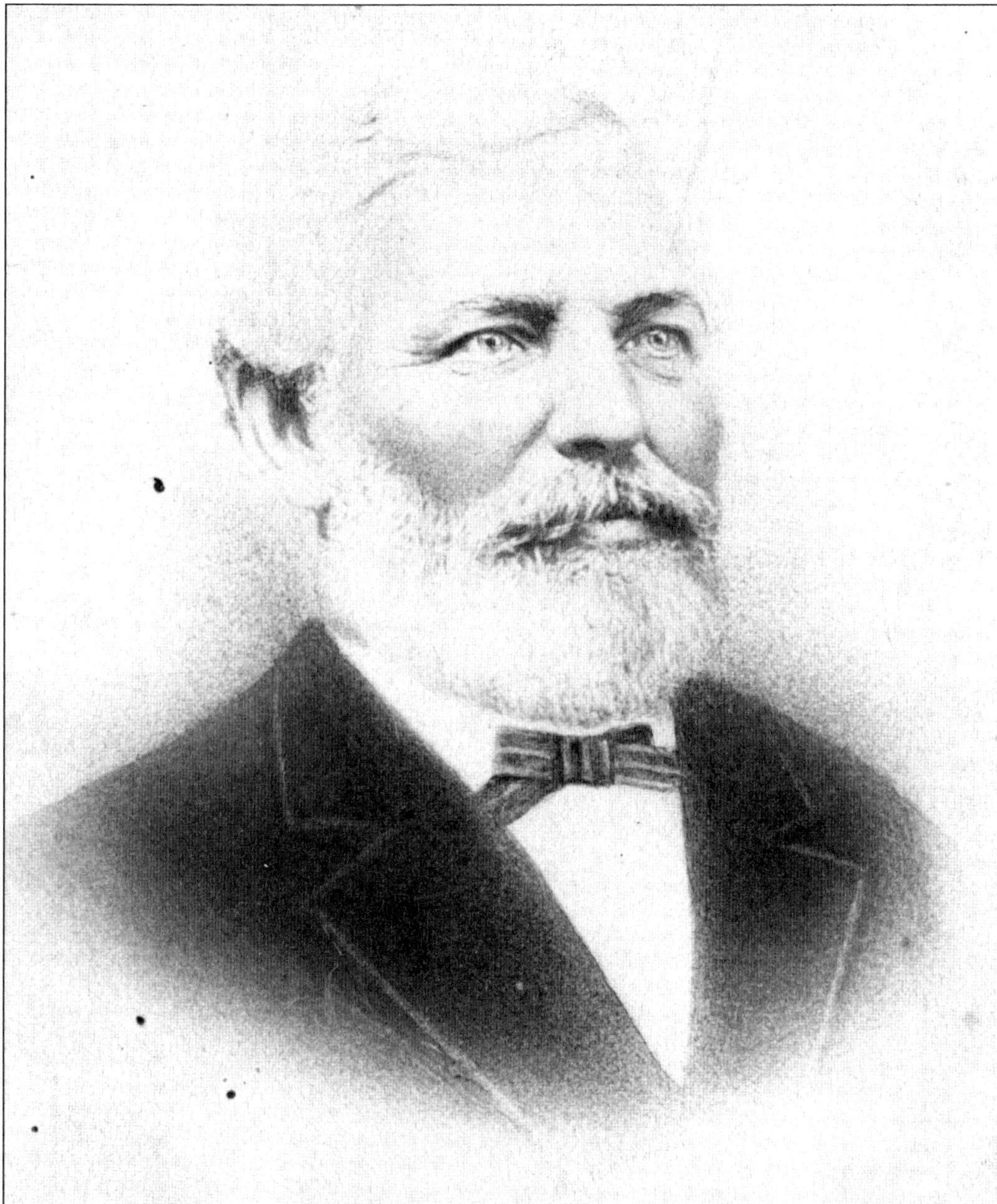

Greenleaf C. George, brother of Jesse George, left Plaistow for Mount Morris, New York, during the 1820s. In a letter dated June 16, 1829, he discussed his recovery from a bout with "the billous fever." Greenleaf George also mentioned the Freemason murders that caused a national scandal in 1826, when William Morgan mysteriously disappeared after purporting to divulge Masonic secrets. Greenleaf recounted that two suspected murderers were convicted and a third was exonerated. (PHS.)

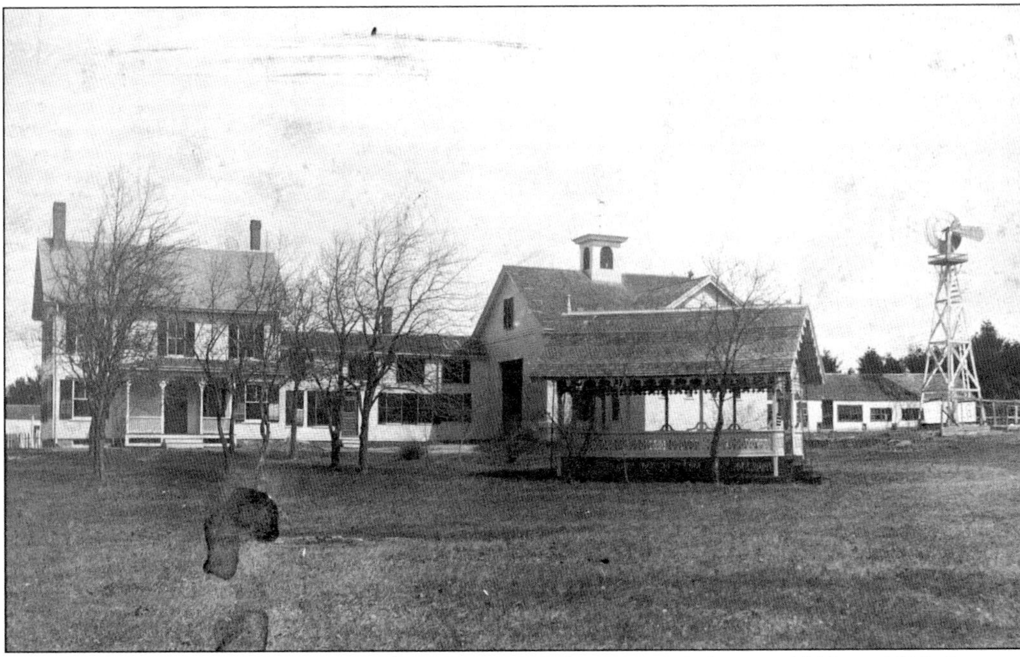

This view of the Palmer Homestead, at 159 Main Street, was taken *c.* 1910 to 1920. Located on the northeast side of the railroad tracks, this connected farmhouse drew water from its well by means of a windmill. In the foreground is the summerhouse. (PF.)

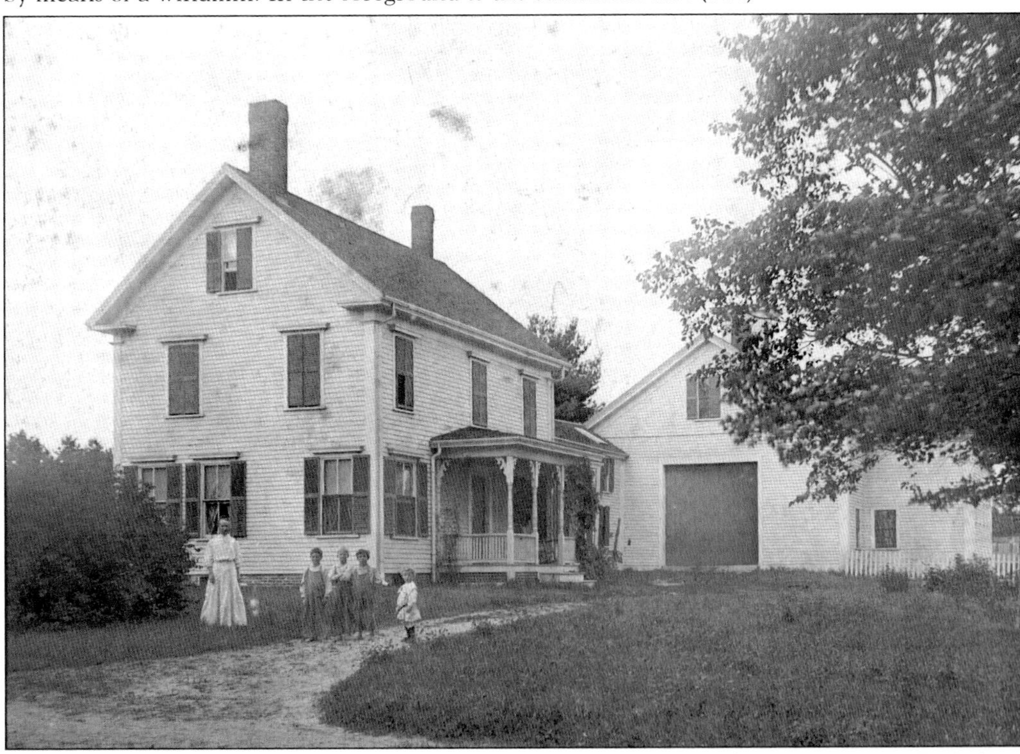

Pictured, from left to right, in this *c.* 1912 view of the Palmer place are Marnie T. Palmer, unidentified, Kelsie Landman, Paul D. Palmer, and John A. Palmer. (PF.)

This structure, at the rear of the old Paul Palmer house on North Main Street, was a short distance from the train station. It housed machinery that carried electricity across the tracks to power streetcars. (PHS.)

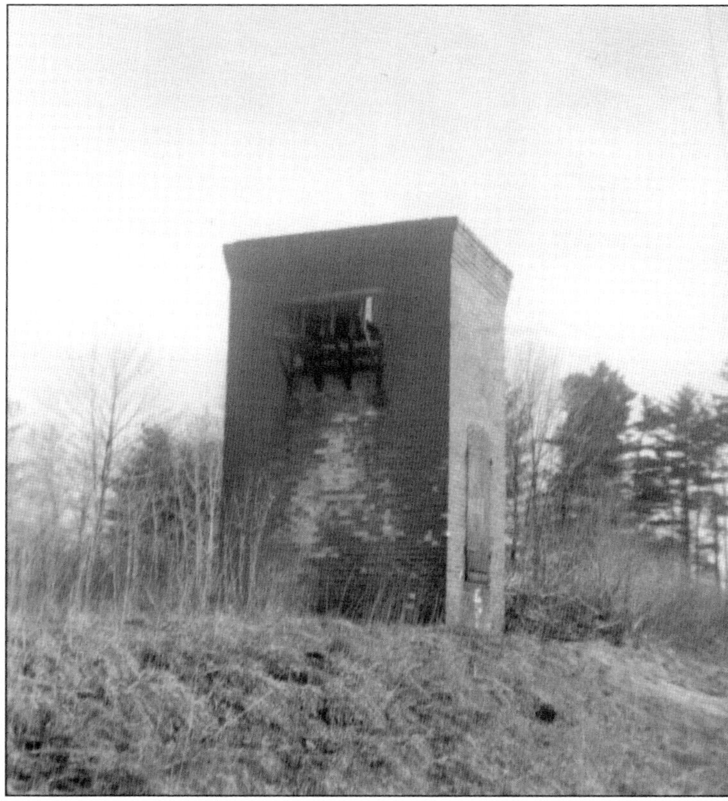

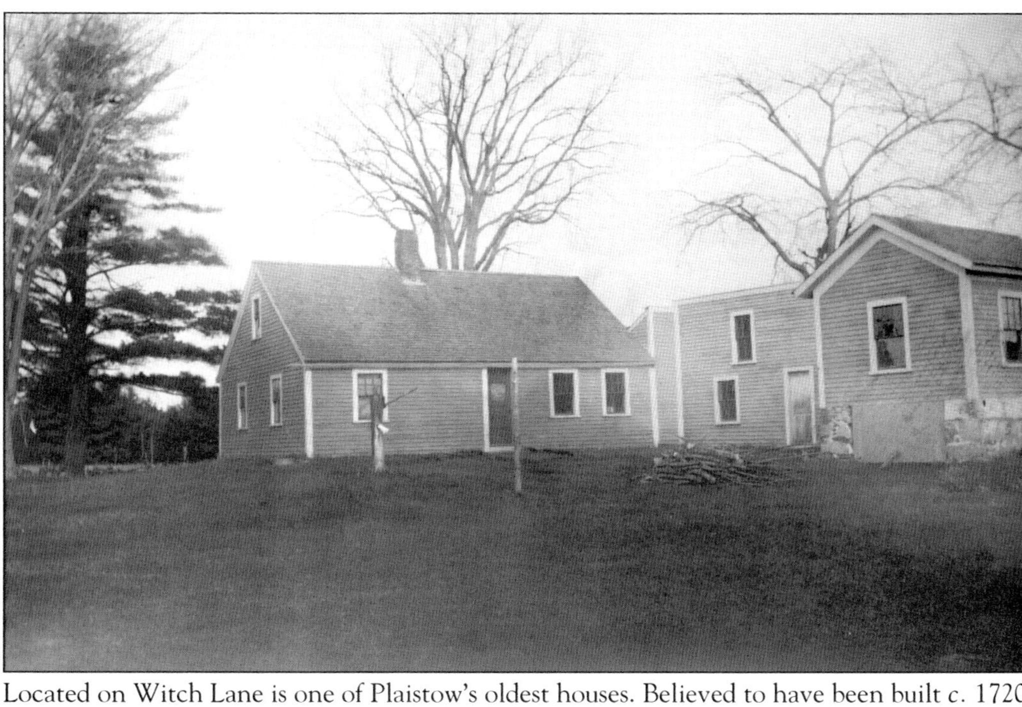

Located on Witch Lane is one of Plaistow's oldest houses. Believed to have been built *c.* 1720, this Cape has been the home of the Sargent, the Williams, and the Ingalls families. (PHS.)

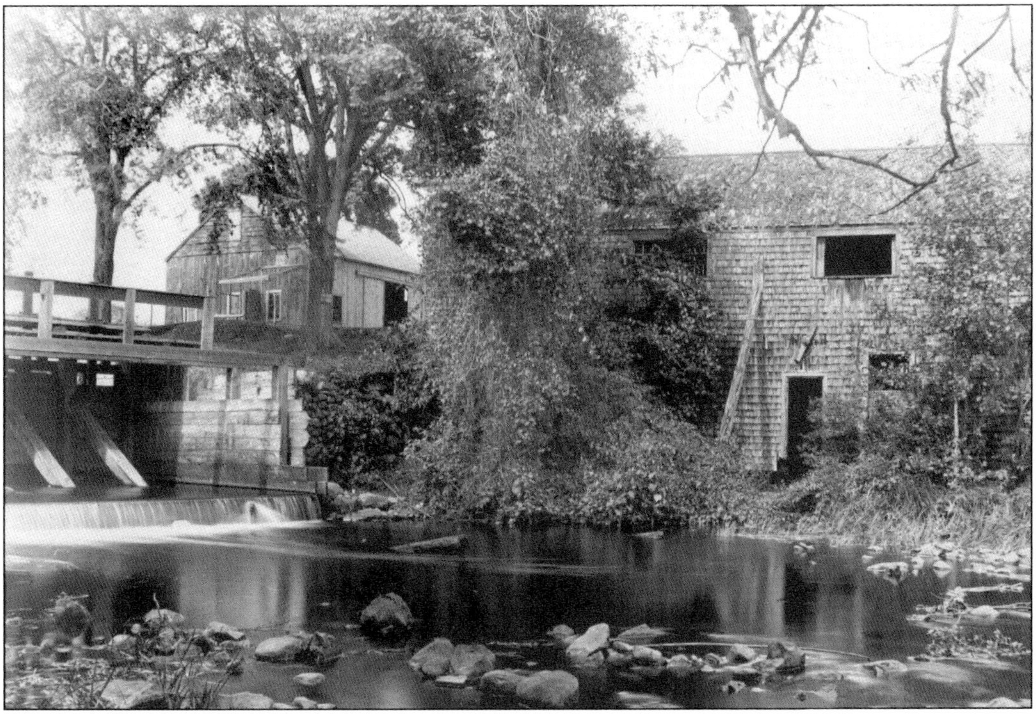

Pollard Mill, shown here in the late 1800s, was powered by a millpond created on Pollard Brook. (PHS.)

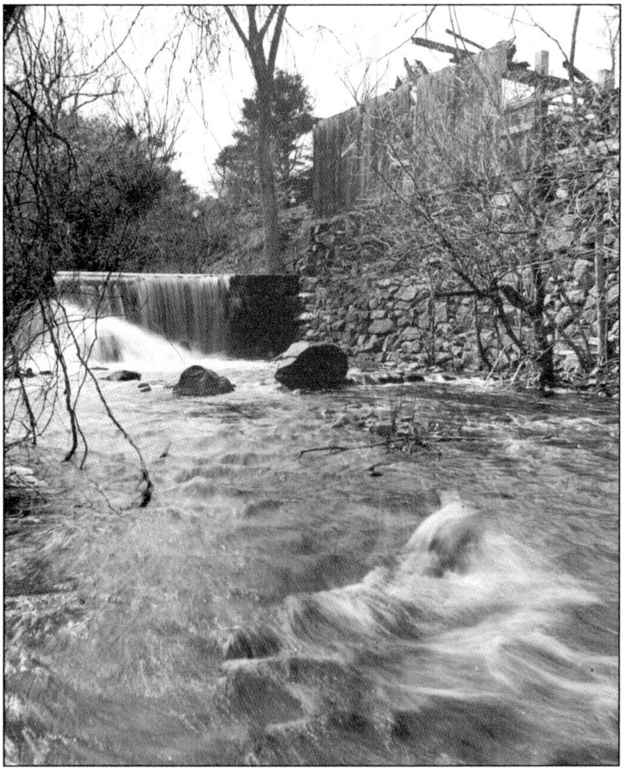

The old Pollard dam is the subject of this image, which also shows the remnants of an earlier mill. The first step in preparing a waterpower site for a mill was to dam a portion of a river to create a steady supply of water to turn the mill's machinery.

Six

WESTVILLE

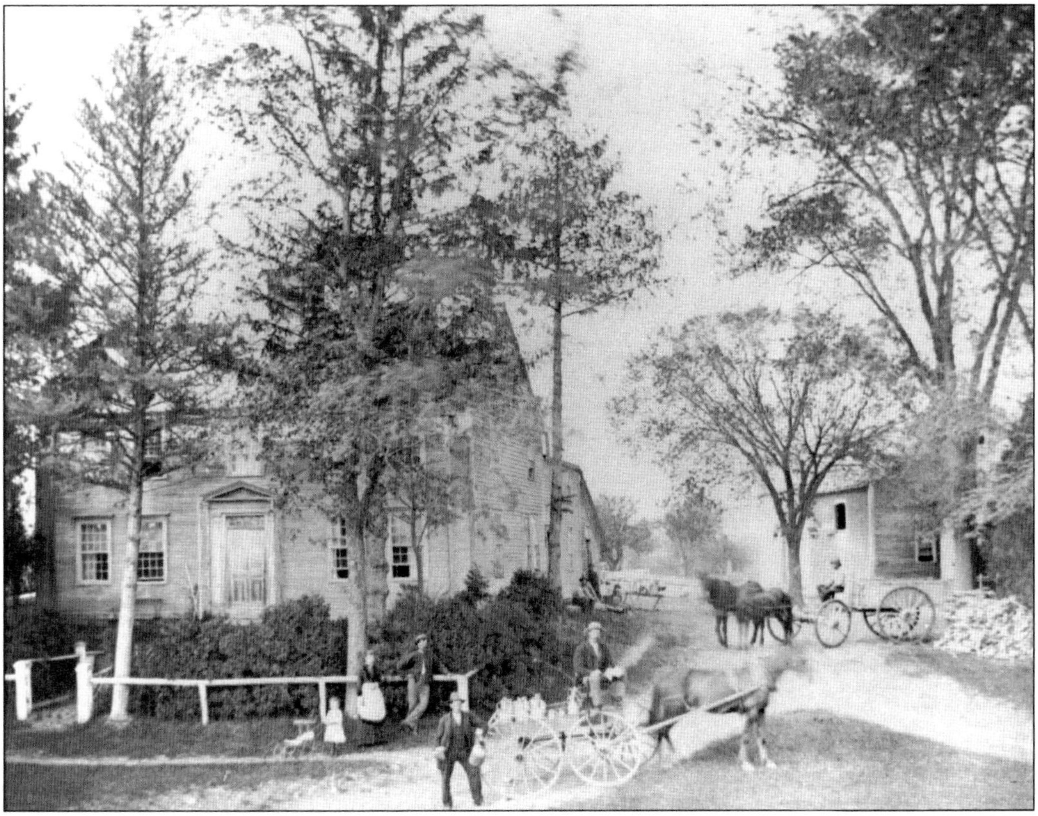

This dwelling, locally known as the Old Welch House, is shown here *c.* 1879. Located on Danville Road near the Pine Street intersection behind the Plaistow Co-op Bank, this house was erected *c.* 1735, making it the oldest surviving structure in Westville. In 1944, it was purchased and restored by Mr. and Mrs. Fred D. Smith. (PHS.)

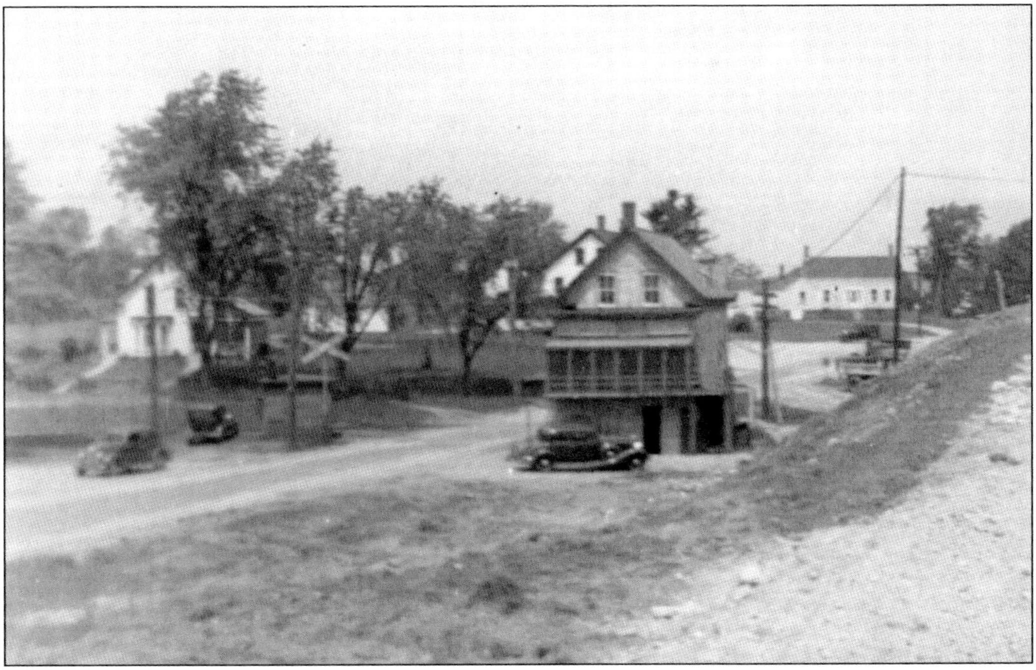

This *c.* 1930 view shows the Westville overpass between the present Wal-Mart and Dunkin' Donuts, and Fecteau's Store (center). Note the railroad crossing, which has since been reconfigured. (PHS.)

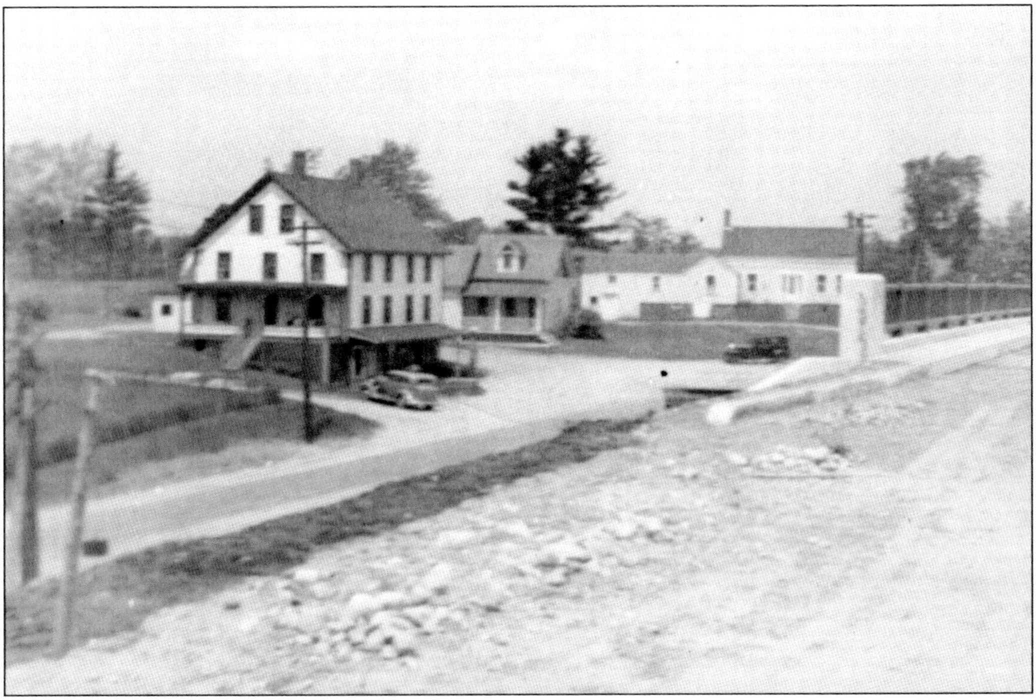

This slightly later view of the same location shows that Fecteau's Store was demolished to make room for an expanded New Deal–era bridge spanning the railroad tracks. This bridge was widened in the 1980s. (PHS.)

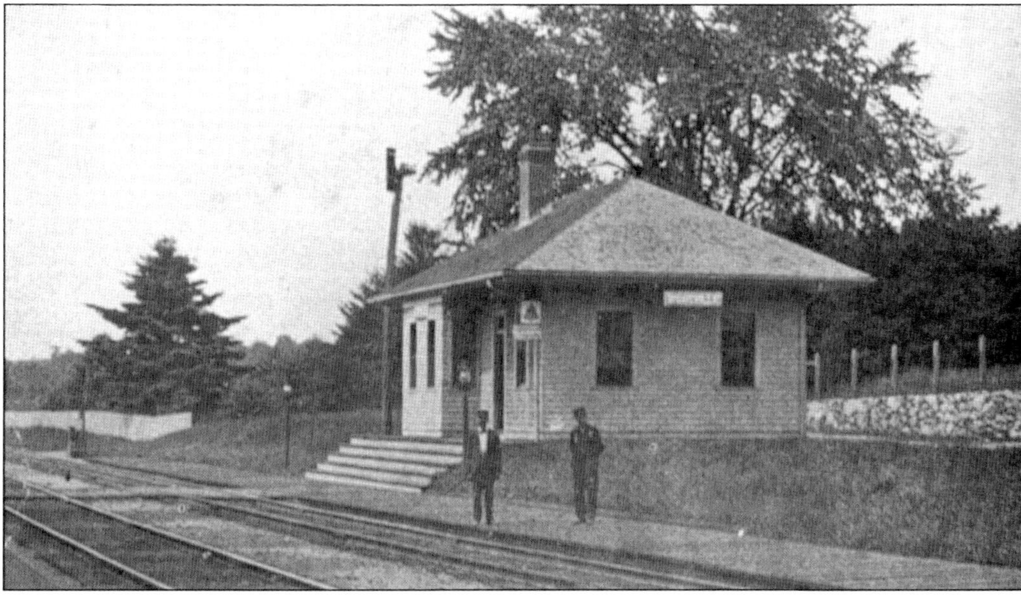

Here is Westville Depot *c.* the 1920s. Built and named by James Newall George, a railroad executive who lived in Plaistow Village, the depot was the center of Westville's activity. Daniel J. Kelleher (left) assumed the position of station agent upon the death of his brother, Gerry Kelleher. (CYR.)

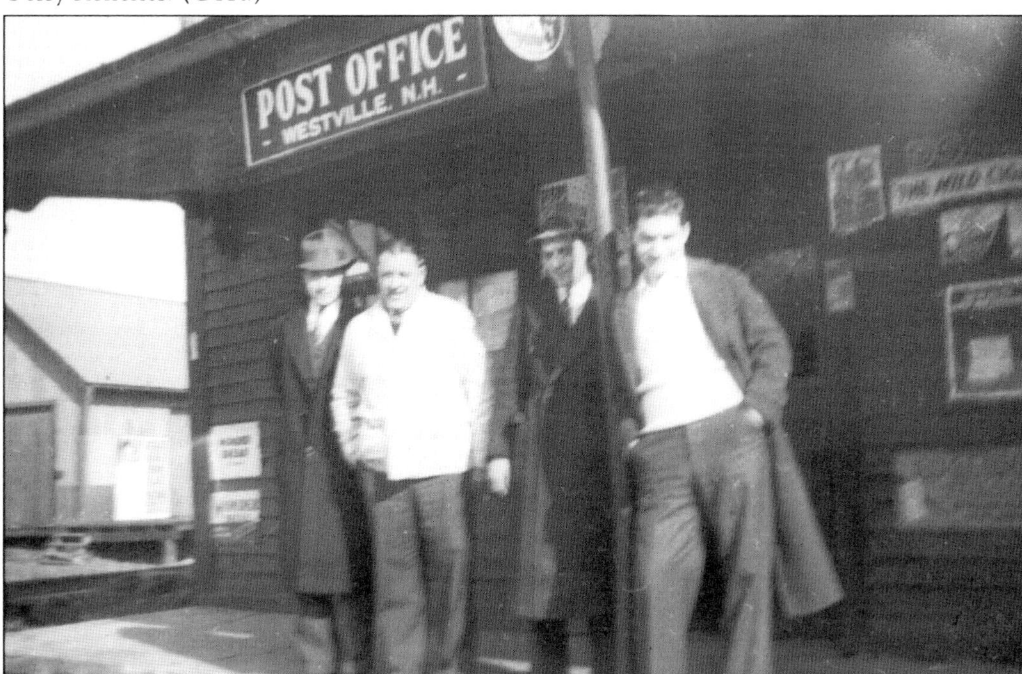

This view of Fecteau's Store, in Westville Depot, was taken *c.* the 1920s. Theodore Fecteau, born in St. Hycinthe, Quebec, came to Plaistow at the age of 12 with his father, also named Theodore Fecteau, a brick maker. Young Theodore operated this store and post office in the early 1900s. He sold the establishment *c.* 1920 to Mike Guard, who is shown here, second from the left. (CYR.)

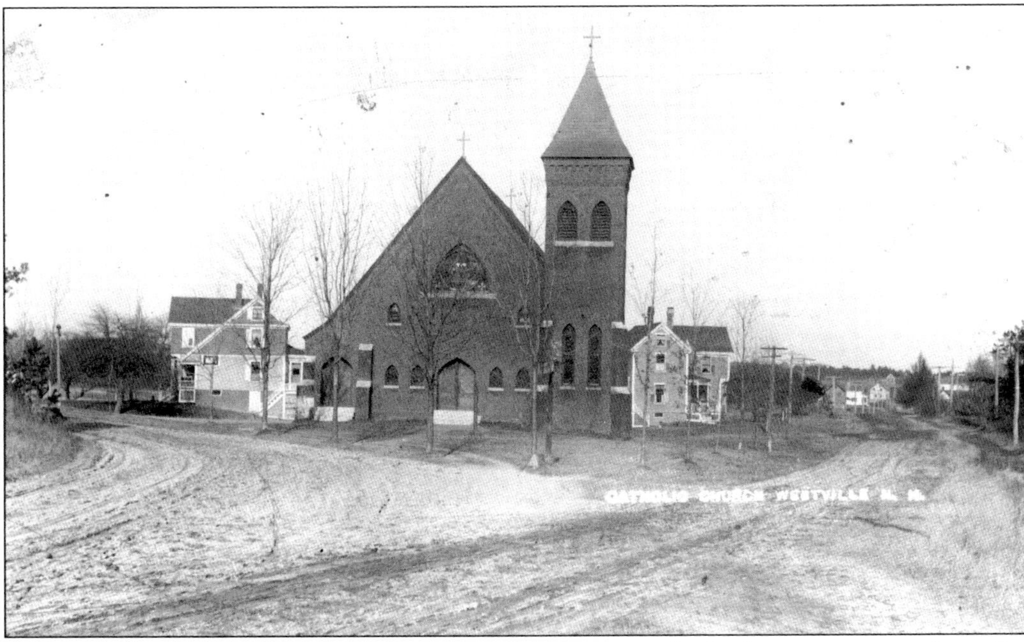

Holy Angels Church, shown here *c.* 1900 to 1914, was established in response to the influx of Roman Catholic French Canadians coming to Westville in the late 1800s to work in area brickyards. The New Hampshire Diocese in Manchester created a Westville parish in 1892 and appointed D. Alexander Sullivan as the church's first pastor; the church was dedicated in 1894. (PHS.)

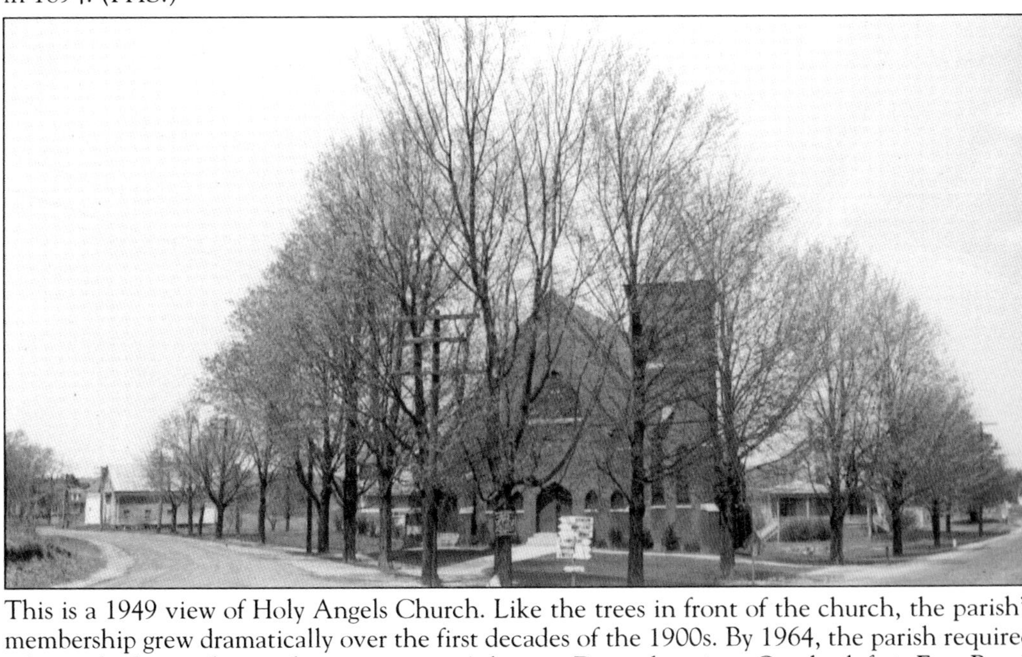

This is a 1949 view of Holy Angels Church. Like the trees in front of the church, the parish's membership grew dramatically over the first decades of the 1900s. By 1964, the parish required a larger facility and moved to its present Atkinson Depot location. On the left is East Road. On the right is the present Route 125, then known as "the Speedway;" although still a straight shot north, by virtue of thick traffic lights and an abundance of cars, Route 125 is now anything but a speedway. (PHS.)

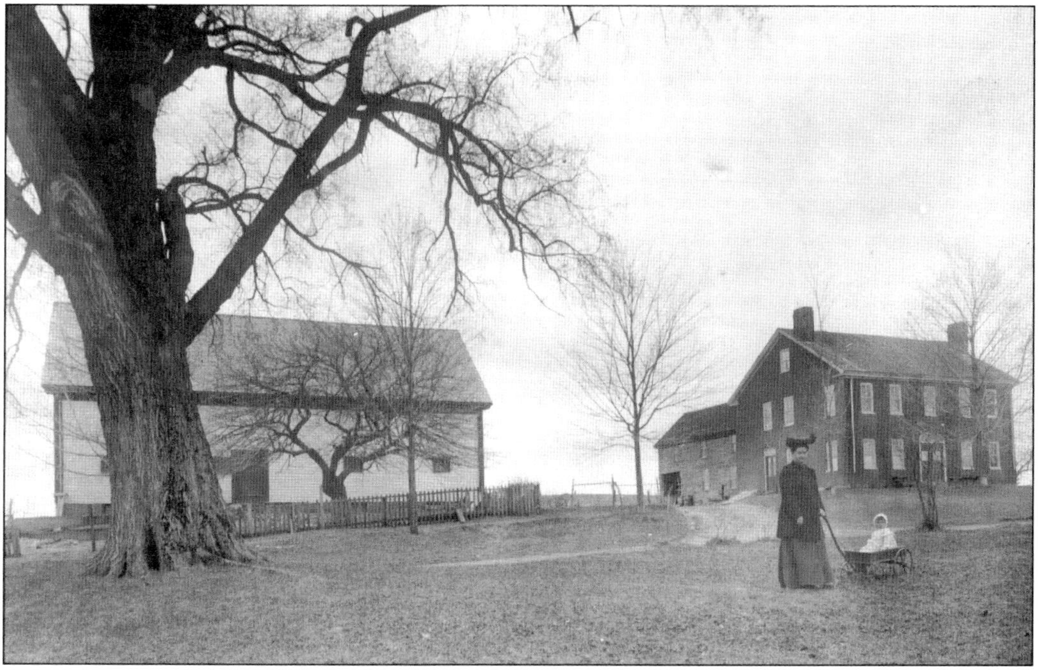

The Veroneau Farm, shown here *c.* 1900, is located on East Road, just to the south of the Holy Angels Cemetery. It was built probably in the mid-1800s. Prior to this, the farm was the property of the Brunelle family. (KV.)

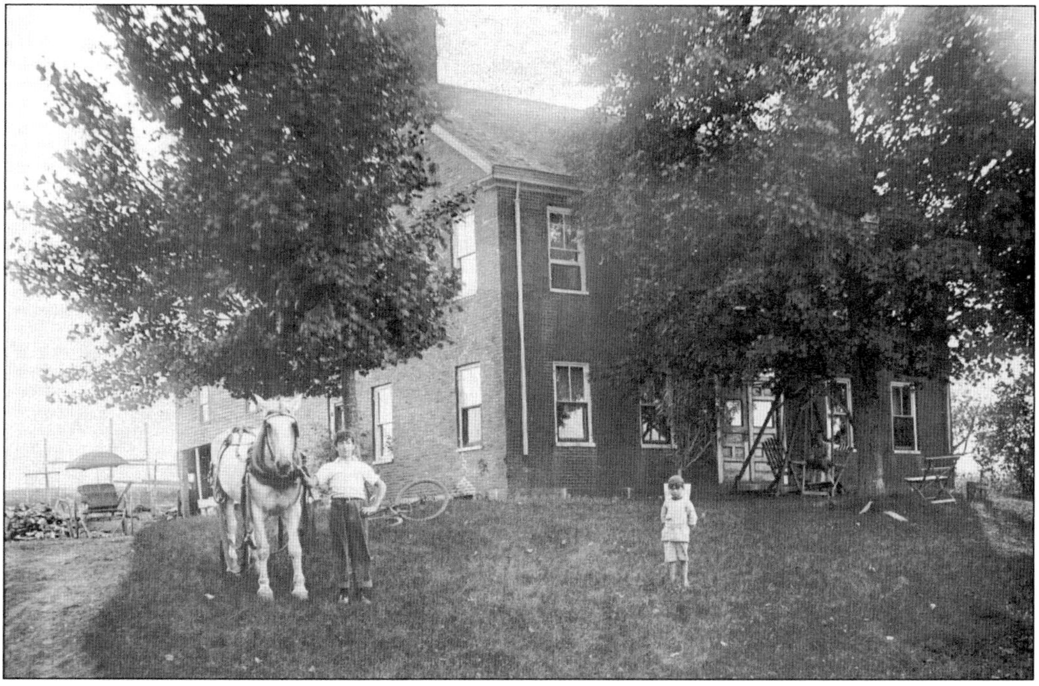

This *c.* 1910 view of the Veroneau Farm shows Frank Veroneau at the horse's side and Alton "Allie" Veroneau on the right. Note the carriage on the left with the makeshift umbrella canopy. (KV.)

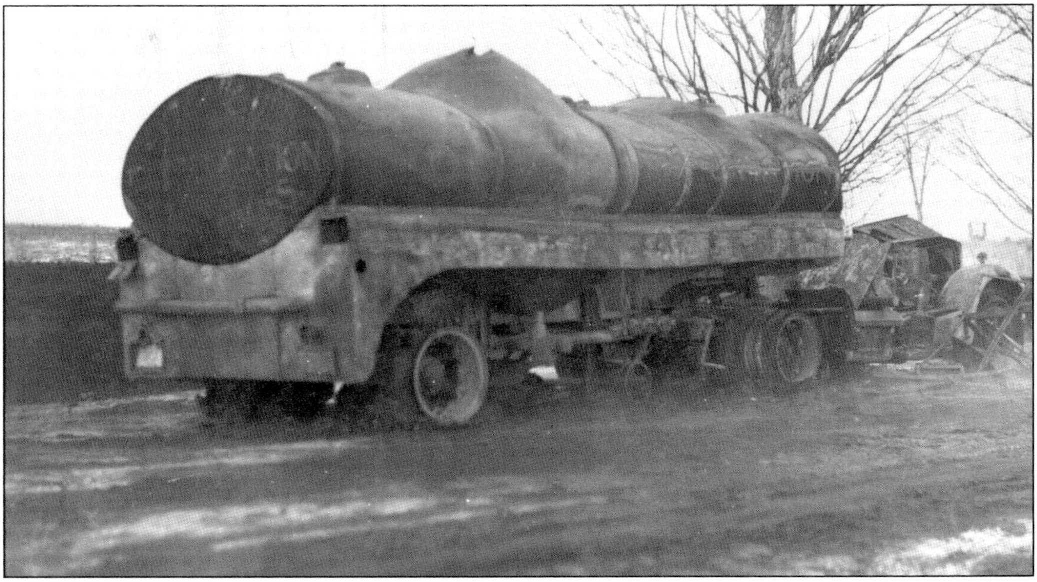

In 1937, this City Oil Transport Company fuel truck, dispatched out of the old trolley carbarn on the corner of Elm Street and Palmer Avenue, caught fire. "Zephy" LeClair drove the burning truck to an open area near the Holy Angels Cemetery on East Road and averted potential disaster. (PHS.)

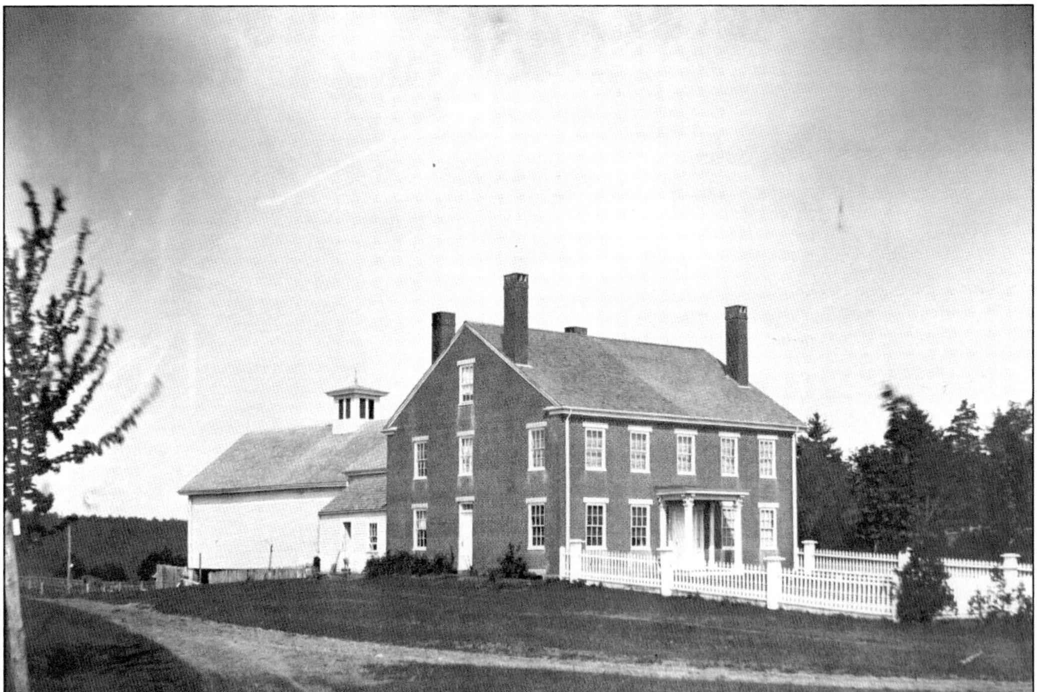

The David Bryant House is pictured in 1879 or 1880. The house, which stood near the present Staples office supply store, was destroyed by fire. Westville, Plaistow, Atkinson, and Haverhill had a disproportionate number of brick houses because of the availability of locally produced brick in the mid-1800s. (HPL.)

The Hotel Maplewood is shown in 1949. Built as a private home in 1920 with timber from all 48 states, it was known as the Birch Tree Inn by 1929. In the 1940s, Mr. and Mrs. William Brennan operated the tavern, by which time it was known as the Hotel Maplewood. In the 1970s, the hotel was converted into apartments. (CYR.)

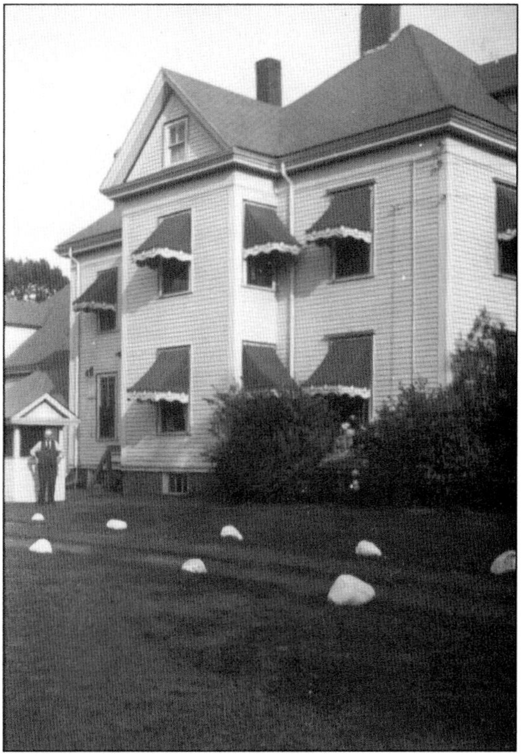

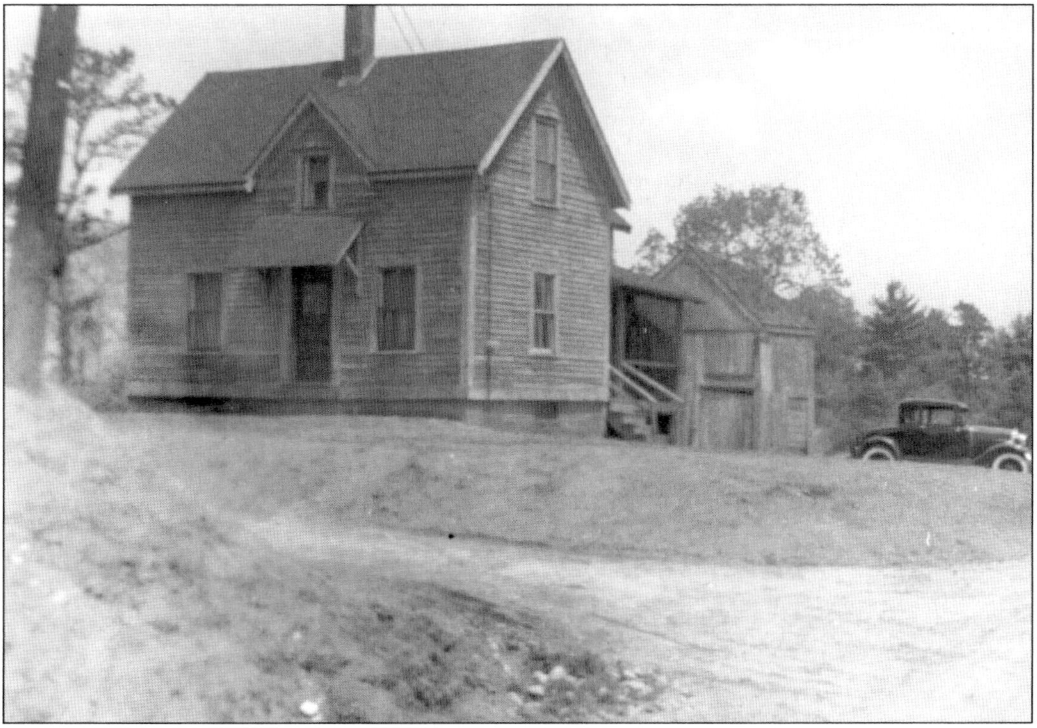

The Gouin House is pictured *c.* the 1930s. According to the notation on the back of the photograph, the structure was "demolished to make room for a large cement building." (CYR.)

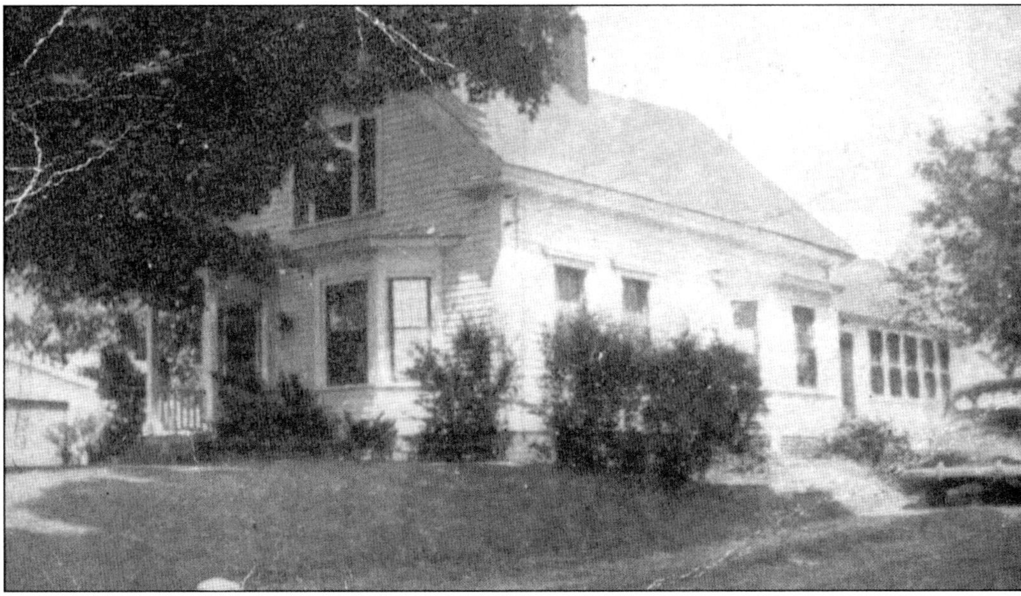

The Yawnitz family acquired this dwelling in 1914 from Daniel Kelleher for $4,000. The property included a 40-acre parcel on which the Yawnitz family raised hogs, cattle, and other livestock. The family sold milk to Westville residents for 6¢ a pint and 12¢ a quart. (CYR.)

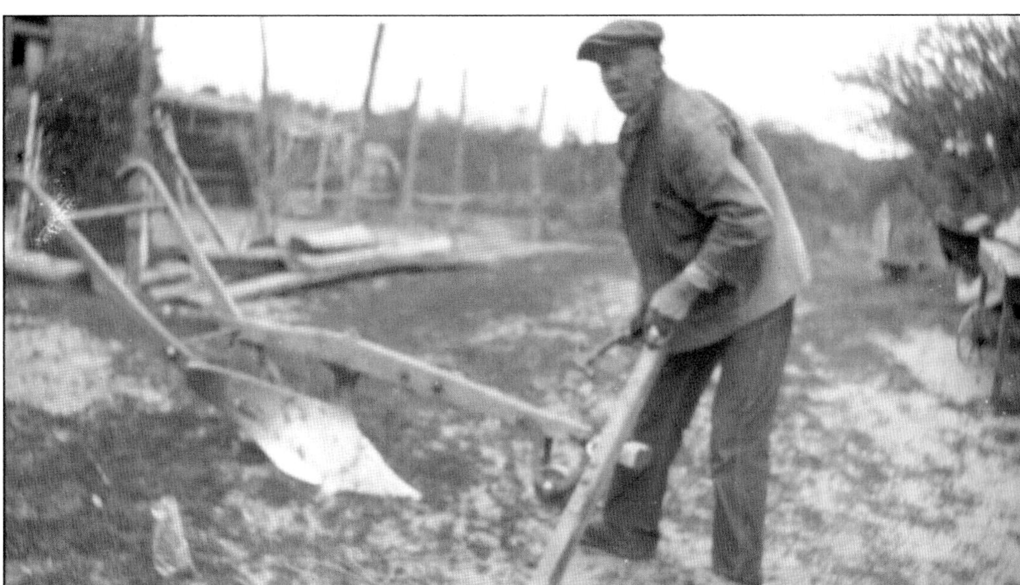

This view shows Yawnitz's Farm in June 1927. George Yawnitz is out from behind the plough. This farm was located near the former Weiner's Furniture warehouse. (CYR.)

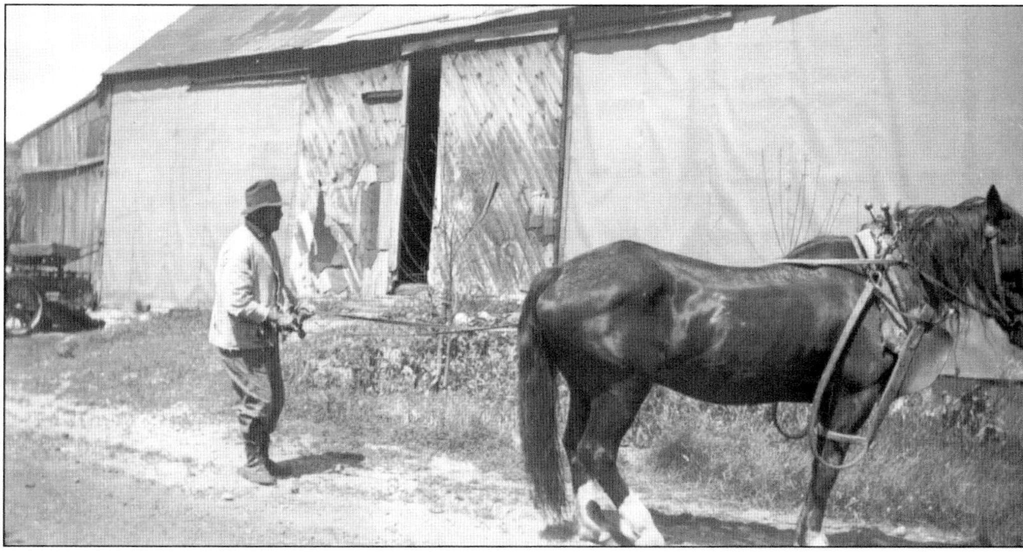

George Yawnitz and his horse Barney retire after a day in the field *c.* the 1920s. (CYR.)

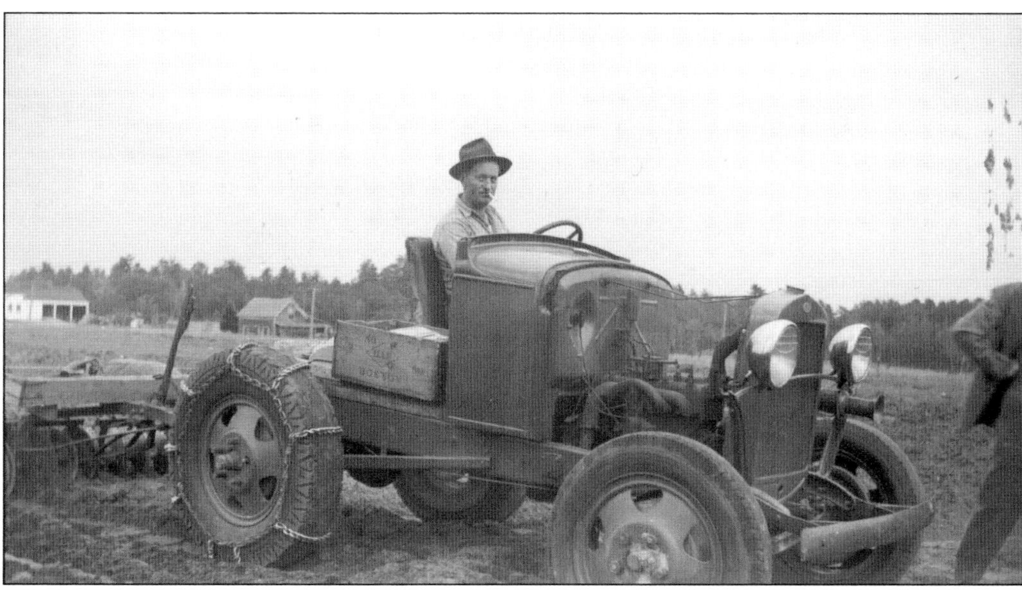

Red Rowell is shown in 1941 with his converted tractor, which he and Eddie Yawnitz fashioned from an old truck. The tractor had attachable blades that were used for mowing hay and cutting wood. (CYR.)

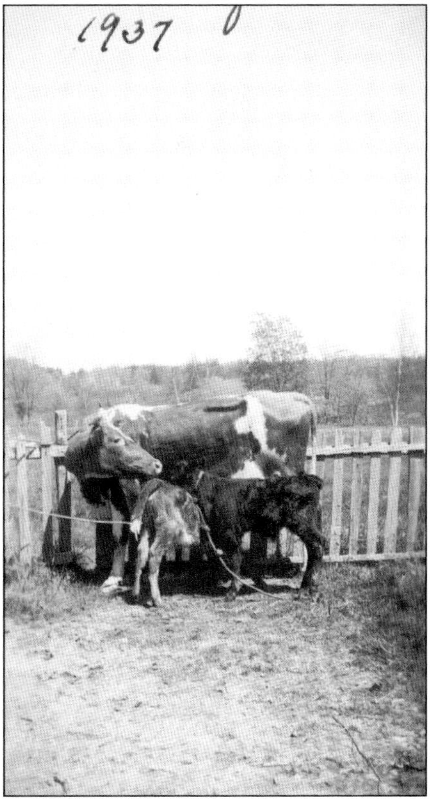

Although Westville is associated with Plaistow's development as an industrial center, it, too, was largely rural in the early 1900s, as this image of twin calves attests. (CYR.)

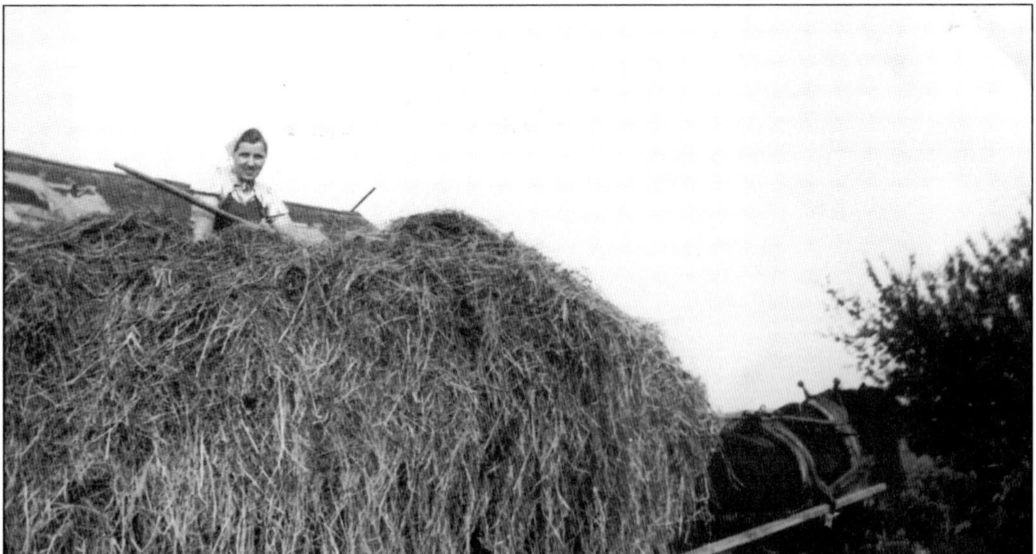

A 14-year-old Katie Yawnitz is shown here making hay on June 5, 1929. (CYR.)

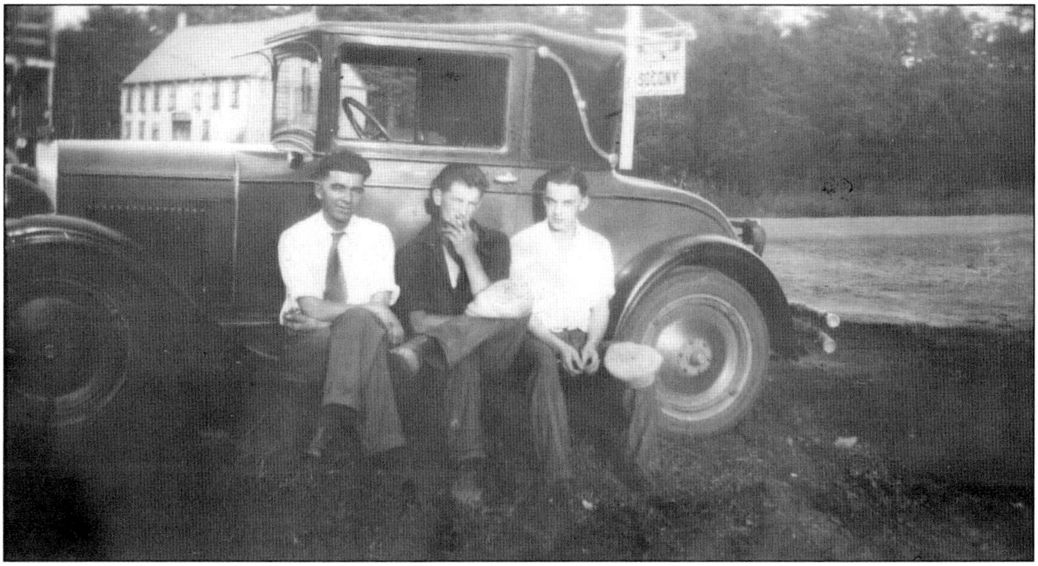

This scene captures a relaxed moment in Westville *c.* 1930. Shown, from left to right, are ? Tozier, Joseph Yawnitz, and Albert Trembley. In the background is a building that functioned as a town hall for the people of the village. (CYR.)

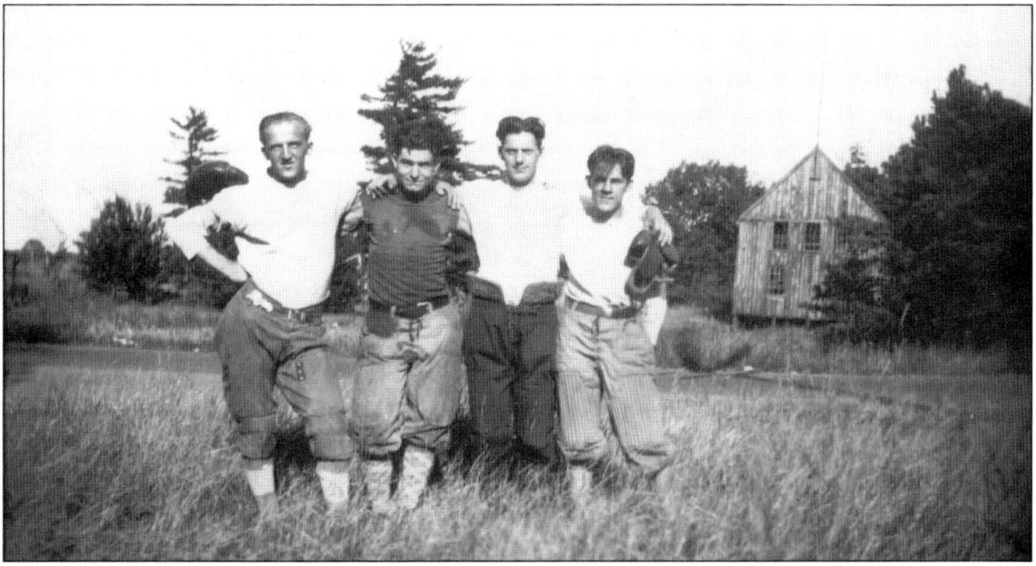

Football was a popular pastime for Westville's youth. This 1929 photograph shows, from left to right, George Yawnitz, Clarence Dion, Richard LaFountaine, and Leon "Fritz" Fuller. Note the dance hall on the right. The location of this picture is the small field kitty-corner from the present Dunkin' Donuts. (CYR.)

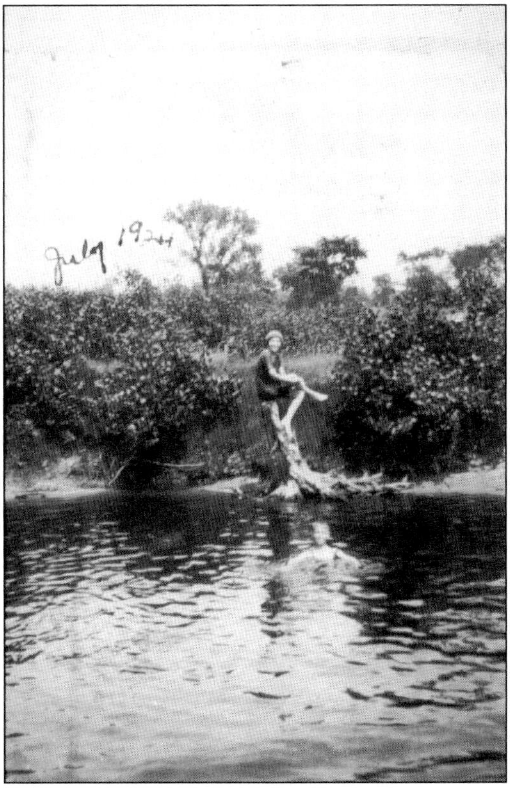

Two 1920s images show a favorite Westville swimming hole. This was a wide spot in the Little River, the unofficial boundary between Plaistow Village and Westville. This spot was located in the vicinity of the Weiner's furniture warehouse. (CYR.)

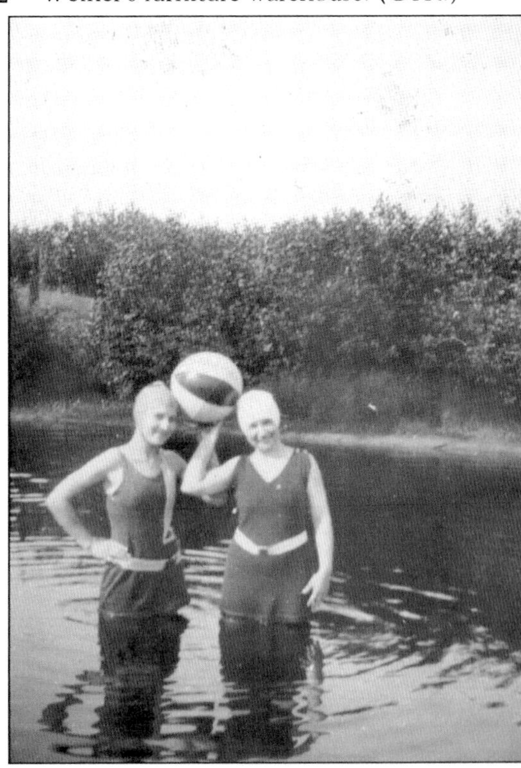

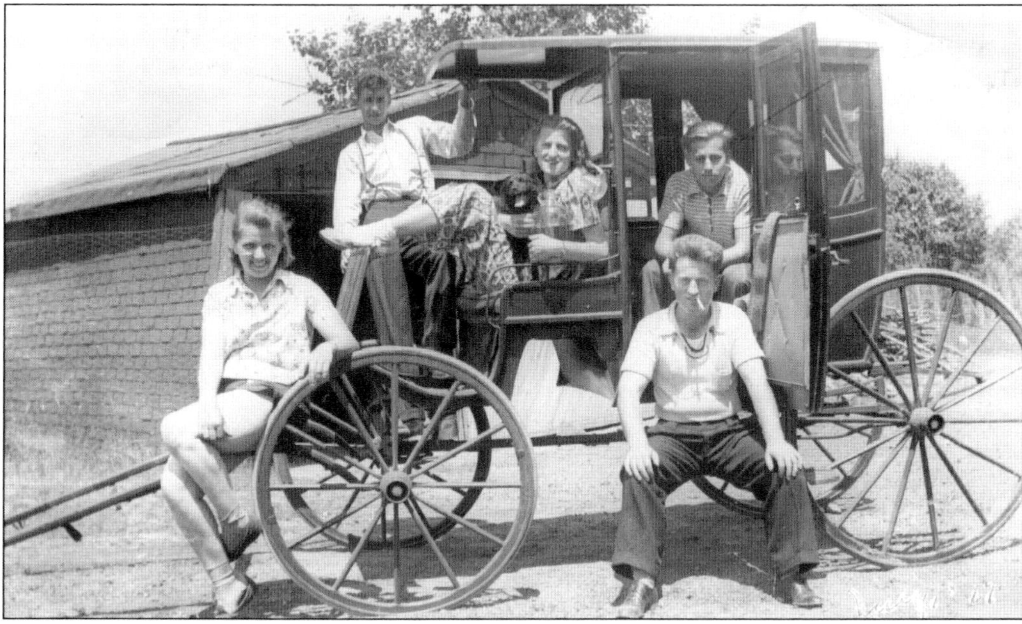

Katie Rowell, Bill Castle, Marianne Yawnitz, Roland LaFountaine, and William "Red" Rowell (with cigarette) relax after a hard day's work in July 1939. (CYR.)

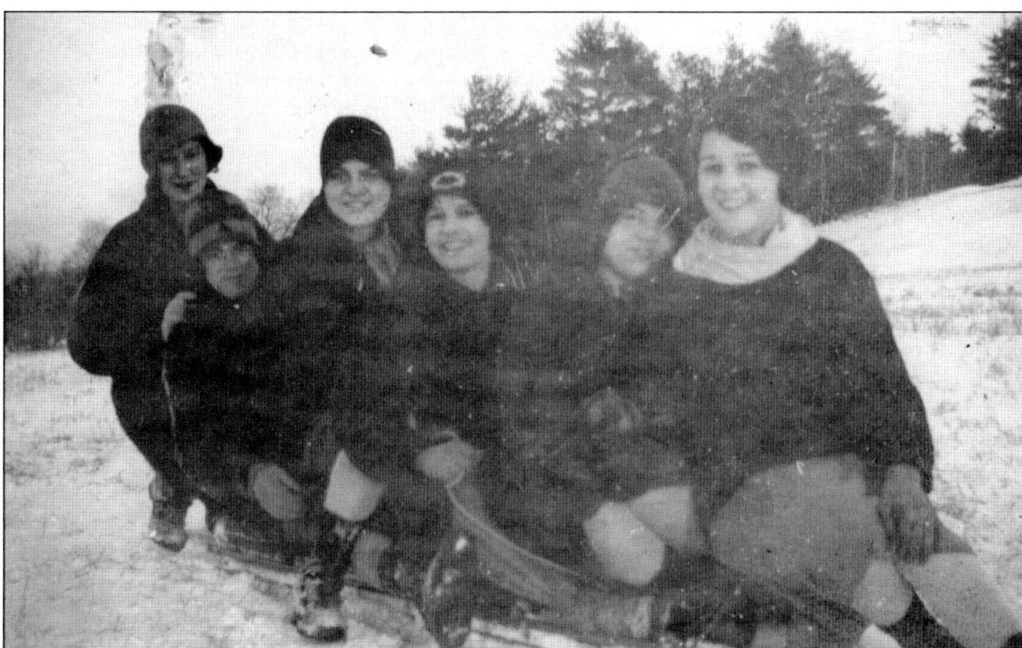

This wintertime scene shows Westville in February 1928. (CYR.)

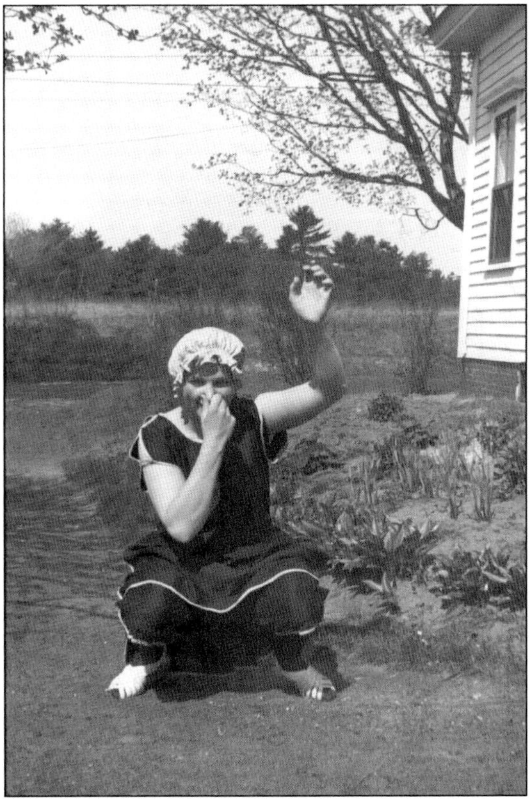

Katie Rowell poses at home before the 1941 Gay Nineties show, held at the Holy Angels Church. (CYR.)

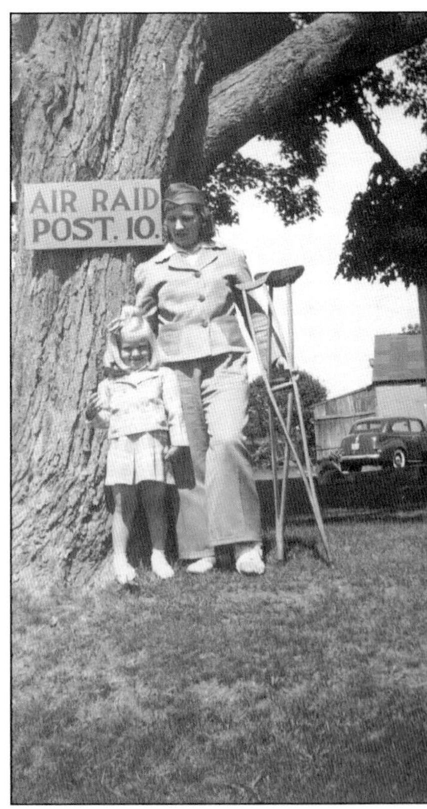

During World War II, local folk such as Katie Rowell expressed their patriotism by helping out on the home front. This 1942 photograph shows Katie Rowell in her capacity as air-raid warden. (CYR.)

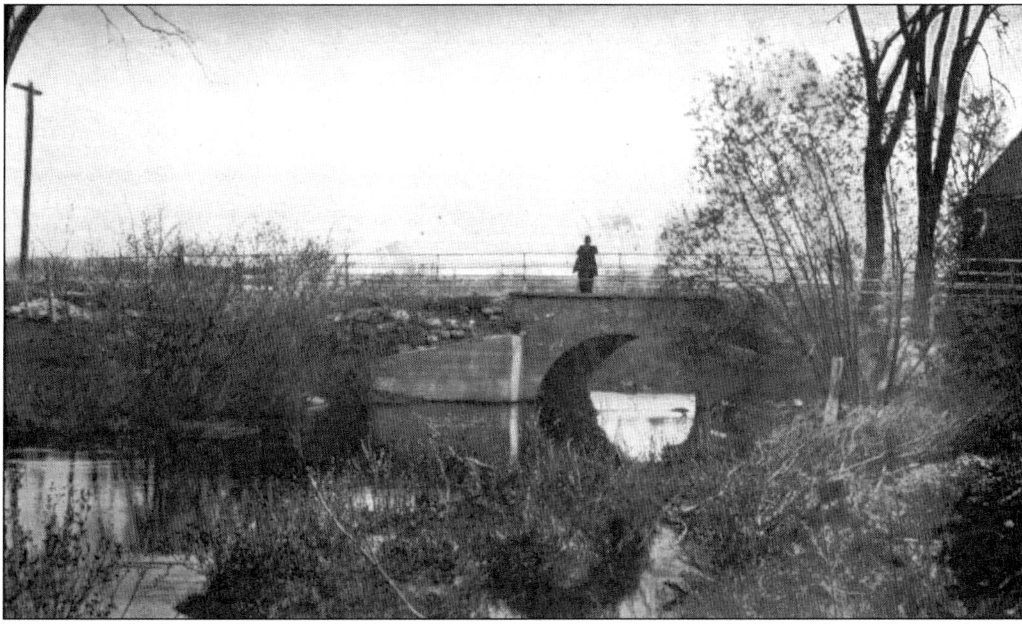

Located behind the present Plaistow Co-operative Bank, the Gilbert Bridge, shown here c. 1930, spanned the Little River, which turned the machinery of the Peaslee Mill. (AC.)

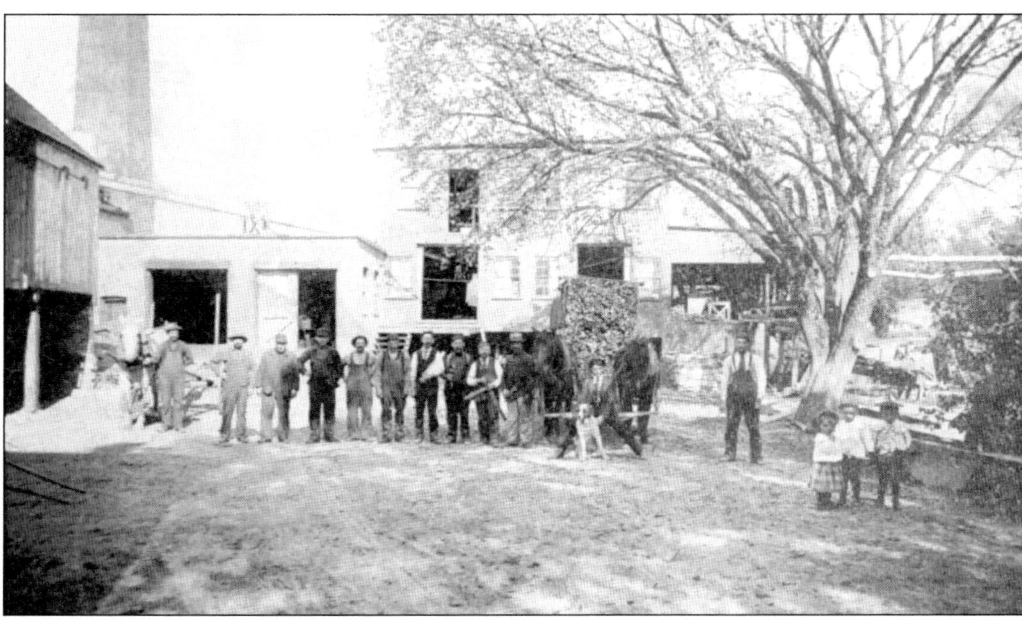

This posed photograph of Peaslee's work force used the lumbermill as a backdrop. Note the seemingly random group of children on the right. (PHS.)

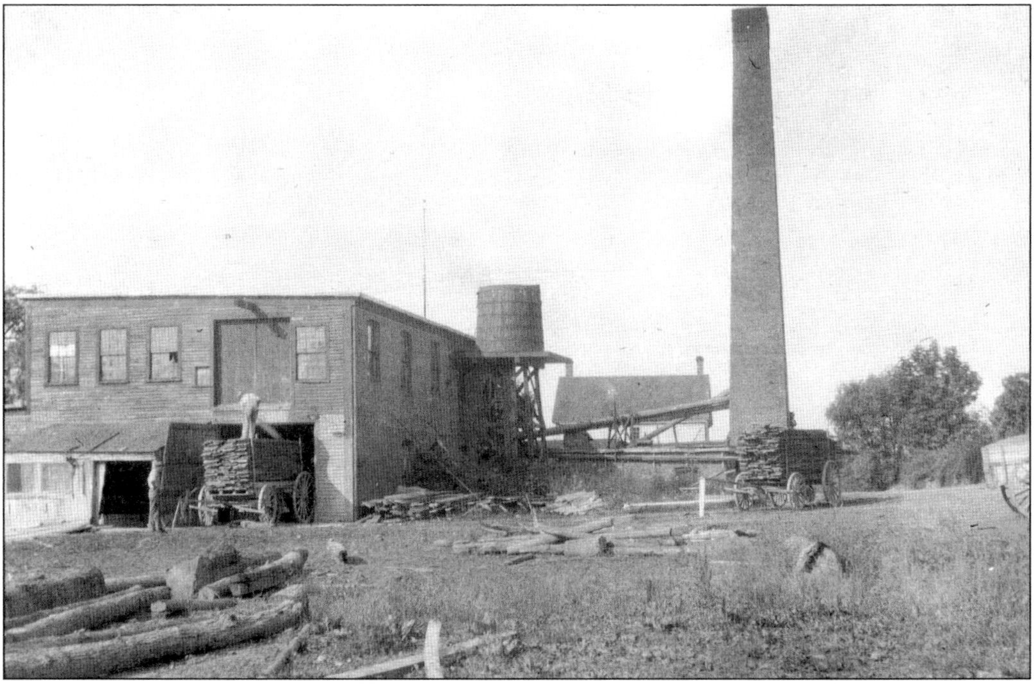

This *c.* 1900 exterior view of the Peaslee Mill shows cut boards leaving the facility. In the late 1800s, this mill employed 15 hands and manufactured 1 million feet of boards annually. (PHS.)

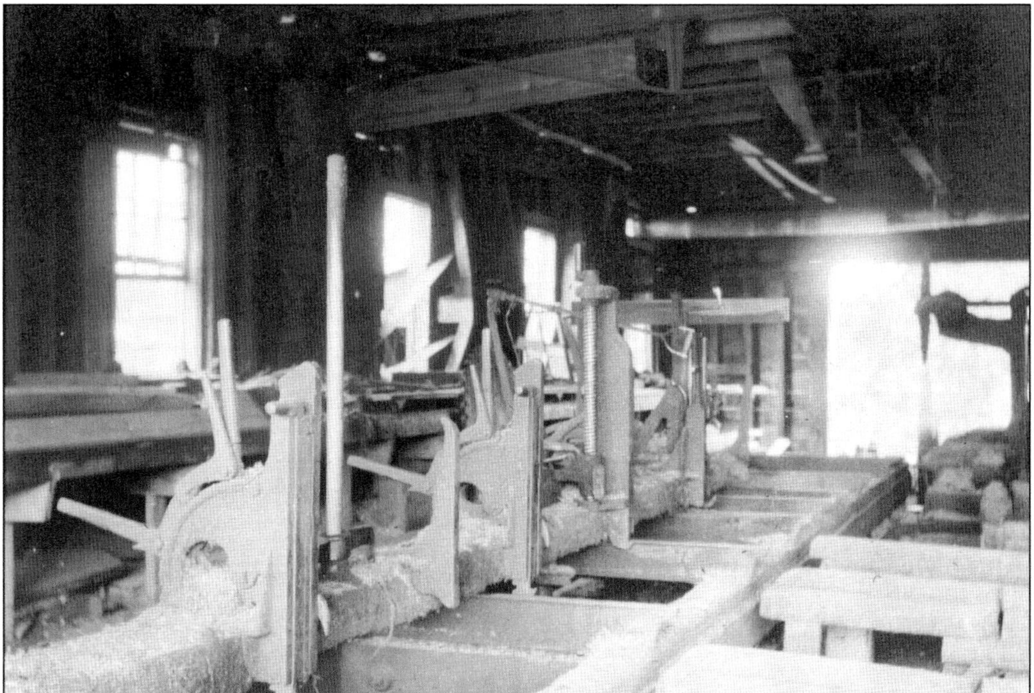

This is a rare photograph of the interior of the Peaslee Mill. The company was operated by Daniel, Edson, and Frank Peaslee, and was later taken over by Edson's son, William Peaslee. According to local tradition, the mill folded in the 1920s. (PHS.)

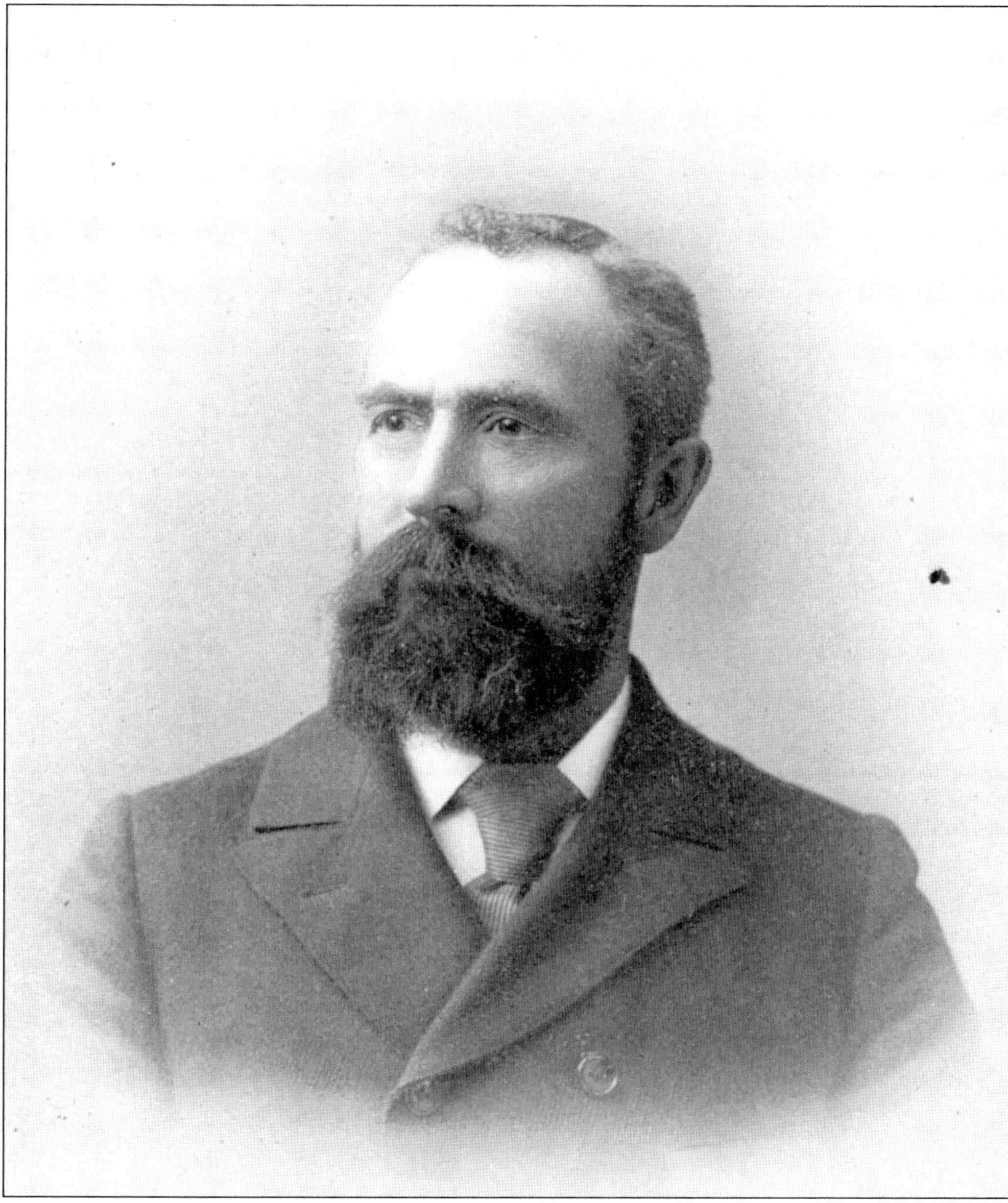

Lumber manufacturer and legislator Edson Peaslee was a lifelong Plaistow resident who was born in 1847. Educated in Plaistow and Connecticut schools, Peaslee learned the lumber business from his father, Daniel Peaslee. Edson Peaslee's "progressive methods and advanced ideas" were considered a boon to the local business community. (NHHS.)

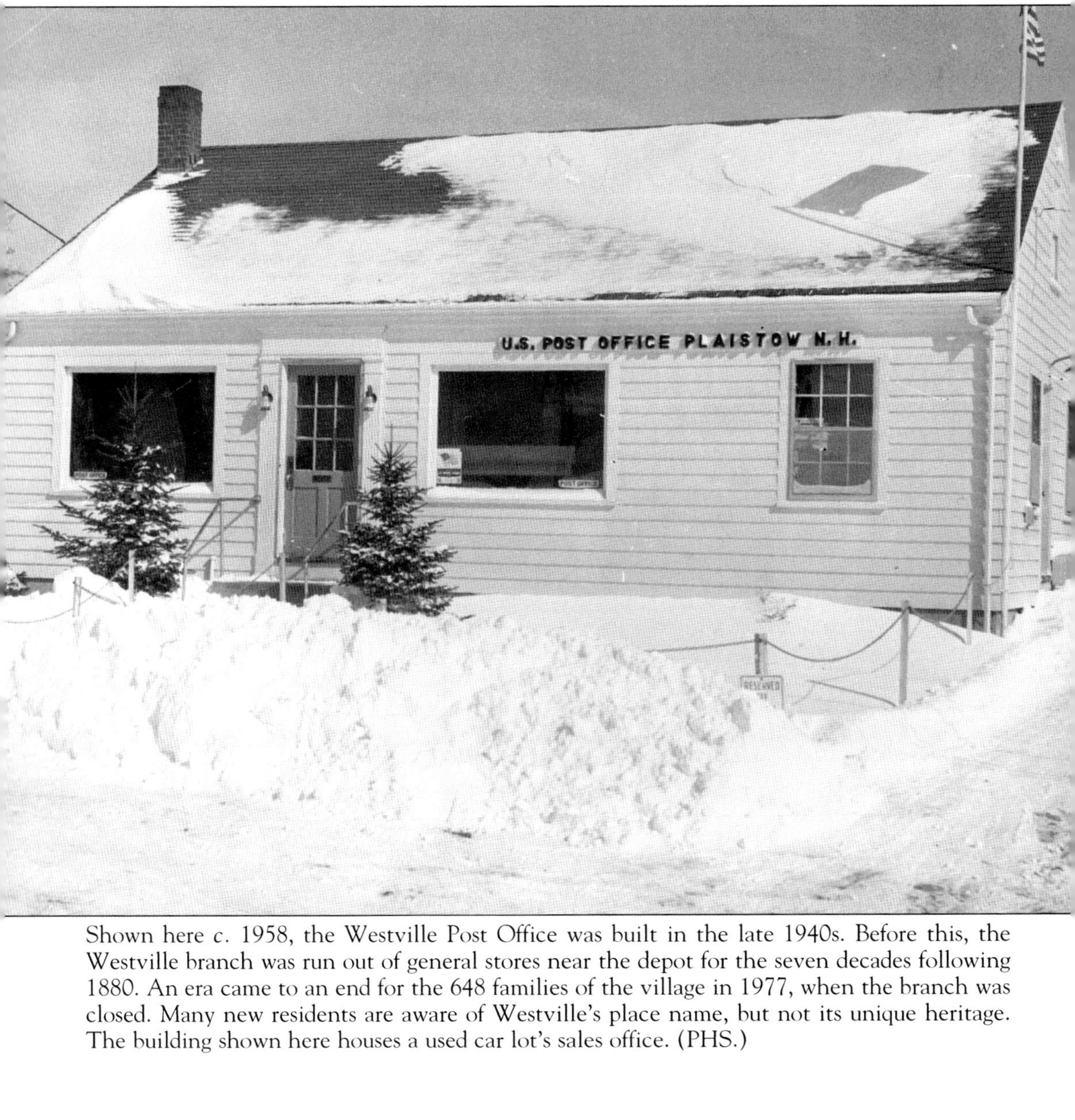

Shown here c. 1958, the Westville Post Office was built in the late 1940s. Before this, the Westville branch was run out of general stores near the depot for the seven decades following 1880. An era came to an end for the 648 families of the village in 1977, when the branch was closed. Many new residents are aware of Westville's place name, but not its unique heritage. The building shown here houses a used car lot's sales office. (PHS.)

Seven

Outlying Areas

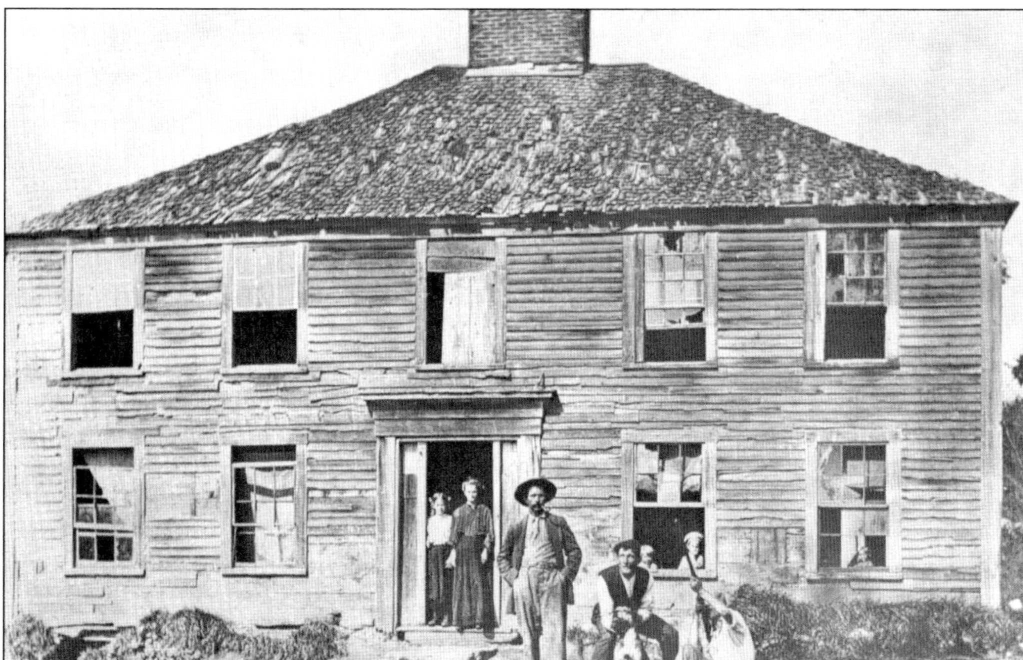

Believed to have been built *c.* 1704, the Hurd House is Plaistow's oldest structure. Shown here in the late 1800s in a state of dilapidation, this house was once a wayside tavern and farmstead that was the home of prosperous people. In the late 1800s, the Hurd House became the temporary residence of a series of tenants and fell into disrepair. Nearly a national headquarters for America's Gypsies, this house was purchased by former Haverhill minister and poet Harry Hurd. Guided by a Colonial Revival aesthetic, he restored the house to its former glory in the 1940s. Hurd, the author of *Yankee Boundaries*, once wrote, "It is probably a good thing that some persons in this progressive world retain a nostalgic feeling for country ways and bygone ways." The preservation of the town's oldest dwelling attests to the veracity of Hurd's statement. (PHS.)

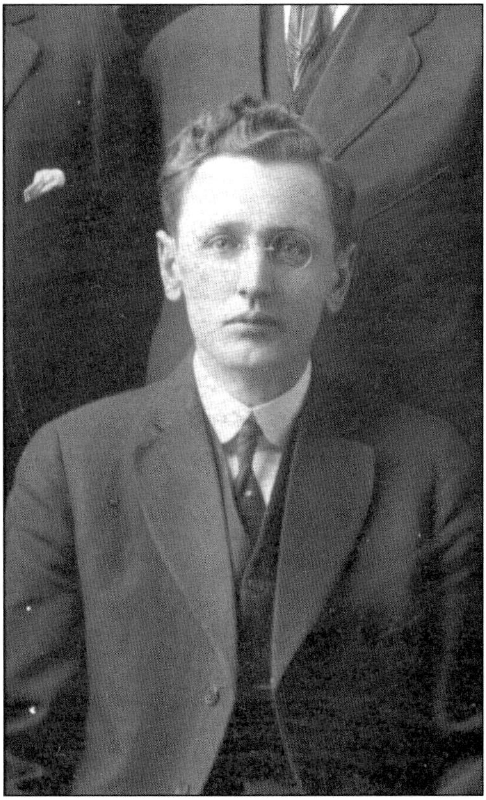

Before moving to Plaistow, Harry Elmore Hurd was the minister of the People's Methodist Church of Haverhill. Later in life, Hurd lent his oratory skills to the people of Plaistow by giving Memorial Day addresses at Pollard Park. Many longtime Plaistow residents still recall his orations. (HPL.)

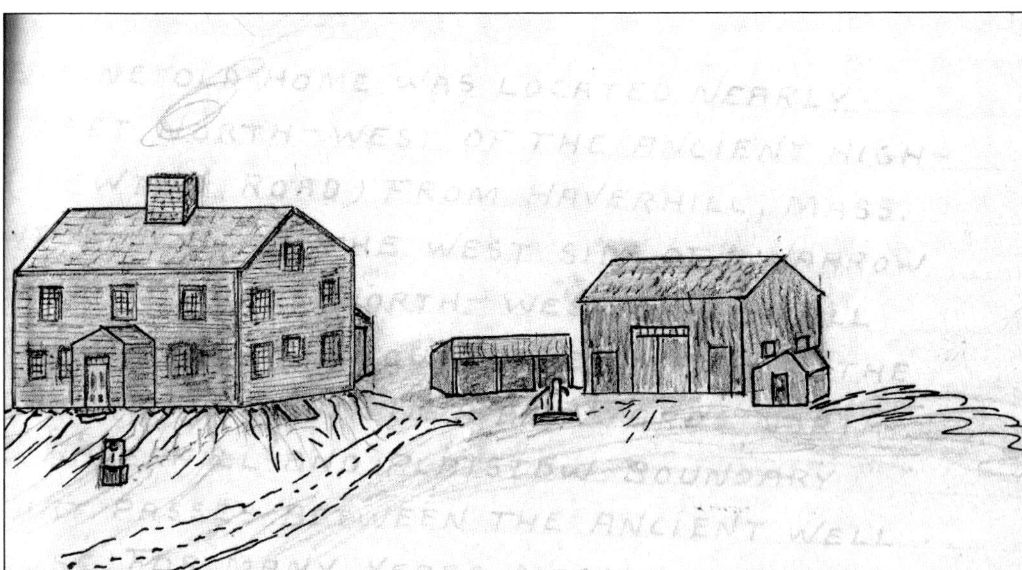

Fred Luce sketched this rendering of the Ayer House in 1947. Now demolished, this house, built before 1725, was located near Lovers' Lane and Ayer's Hill. The structure was on land disputed by Plaistow and Haverhill until Plaistow prevailed in 1877. The earliest owners of this house are lost to the historical record. The earliest known inhabitant whom Luce recalled was John Moulton, a shoe manufacturer of the 1800s. (HPL.)

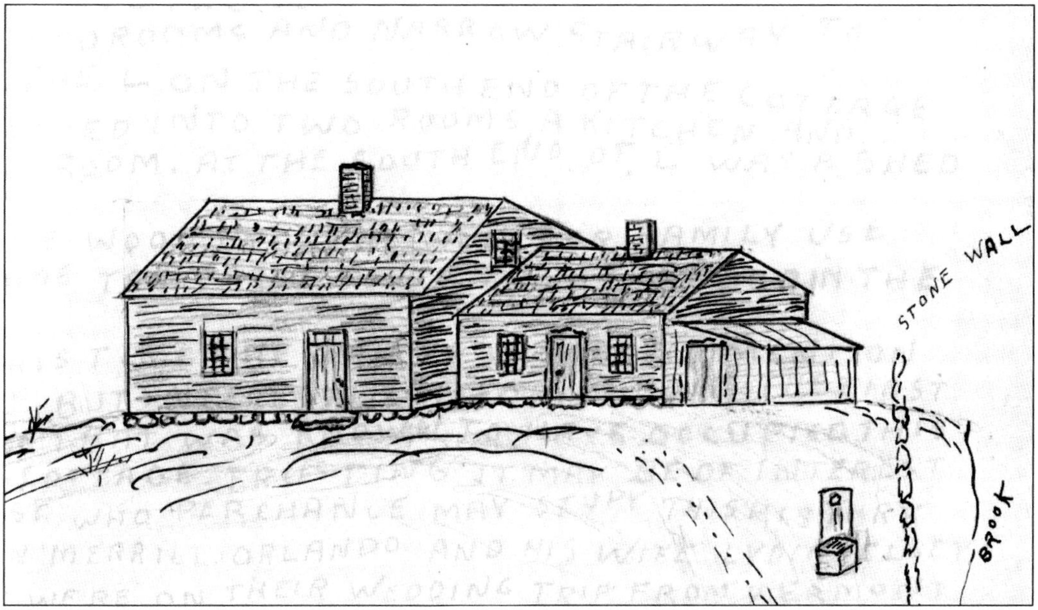

This is a view of the Ayer Cottage, located near the Ayer House. It is not known when this structure was erected or demolished. The first known inhabitants were the Smiths, known in the vicinity as the "Rummy" Smiths because of their reputation as purveyors of strong drink. In the late 1800s, there were a racetrack and several taverns in the Newton Road area. (HPL.)

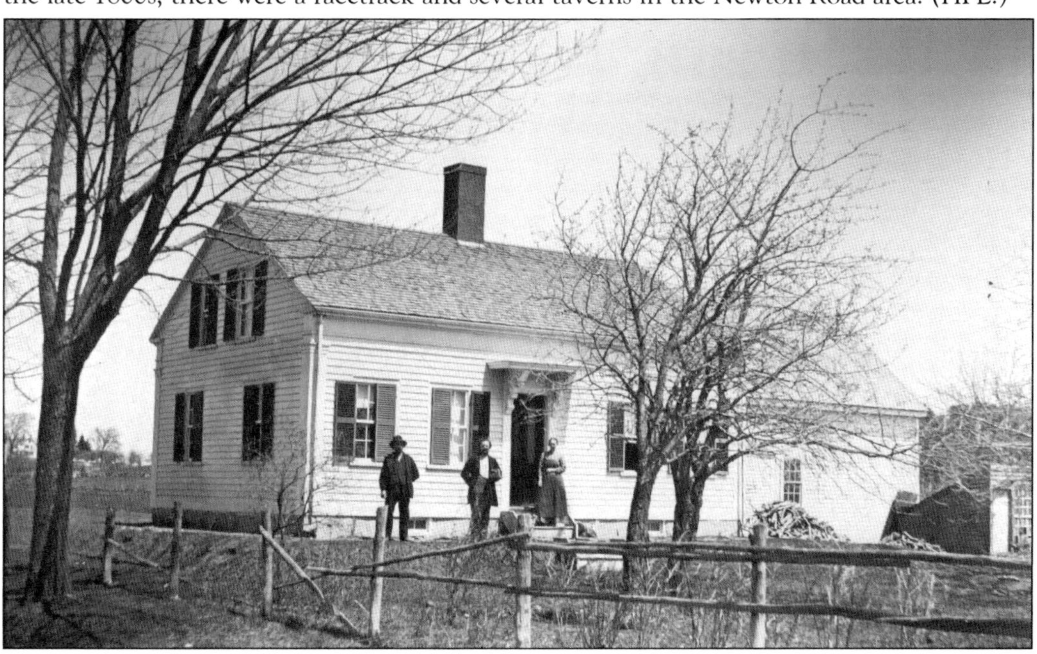

The Simonds House is pictured in 1879 or 1880. Located near the intersection of Newton Road and Forrest Street, this farmstead was improved after 1880 by the relocation of an outbuilding from the Carlton House to Simonds's grounds; the outbuilding was used as a shoe shop by Louis Simonds. Later, this was the home of Mr. and Mrs. Marconi DiFatta, who were retired circus acrobats. The DiFattas raised English setters and maintained a small garden to supplement their savings. (HPL.)

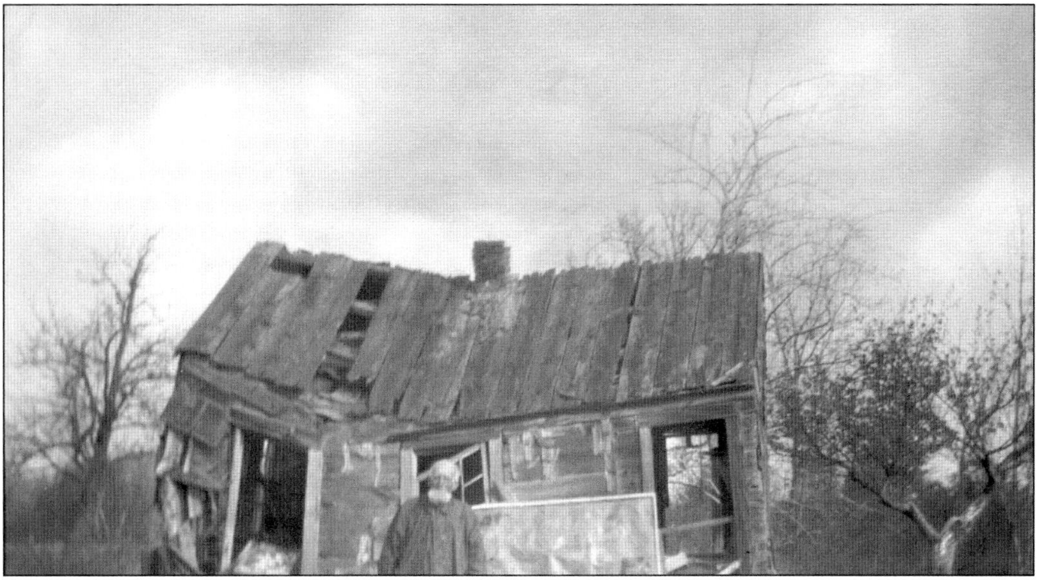

Dean Harriman poses in front of the remains of his shoe shop in 1934. Harriman lived with his brother Ira Harriman in their home near Tootenham Corner—the intersection of Sweet Hill Avenue and Newton Road. The Harriman brothers' relationship was marked by acrimony. When Ira Harriman disappeared and selectmen came to investigate after two weeks, they found him dead in a field. His brother seemed nonplussed and shrugged, "He's been lying there a couple of weeks." (HPL.)

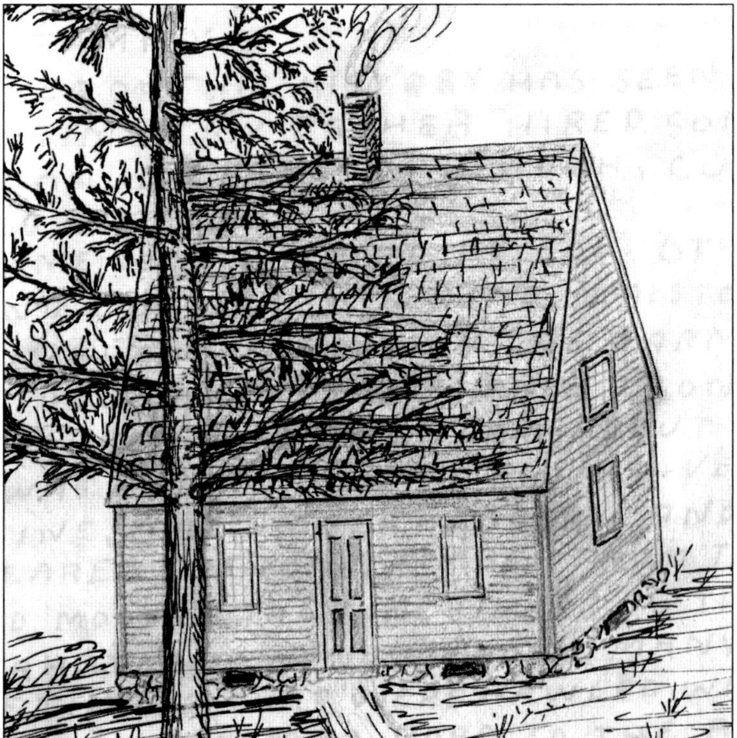

This sketch shows the Lightning Splitter, home of Symeon "Cripple" Thompson and his family, near Brandy Brow. The image, taken from Fred Luce's *Newton Road and Kenoza Avenue*, is the only surviving picture known of this distinctive structure. According to Luce, the whole family made shoes at home from stock provided by Frank Hatch, who brought shoe stock to Newton Road families. Luce notes that Symeon married his cousin, "a cripple," and that "the entire family had deformed feet." (HPL.)

Ed McKenzie skis on Sweet Hill *c.* 1940. Prior to the development of Sweet Hill, this was a popular destination for sledders, tobogganers, and skiers. (PH.)

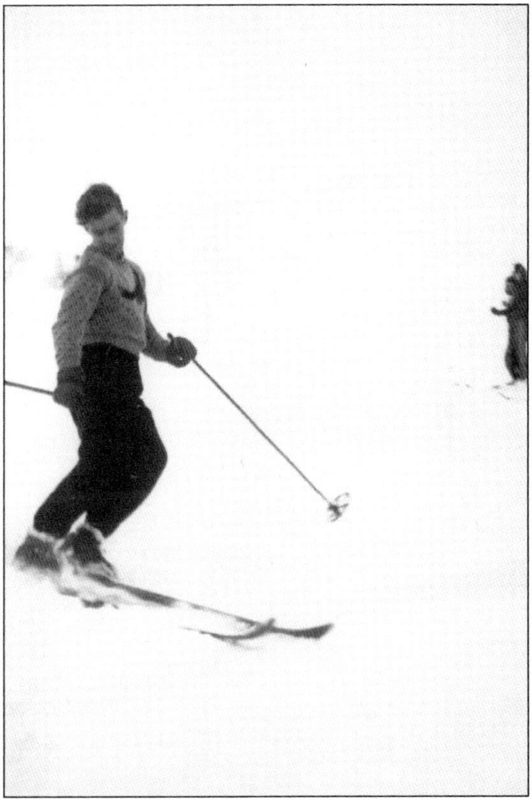

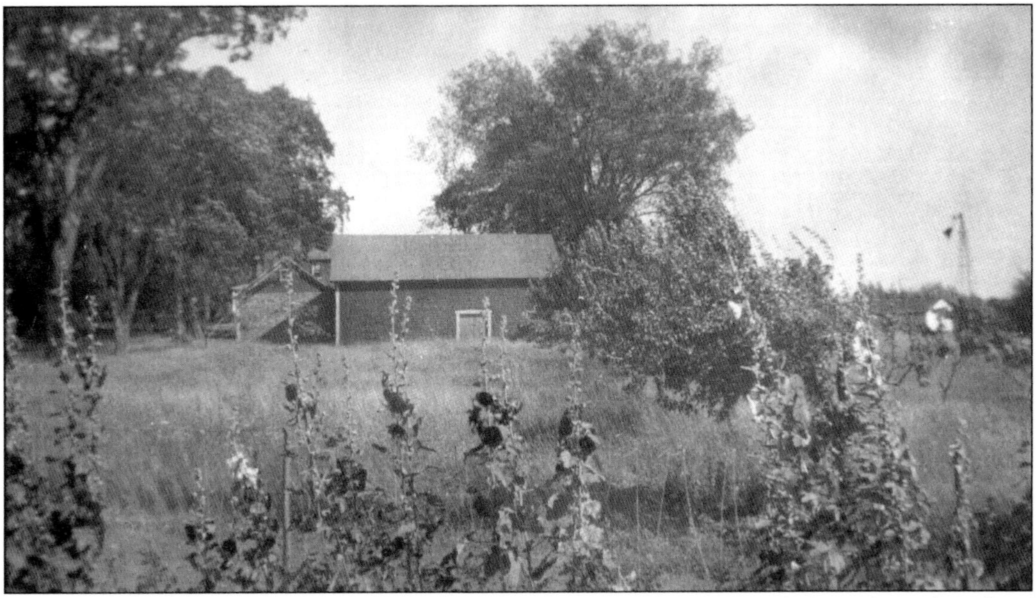

The Lloyd Mitchell Farm is shown *c.* 1930. Sweet Hill Road is concealed on the right side of the image by a row of elm trees. The farmstead, partially hidden by outbuildings, is the only pre–World War I brick structure in the eastern part of town. At the time of this photograph, the grounds boasted two barns, a garage, a tool shed, three wells, a 60-foot chicken house, meadows, an apple orchard, a 50-acre woodlot, and a windmill (right). (PH.)

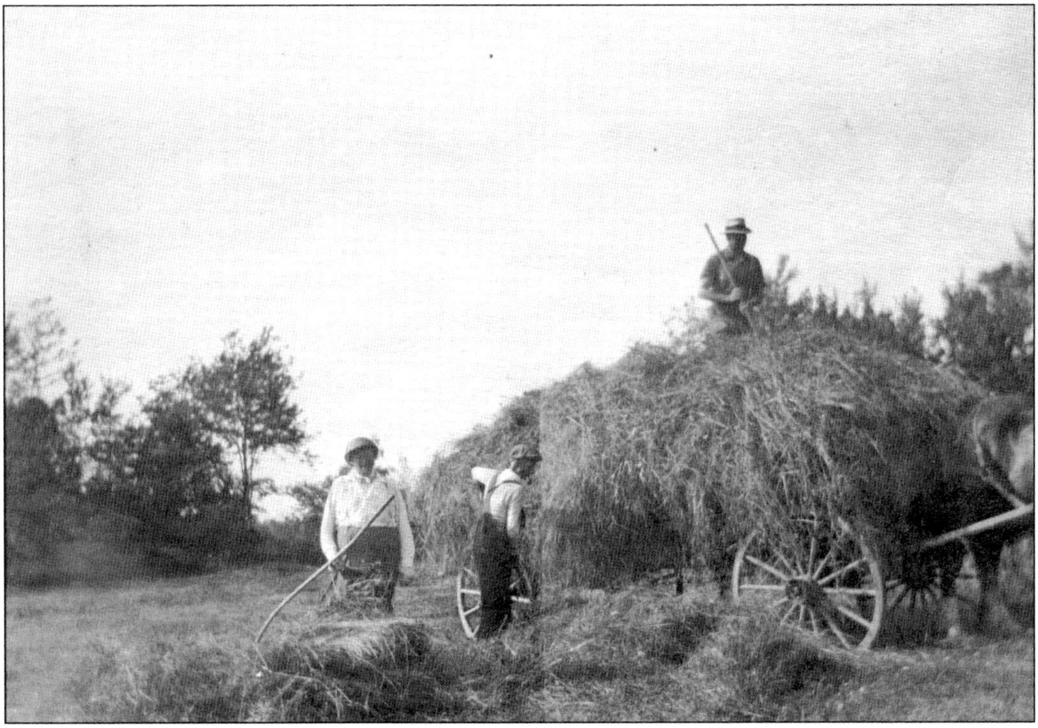

It is haying time on Sweet Hill, *c.* the 1920s or 1930s. (PHS.)

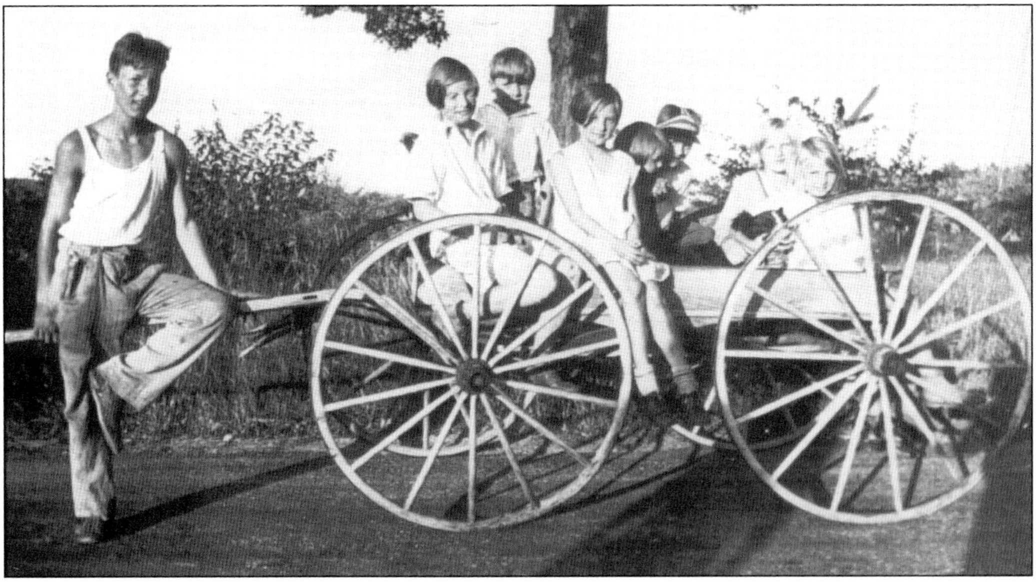

Connecticut tourists captured this *c.* 1928 Sweet Hill Road image. Pictured, from left to right, are Harold Gebow, Robert Gebow, Paul Holmes, Gladys G. Libby, Constance Cullen, Norman Gebow, Chummy the dog, Janette G. Warchut, and Harriet H. Ingalls. The slant of the photographer's shadow (lower right) suggests that the picture was taken early or late in the day. (PH.)

This is a view of St. Christopher's Episcopal Church, now demolished. This parish came into being when five families of Plaistow decided there was a need for an Episcopal church closer than Exeter or Haverhill. The first service was held here in 1967. The site of this building, the northeastern corner of the intersection of Old County Road and Route 125, is now occupied by Dodge's Agway. (PHS.)

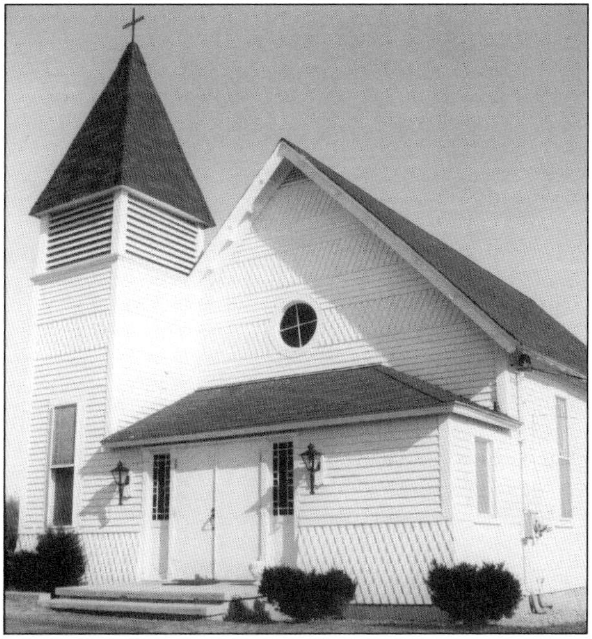

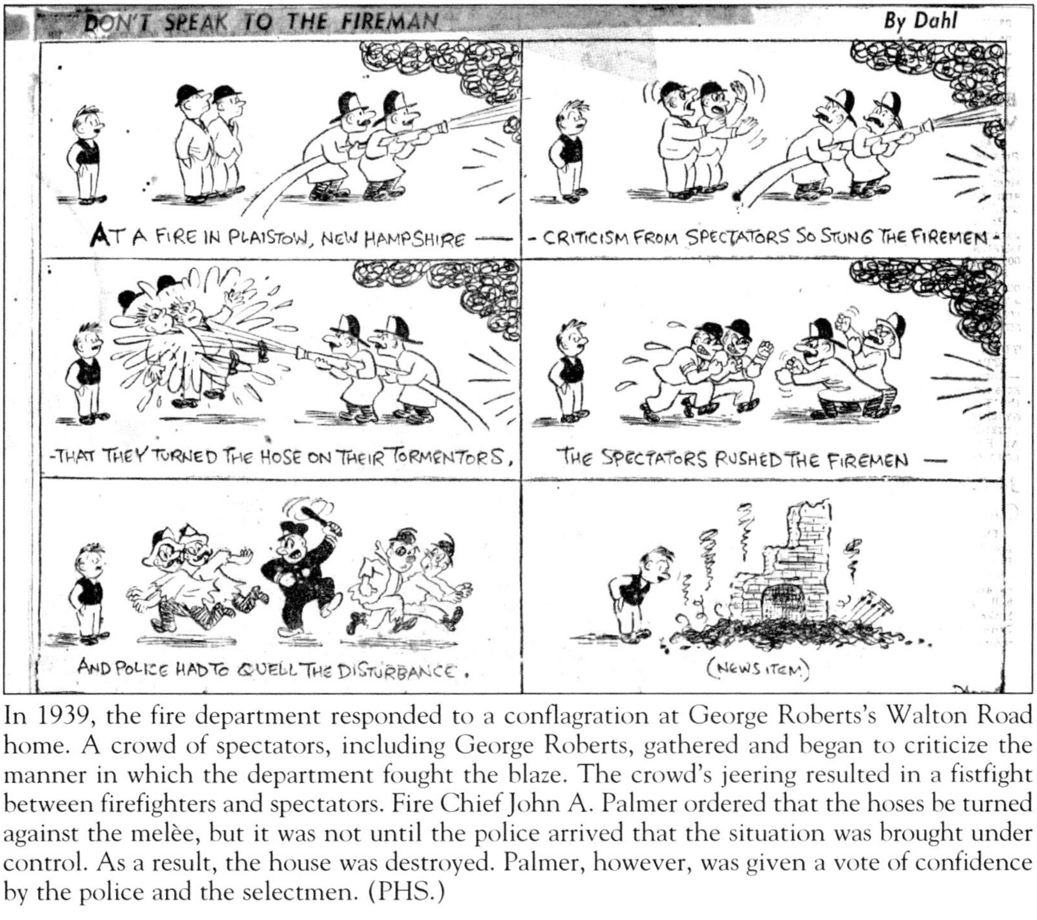

In 1939, the fire department responded to a conflagration at George Roberts's Walton Road home. A crowd of spectators, including George Roberts, gathered and began to criticize the manner in which the department fought the blaze. The crowd's jeering resulted in a fistfight between firefighters and spectators. Fire Chief John A. Palmer ordered that the hoses be turned against the melèe, but it was not until the police arrived that the situation was brought under control. As a result, the house was destroyed. Palmer, however, was given a vote of confidence by the police and the selectmen. (PHS.)

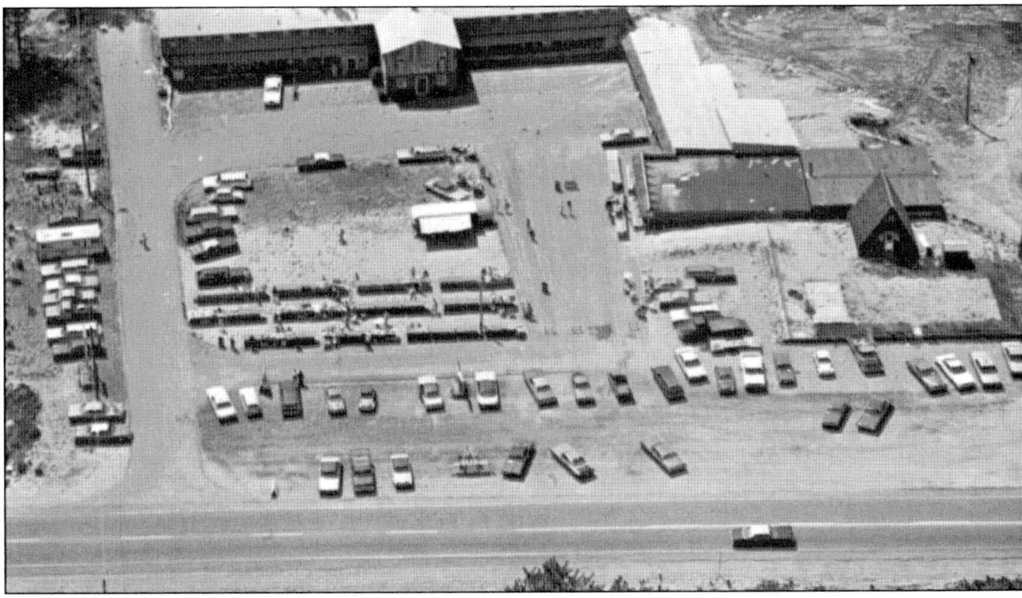

Although this has not been the site of flea markets since the early 1980s, the Little River Motel still houses lodgers. Located on the Kingston-Plaistow line on Route 125, this complex is mere walking distance from the area's most significant Native American archaeological site, which has yielded dozens of artifacts dating back thousands of years. (AC.)

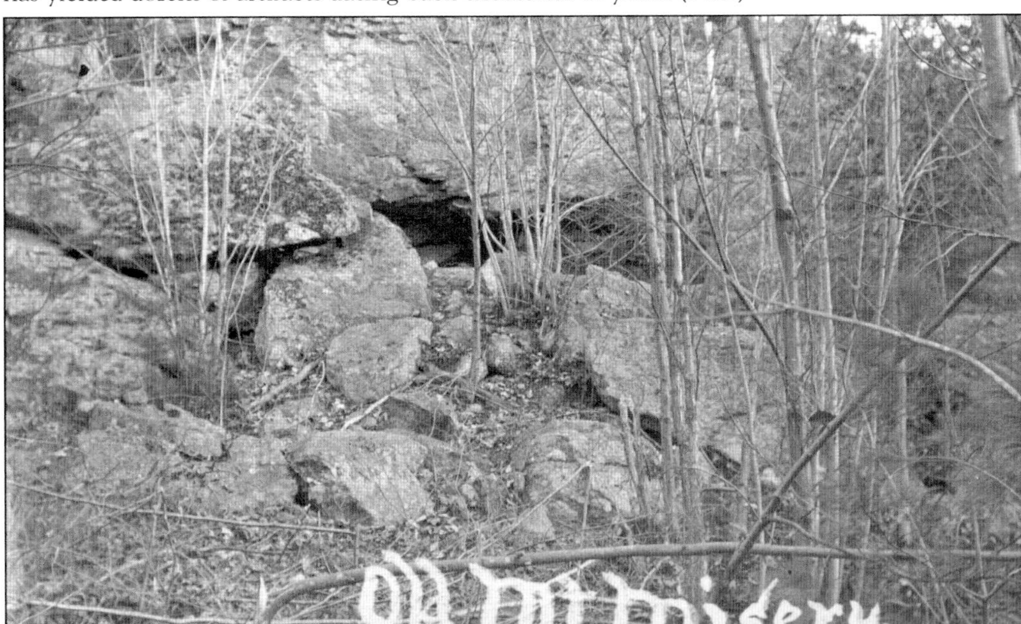

Mount Misery, at an elevation of 384 feet, is Plaistow's highest point. Once part of an unfortunate farmer's unyielding holding (hence the name), Mount Misery is also believed to have been a rendezvous point for horse thieves and bootleggers, known to Plaistow folklore as the "Barcelona Boys." The wooded areas in the mount's vicinity provided fuel for local families' stoves well into the 20th century. This image shows the large cave on the mountain's western side. (PHS.)

Eight

GOING TO SCHOOL

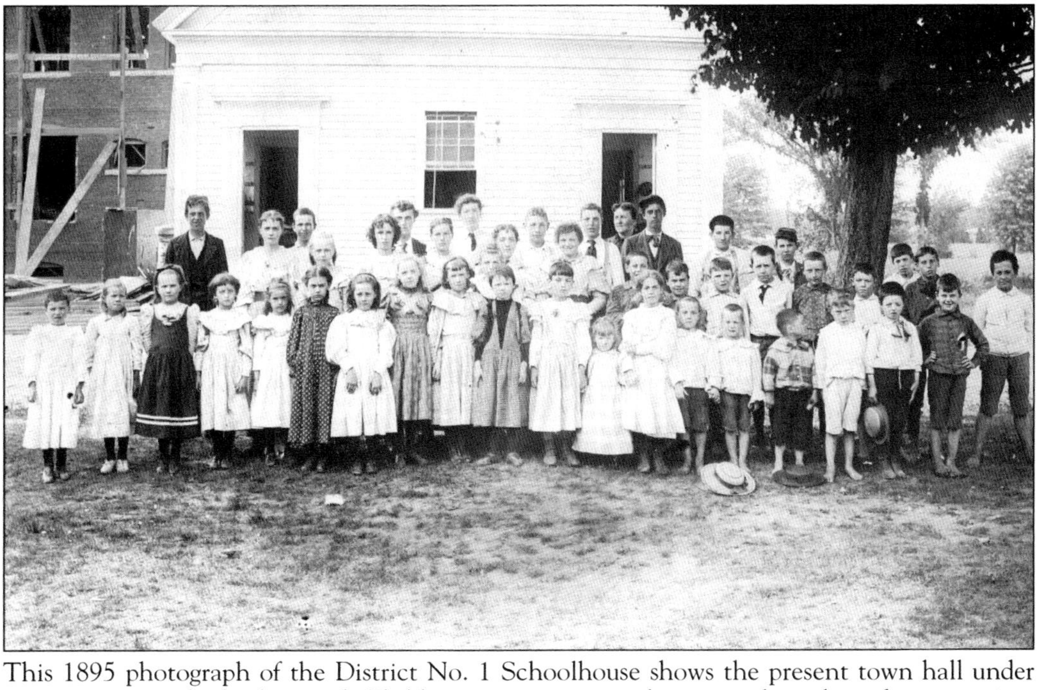

This 1895 photograph of the District No. 1 Schoolhouse shows the present town hall under construction in the background. Children were encouraged to spare their shoes for wintertime use; thus, the number of barefoot schoolchildren here suggests that this photograph was taken during the late spring or the summer. (PHS.)

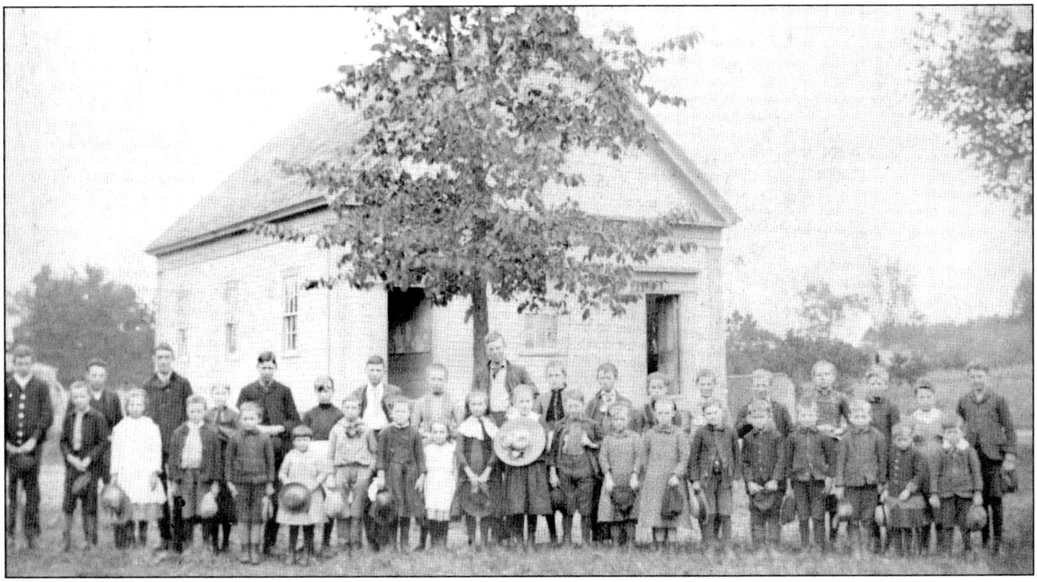

The District No. 1 Schoolhouse, located on Plaistow Common, is pictured *c.* the 1880s. Note the disparity in the age of the pupils. This school, like the town's other three, served multiple grades in a single room. The schoolmaster, who taught every grade, is shown in the center, to the right of the tree. To the left of him is Anna George, who lived at the old Tucker Tavern, on the corner of Main Street and Westville Road. (PHS.)

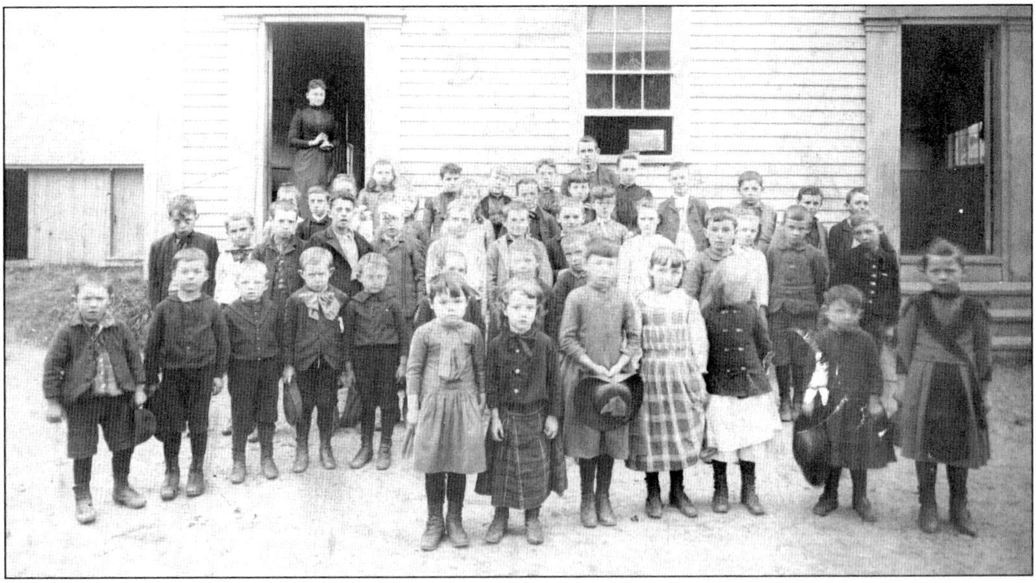

The District No. 1 Schoolhouse is shown *c.* the 1870s. This was a grade one-through-eight school; yet, observe the small number of older students, suggesting the level of education obtained by Plaistow children in the 1870s was fairly low. In 1875, the school superintendent, Ruben Peaslee, noted, "Of the 195 scholars in town, the average daily attendance is a small portion over 26. This is a sorrowful exhibit of the interest taken by our people in the education of their children." (PHS.)

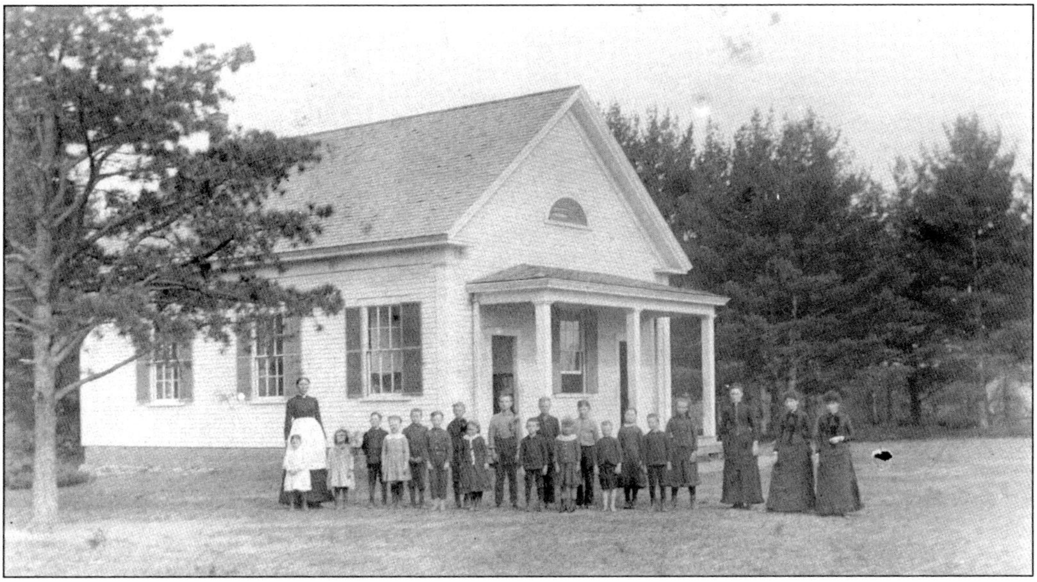

This schoolhouse stood near Kelley's Corner, on the east side of Main Street. The photograph dates from *c.* 1874. Before the 20th century, towns were not directly responsible for the education of their young; this responsibility fell to neighborhoods within each town. Plaistow contained four school districts until consolidation began to occur in the early 1900s. (PHS.)

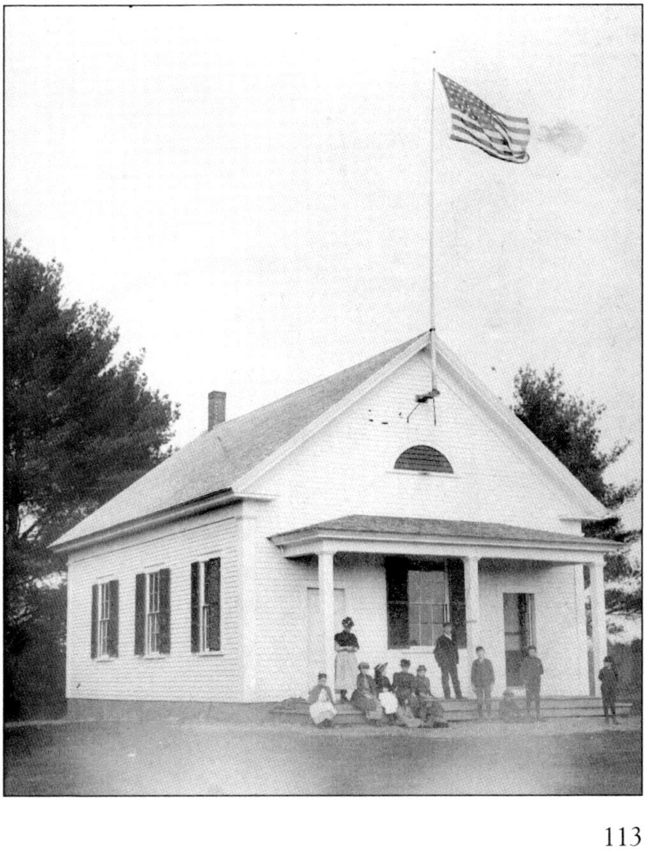

The old District No. 2 School was also known as the Kelly Corner School. This school was located near the intersection of North Main Street and Kelly Road and served children in the town's northern section. (PHS.)

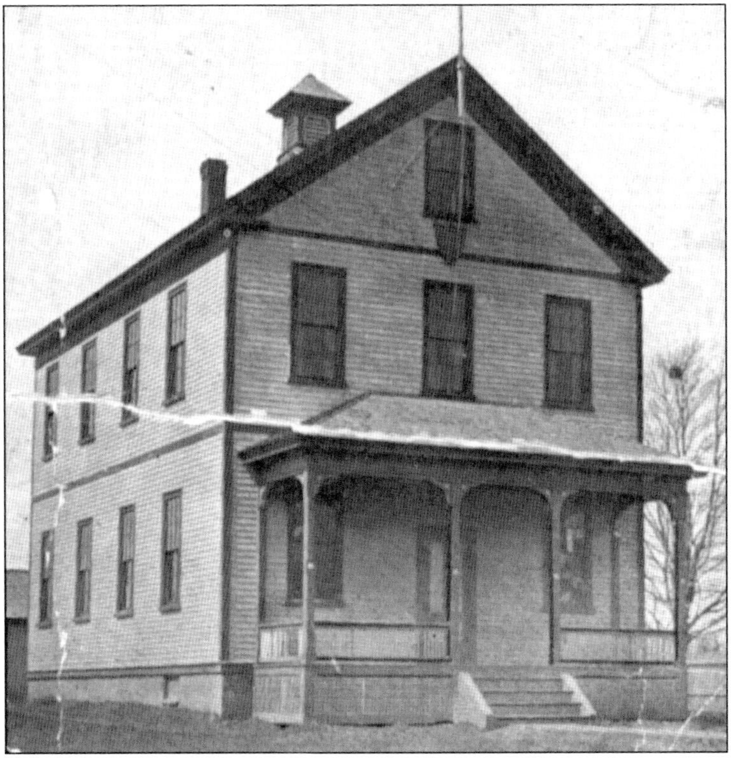

The old Pollard School is pictured *c.* 1896. By the 1890s, the school on the common became increasingly inadequate for the district's "scholars." Arthur G. Pollard gave the town land upon which to build a larger school. Unlike earlier schoolhouses, the Pollard School did not have separate entrances for boys and girls, and had multiple rooms and teachers for children of different age groups. This facility was used until 1911, when it was razed to make room for a larger school of the same name. (PHS.)

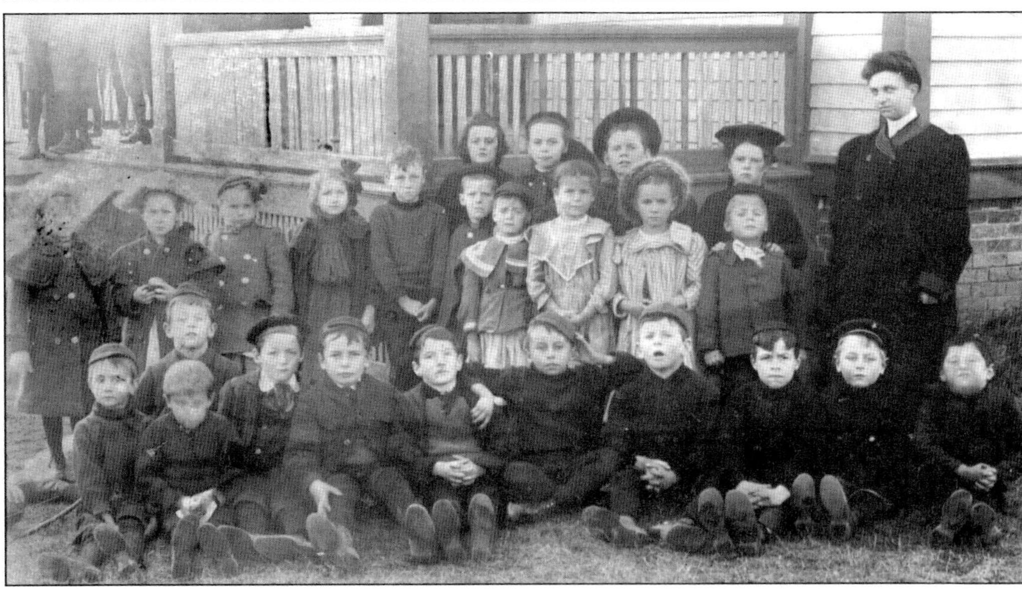

This view shows the old Pollard School in 1906 or 1907. The teacher is Alice Messer. The pupils are, from left to right, as follows: (front row) Nelson Fecteau, Philip Davis, Raymond Seaver, Albert Davis, two unidentified, Oscar Fecteau, unidentified, Newman Sleeper, Paul Dearborn, and Bernard Merrick; (middle row) Reva Gates, Amber Russell, Florence Kelly, Elizabeth Sultaire, George Alden, Merriden Crockett (standing in front), Marion Spear, Cora Andrews, Dorothy Sawyer, and Fred Andrews; (back row) Donna Hall, Dorothy Cushing, Bernice Sawyer, and Ruth Mansell. (PHS.)

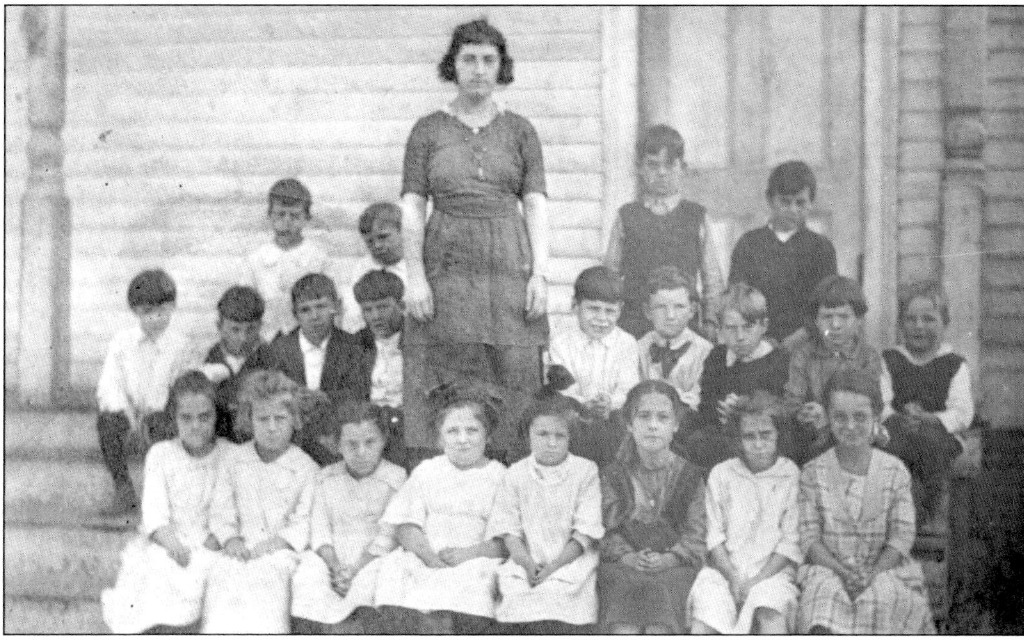

The Westville School accommodated grades one to four. Pictured *c.* 1920, from left to right, are the following: (front row) Helen Castle, Veronica Yawnitz, Irene Gouin, Verna Leavitt, Delores Dion, Gloria LaBonte, Ida Shaw, and Eunice Smith; (middle row) four unidentified, Mrs. Bouchard, Earle Tozier, Robert Mayo, Norman Shaw, Clarence Dion, and Clifton Sargent; (back row) Emile Cote, unidentified, Charles Tremblay, and Richard LaFountain. (PHS.)

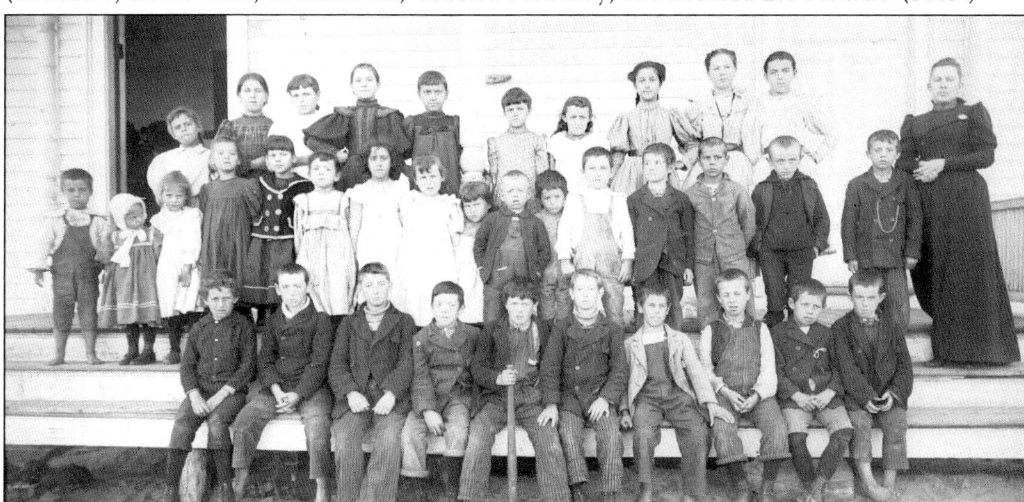

The District No. 3 School of Westville held grades one through four. This schoolhouse served about two dozen pupils until it burned in the spring of 1939. A single-room building, it featured no modern facilities. Posted on the building was a sign that read: "$56 reward, the Town of Plaistow will pay the above sum for information leading to the arrest and conviction of any persons breaking glass or other damaging this property. Per order Selectmen." Among those pictured *c.* 1917 to 1920 are Marie Cote, second row, fifth from left; George Yawnitz, Joseph Yawnitz, and Leo Cote, 12th through 14th from left; and Louise Tremblay, third row, fifth from left. (PHS.)

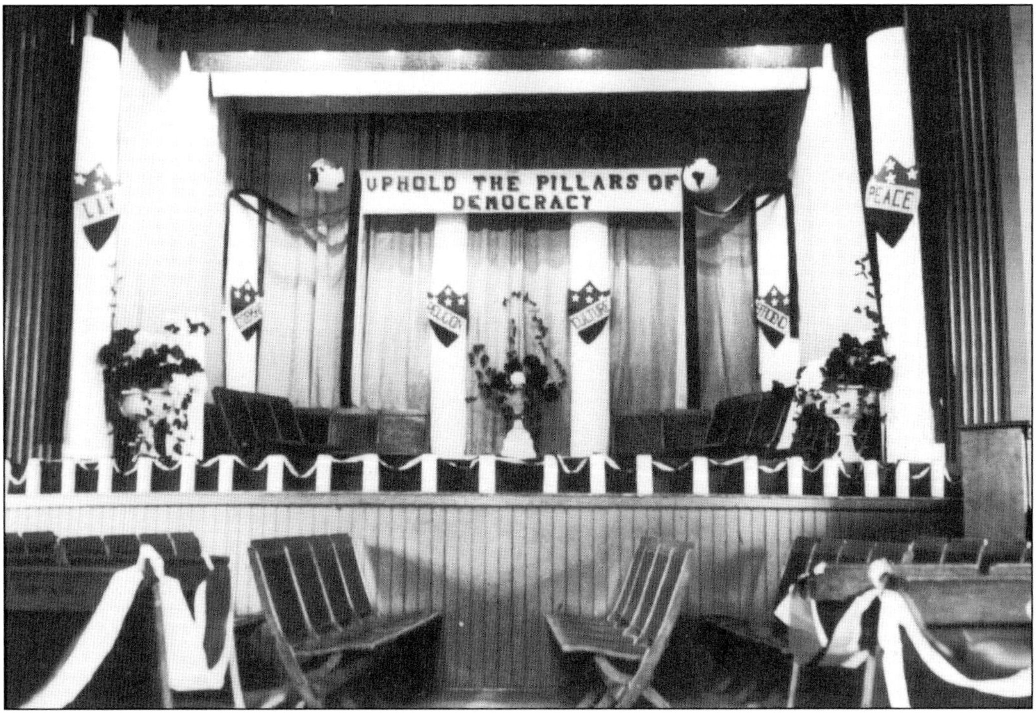

This World War I–era image of the Pollard School graduation held in the town hall is a study in the civic virtues that local schools upheld in the first quarter of the 20th century. The banner reads, "Uphold the pillars of democracy." Each of these "pillars" is identified on a shield, from left to right, law, citizenship, religion, culture, efficiency, and peace. (PHS.)

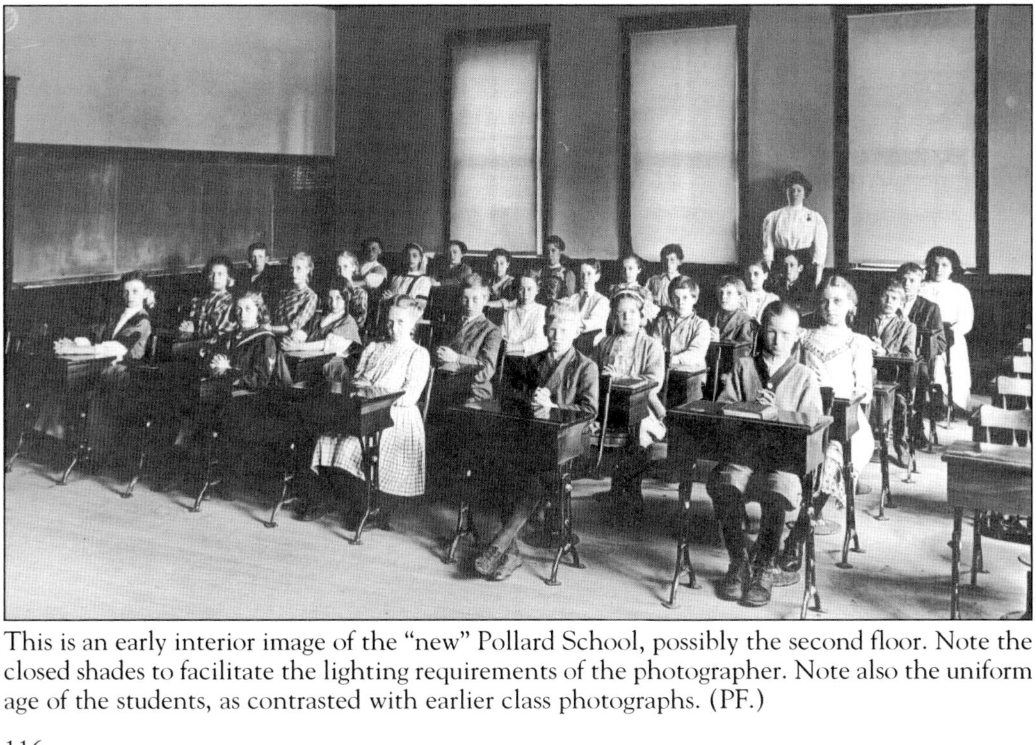

This is an early interior image of the "new" Pollard School, possibly the second floor. Note the closed shades to facilitate the lighting requirements of the photographer. Note also the uniform age of the students, as contrasted with earlier class photographs. (PF.)

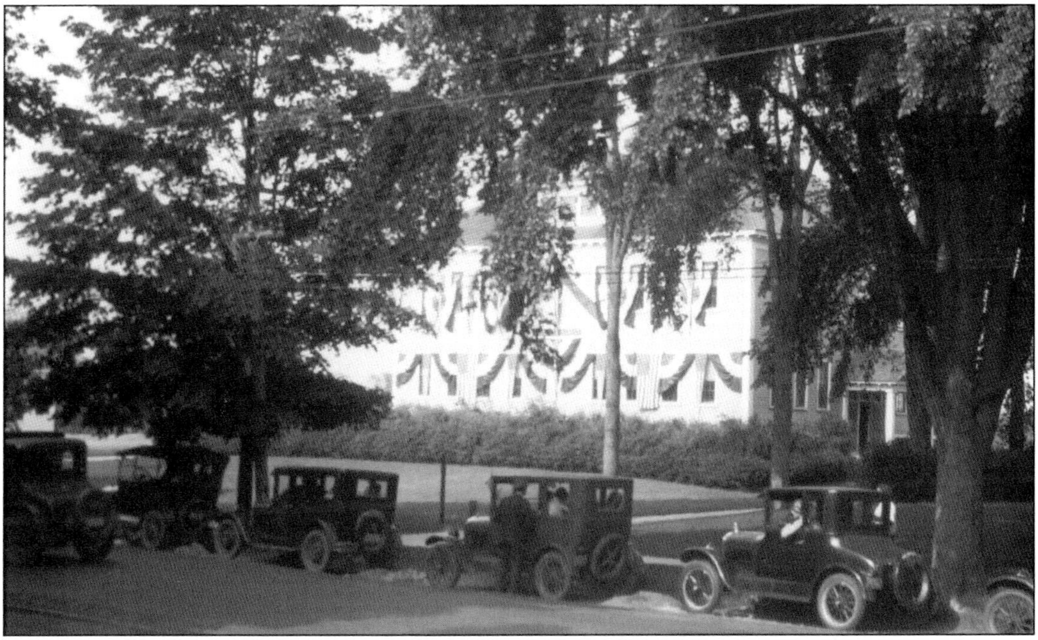

The present Pollard School is draped in flags and bunting on July 4, 1928. (PHS.)

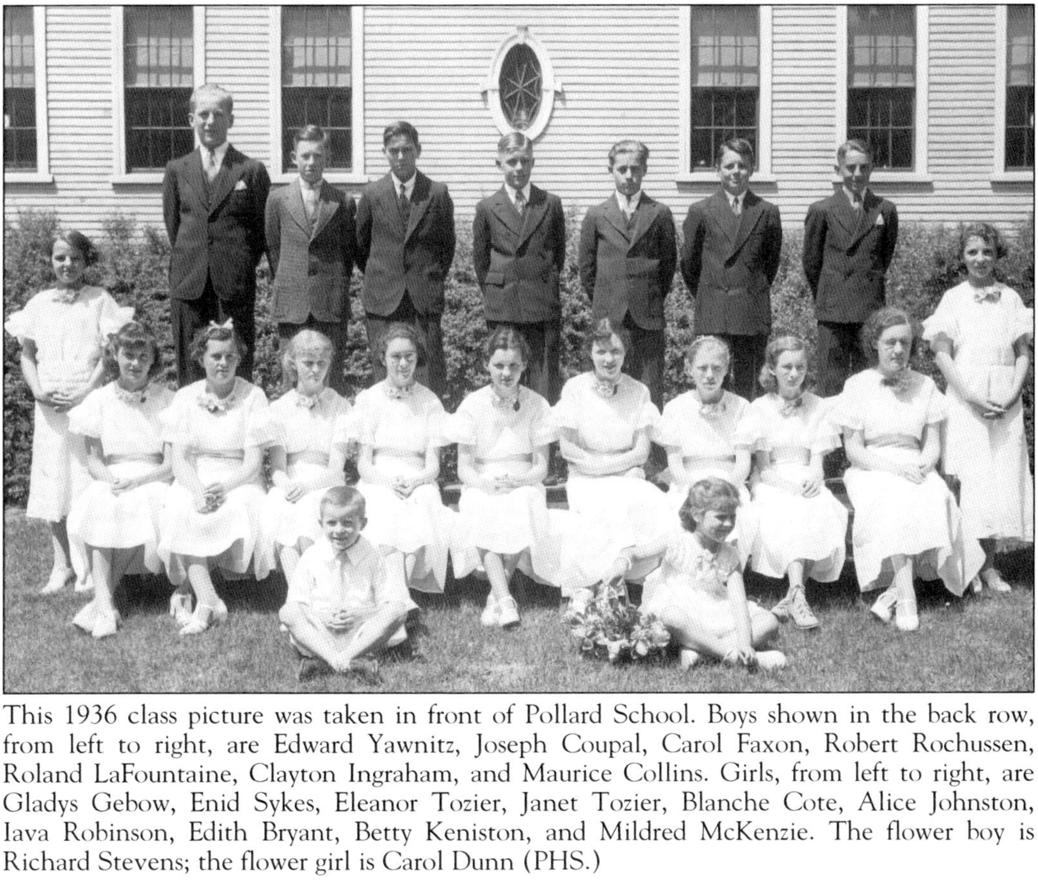

This 1936 class picture was taken in front of Pollard School. Boys shown in the back row, from left to right, are Edward Yawnitz, Joseph Coupal, Carol Faxon, Robert Rochussen, Roland LaFountaine, Clayton Ingraham, and Maurice Collins. Girls, from left to right, are Gladys Gebow, Enid Sykes, Eleanor Tozier, Janet Tozier, Blanche Cote, Alice Johnston, Iava Robinson, Edith Bryant, Betty Keniston, and Mildred McKenzie. The flower boy is Richard Stevens; the flower girl is Carol Dunn (PHS.)

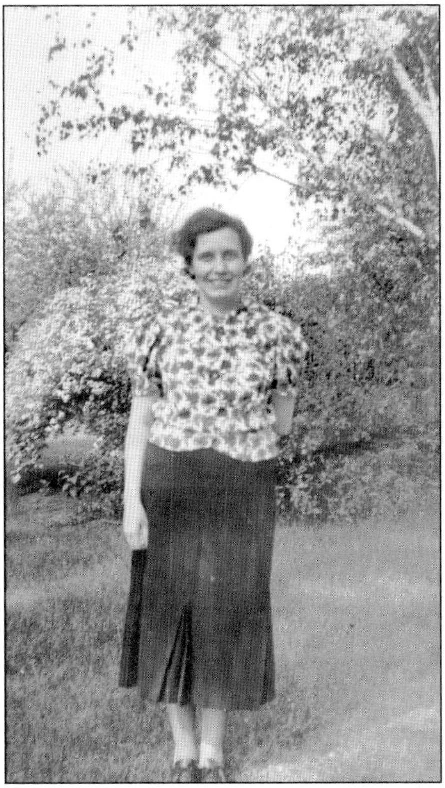

Mary Priest was a Pollard School teacher in the 1930s. (PHS.)

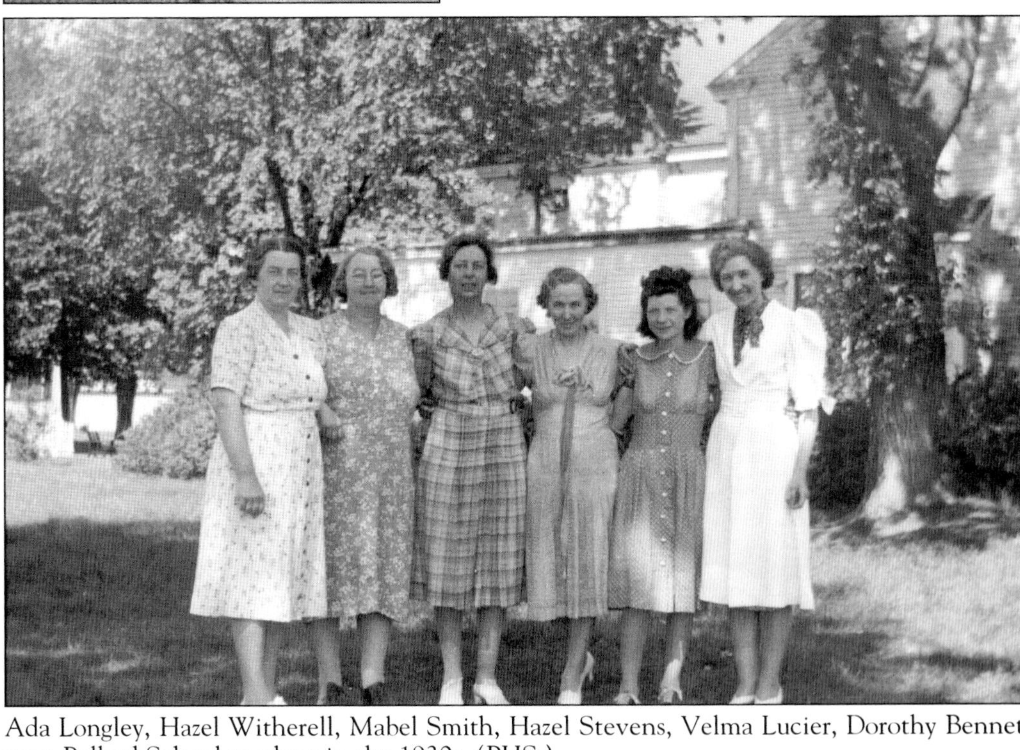

Ada Longley, Hazel Witherell, Mabel Smith, Hazel Stevens, Velma Lucier, Dorothy Bennett were Pollard School teachers in the 1930s. (PHS.)

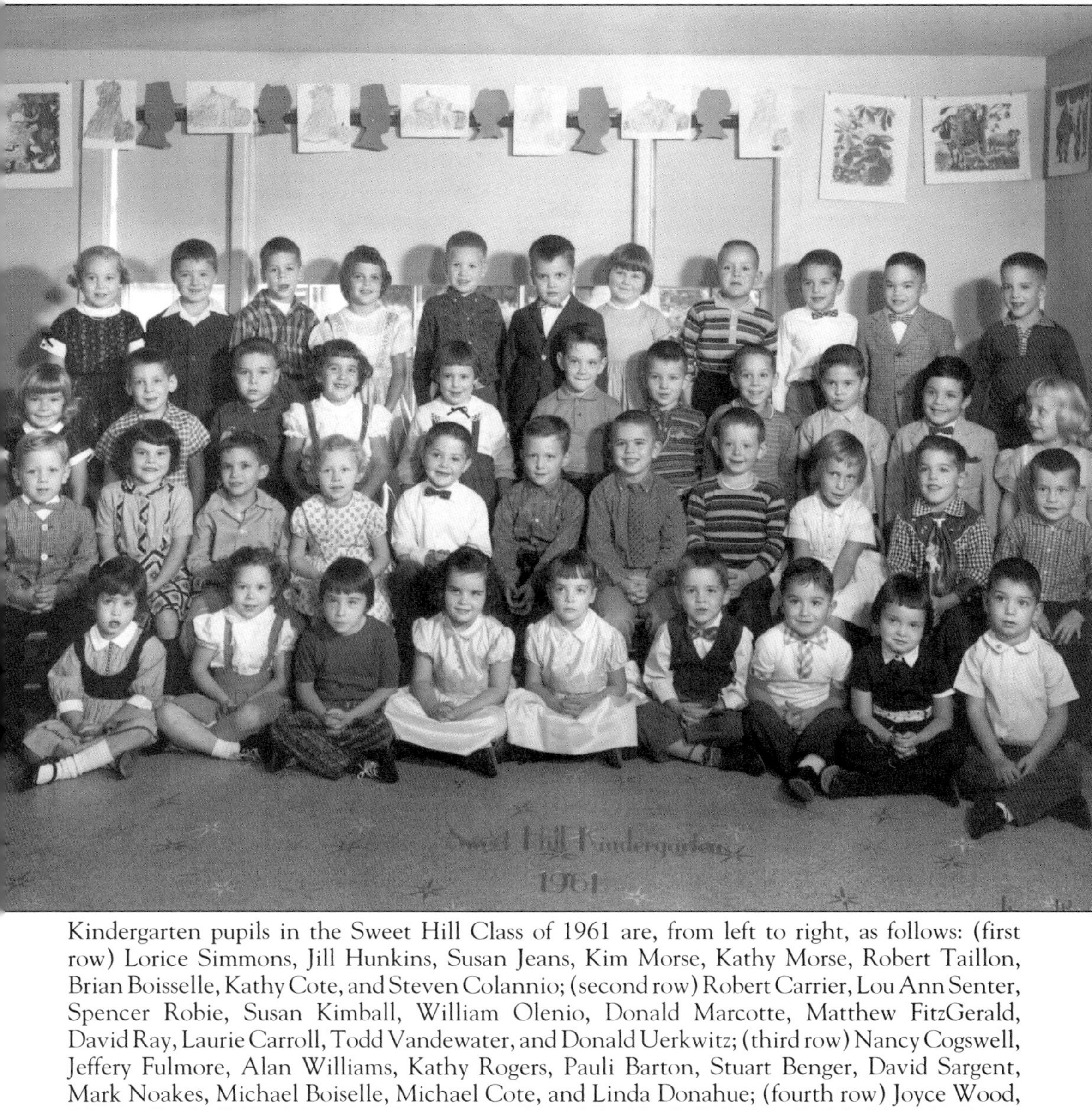

Kindergarten pupils in the Sweet Hill Class of 1961 are, from left to right, as follows: (first row) Lorice Simmons, Jill Hunkins, Susan Jeans, Kim Morse, Kathy Morse, Robert Taillon, Brian Boisselle, Kathy Cote, and Steven Colannio; (second row) Robert Carrier, Lou Ann Senter, Spencer Robie, Susan Kimball, William Olenio, Donald Marcotte, Matthew FitzGerald, David Ray, Laurie Carroll, Todd Vandewater, and Donald Uerkwitz; (third row) Nancy Cogswell, Jeffery Fulmore, Alan Williams, Kathy Rogers, Pauli Barton, Stuart Benger, David Sargent, Mark Noakes, Michael Boiselle, Michael Cote, and Linda Donahue; (fourth row) Joyce Wood, Clayton Birdsall, Keith Pearson, Patricia Vaughn, Philip Kimball, Robert Dolph, Rhonda Chase, Steven Guscora, Raymond Marquis, and Norman LeBlanc. (PHS.)

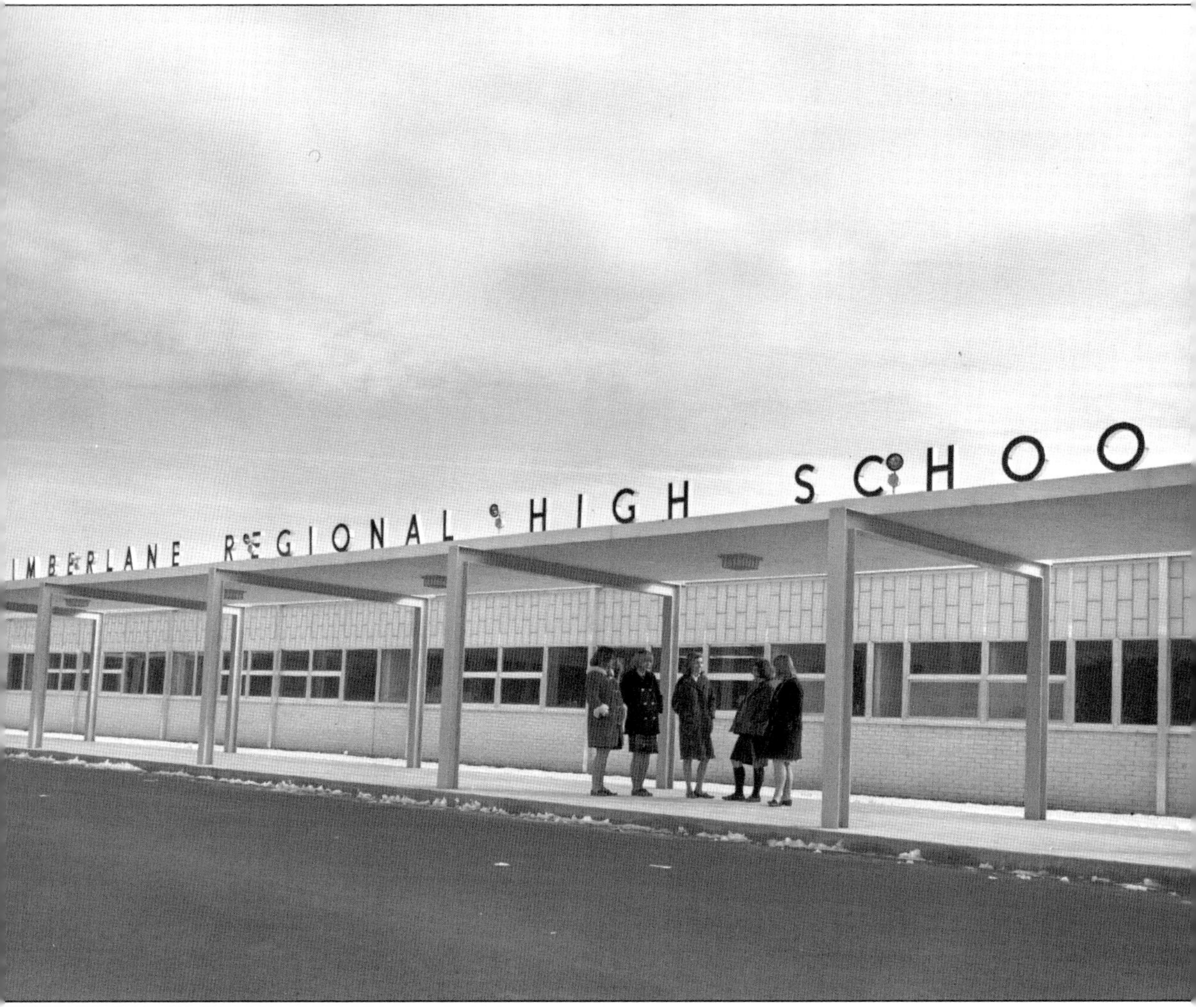

Timberlane High School is shown here in the late 1960s. When this regional high school opened in September 1966, it was a cutting-edge facility whose progressive pedagogic approach brought considerable acclaim from educators statewide. The 1970s proved tumultuous when a strike rocked the district. (PHS.)

Nine

Recreation, Celebration, and Fraternity

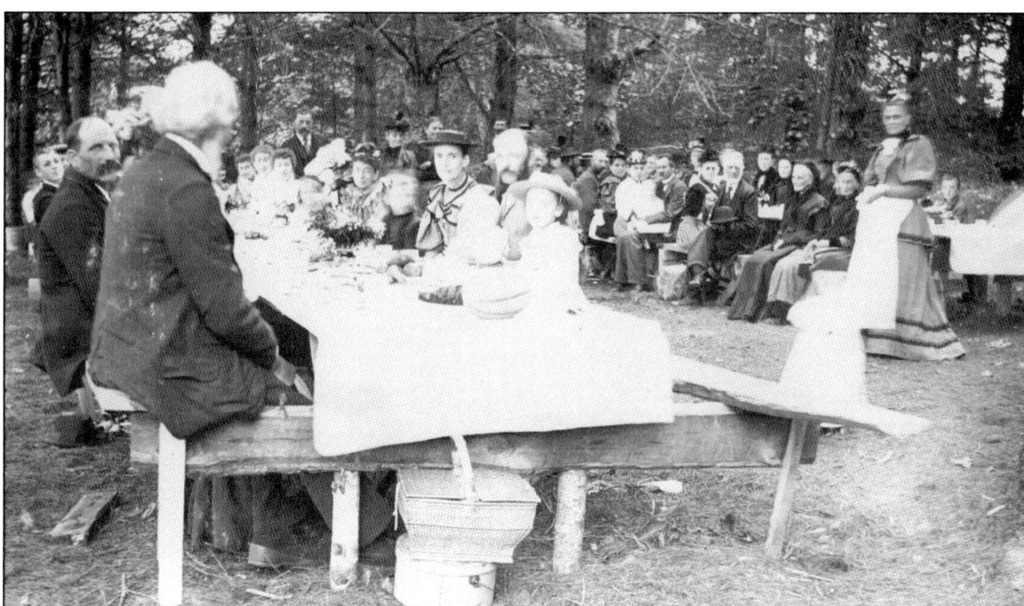

Shown is the Peaslee family reunion *c.* 1900. A newspaper account, presumably from the Haverhill *Gazette*, describes in minute detail this gathering of over 150 Peaslees from throughout the region. The meal consisted of a "rich chowder," which ensured that "none departed hungry." Although a late summer rain threatened to dampen the day's festivities, "hearts still glowed with joy" as the "party was entertained by sweet singers for a time." (PHS.)

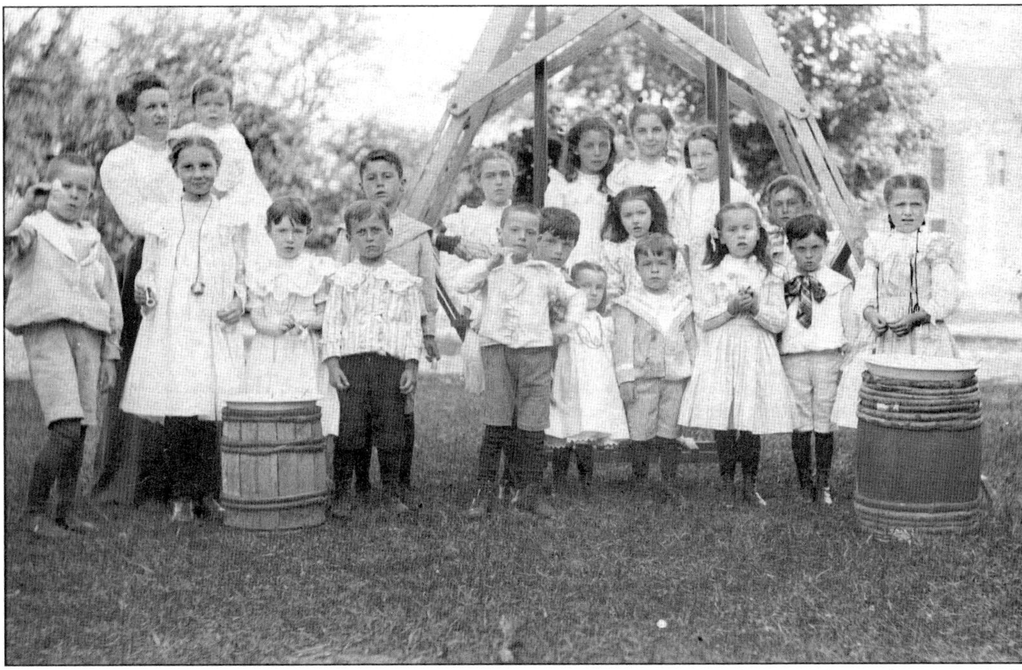

This was John Wilder Sleeper's birthday *c.* 1902. The Sleepers lived across from the town hall. Reva Gates is the smallest child standing. Note the bubble pipes that were given to guests as party favors. (PHS.)

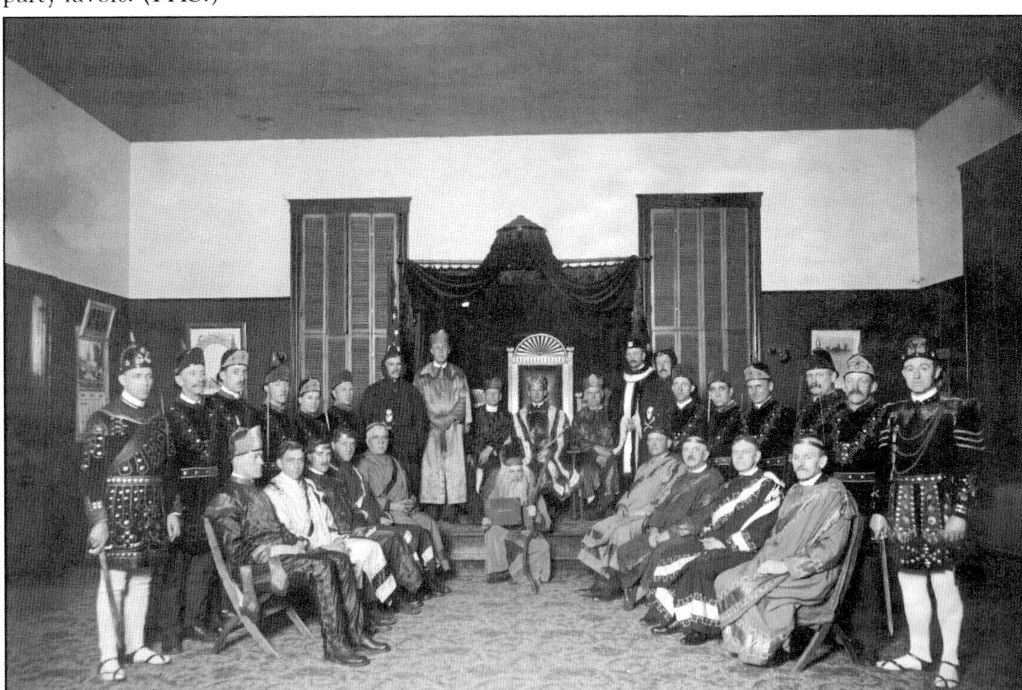

The Knights of Pythias pose for a formal group photograph in the grand room of the Crown Building. The Pythians used the upper story of this building as a gathering place and leased the ground floor to store proprietors.

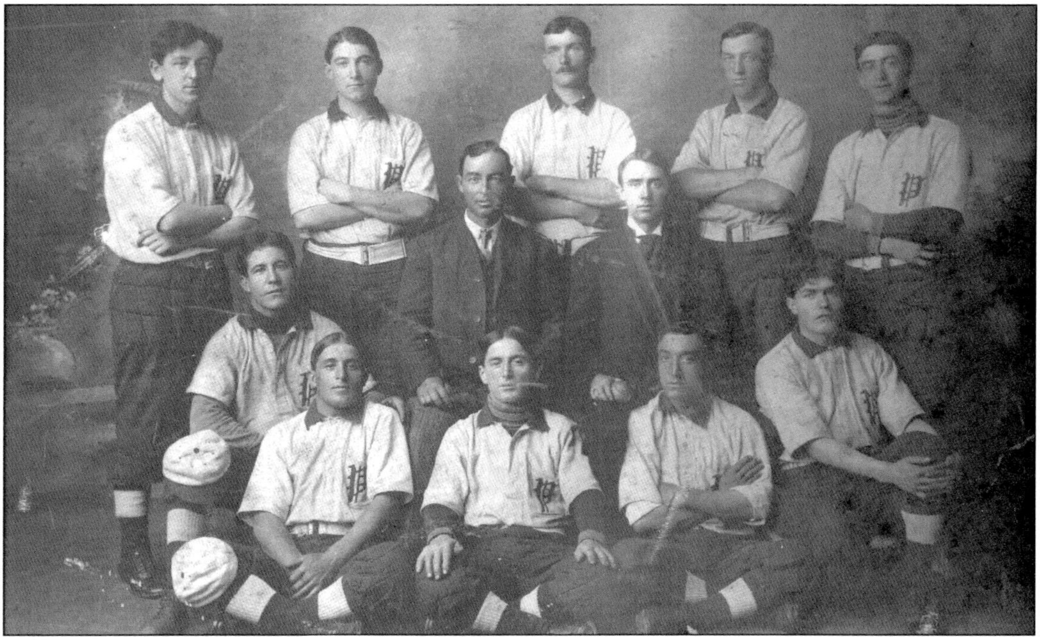

Like many towns, Plaistow has a local ball team, sponsored by area merchants and fraternal organizations. This picture shows the Plaistow baseball team *c.* the late 1800s or early 1900s. Members are, from left to right, as follows: (front row) Pete Dupont, Philip Dupont, Henry Gosselin, and Louis Dion; (middle row) Jack Lucier, Charles Denoncour, and Dr. Bailey; (back row) Jack Newcomb, unidentified, William Johnson, and Henry Fountaine. (PHS.)

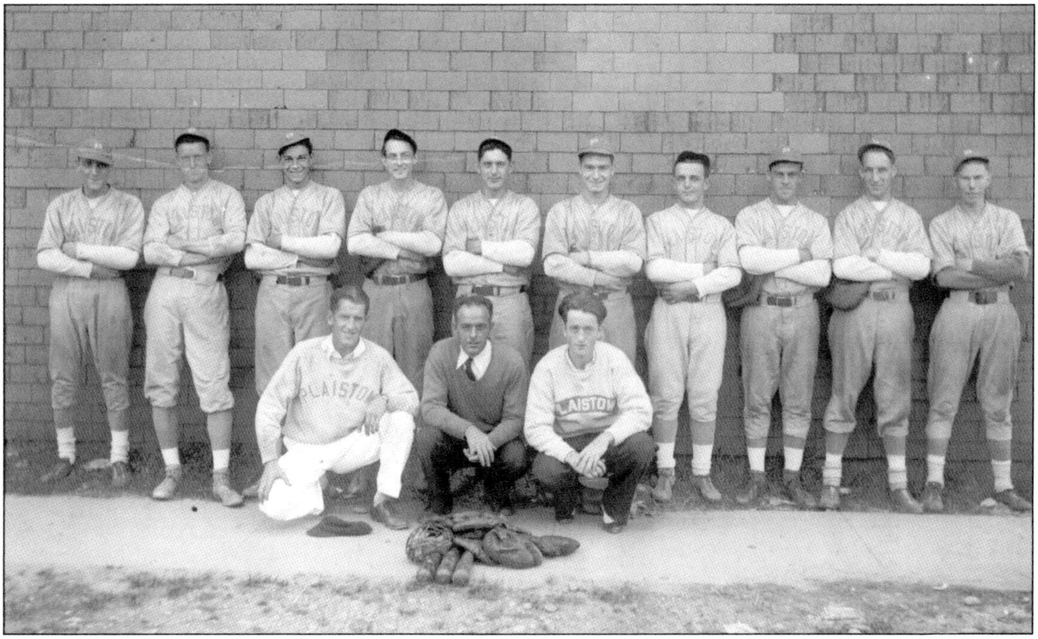

In 1933, the Plaistow baseball team consisted of the following, from left to right: (front row) Joseph Yawnitz, ? Dion, and William "Red" Rowell; (back row) "Chi Chi" Yannalfo, Joe Klimavich, Victor Aucoin, Joseph Gauron, Richard LaFountain, Clarence Dion, Emile Cote, Clifton Sargent, and Orra Robinson. (CYR.)

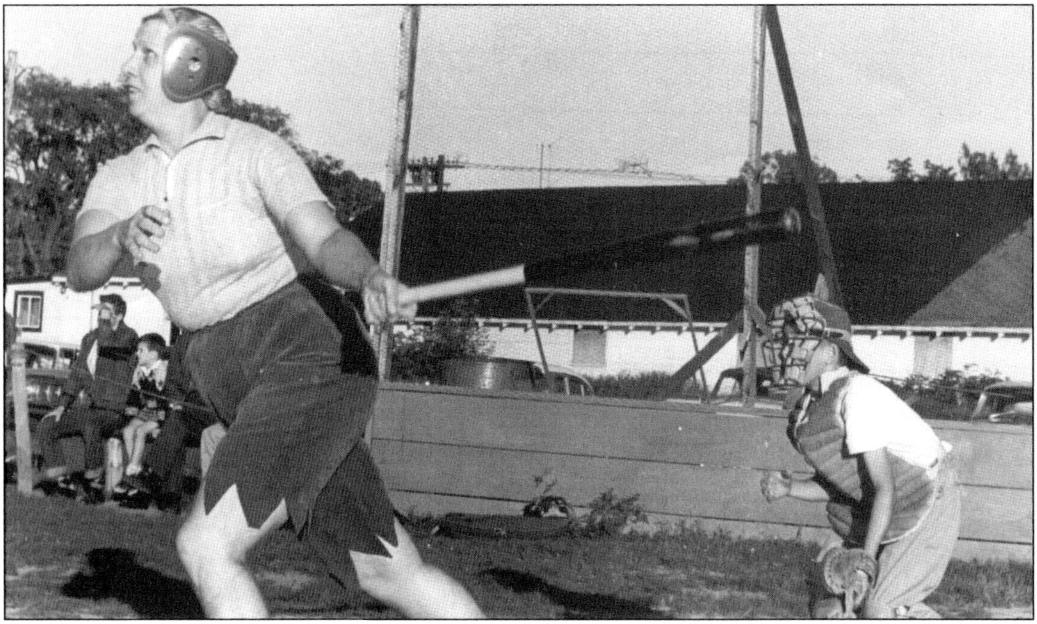

Katie Rowell is pictured at Landman's Field at the 1960 Mother and Son Game. Her inscription on the back of the photograph claims, "I hit a home run when this picture was taken." Note the bowling alley in the background. (PHS.)

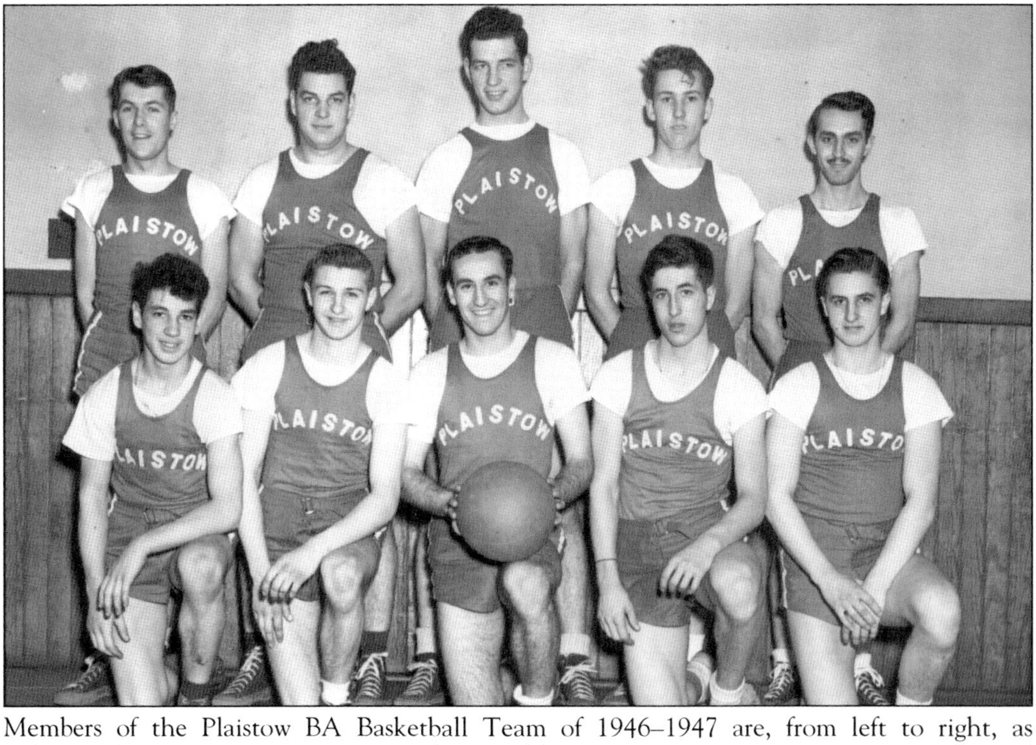

Members of the Plaistow BA Basketball Team of 1946–1947 are, from left to right, as follows: (front row) Leo Doton, Dick Trombley, Don Clement, Norman Mercier, and Bob Trombley; (back row) Bob Rochussen, Jerry Doyon, Ray "Shorty" Doyon, Rod Moore, and Maurice "Jake" Collins. (PHS.)

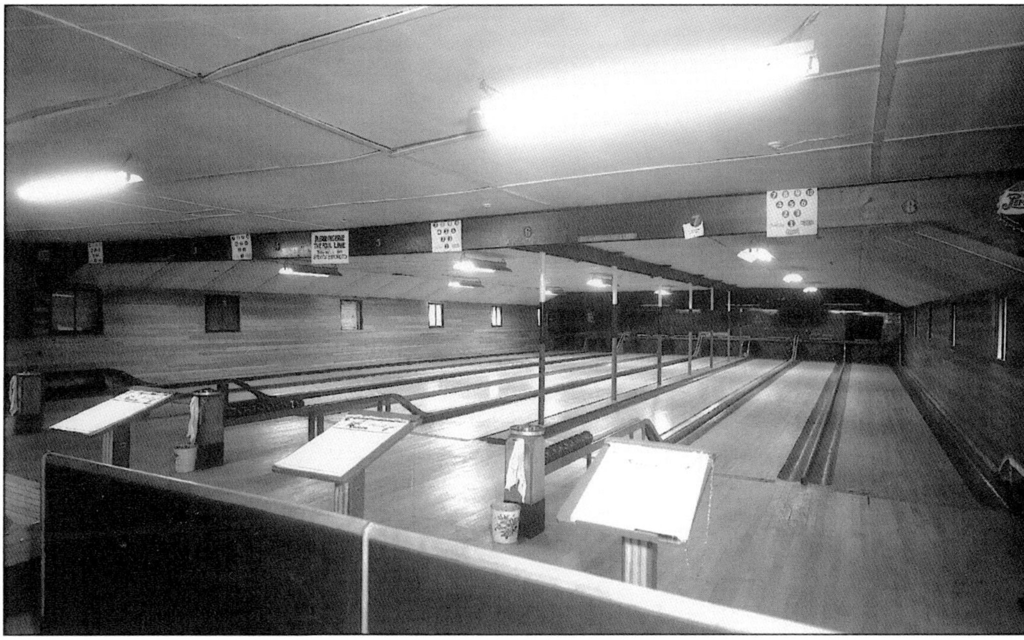

The Plaistow bowling alley was located near the entrance of Process Engineering. Now demolished, the bowling alley provided many Plaistow boys with their first jobs. Employed as pin boys, local youths aged 12 to 14 years could make up to 50¢ a night setting up pins. The work was not without its hazards. Older boys hoping to show off in front of their friends used to purposefully try to peg pin boys with fastballs and ricocheting pins. (HPL.)

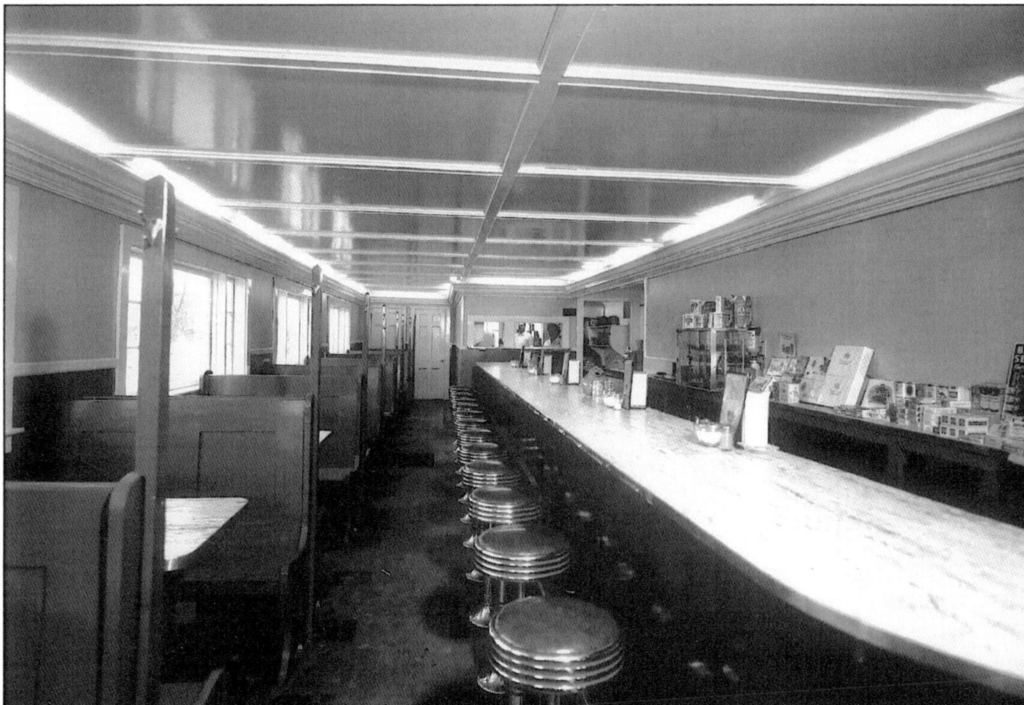

This is an interior view of a Plaistow diner *c.* the late 1950s or early 1960s. (HPL.)

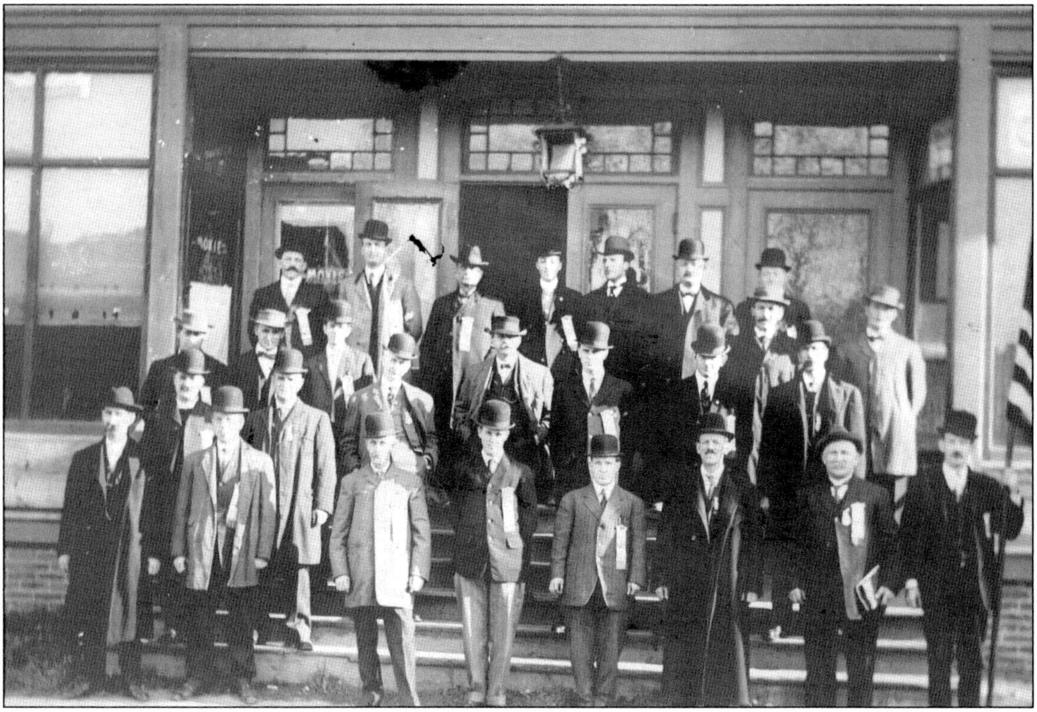

Members of the Junior Order of United American Mechanics pose for a photograph in front of Dustin's Store c. the 1920s. In the front row, beginning with the fifth person from the left, are "Pug" Tozier, Ed Carter, Eugene Davis, and Harry Flanders. Third from the left in the fourth row is George Gates. The Junior Order was a fraternal and mutual aid society that provided insurance benefits to members. (PHS.)

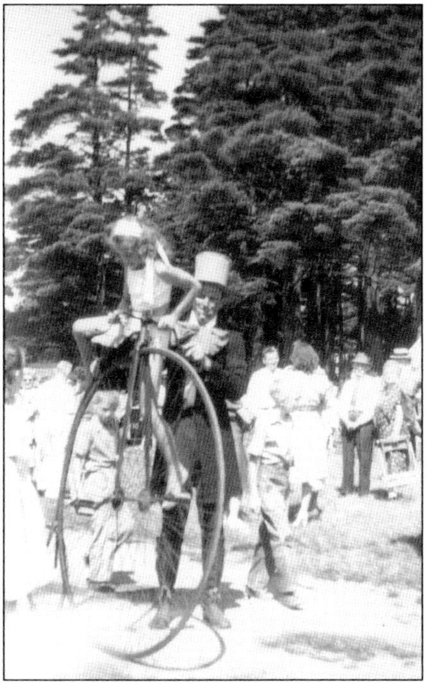

This was Field Day of 1947, sponsored by the Junior Order of United American Mechanics. Held at Landman's Field near the old bowling alley, this annual event was a major fund-raiser for the organization. (PHS.)

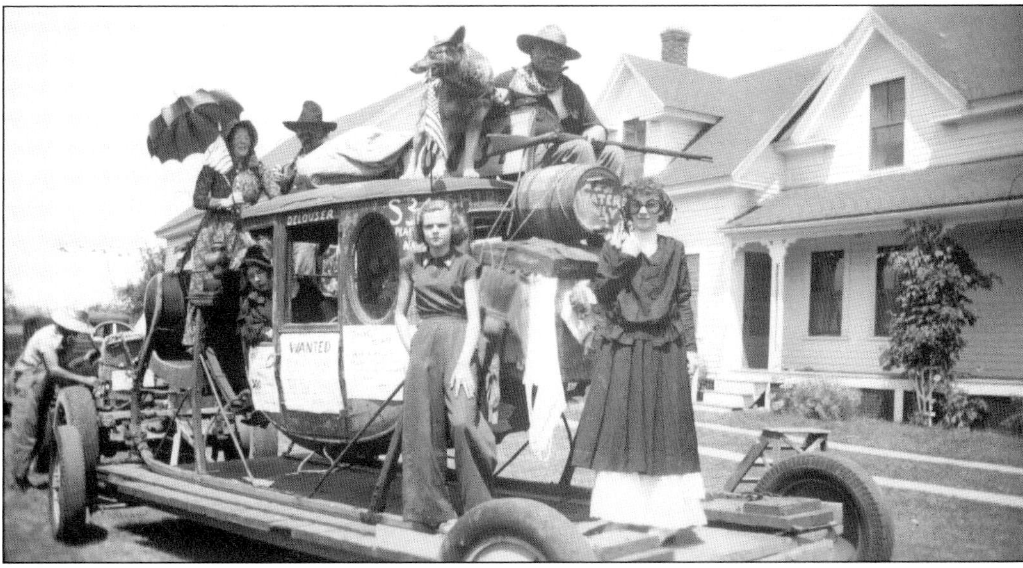

This creative adaptation of a Concord Coach was compliments of the Delouser family, who entered this float in the town's 250th anniversary parade in 1949. The barrel at the front reads "Water Only," perhaps as a parody on the temperance movement that was strong in the North Parish section. (PHS.)

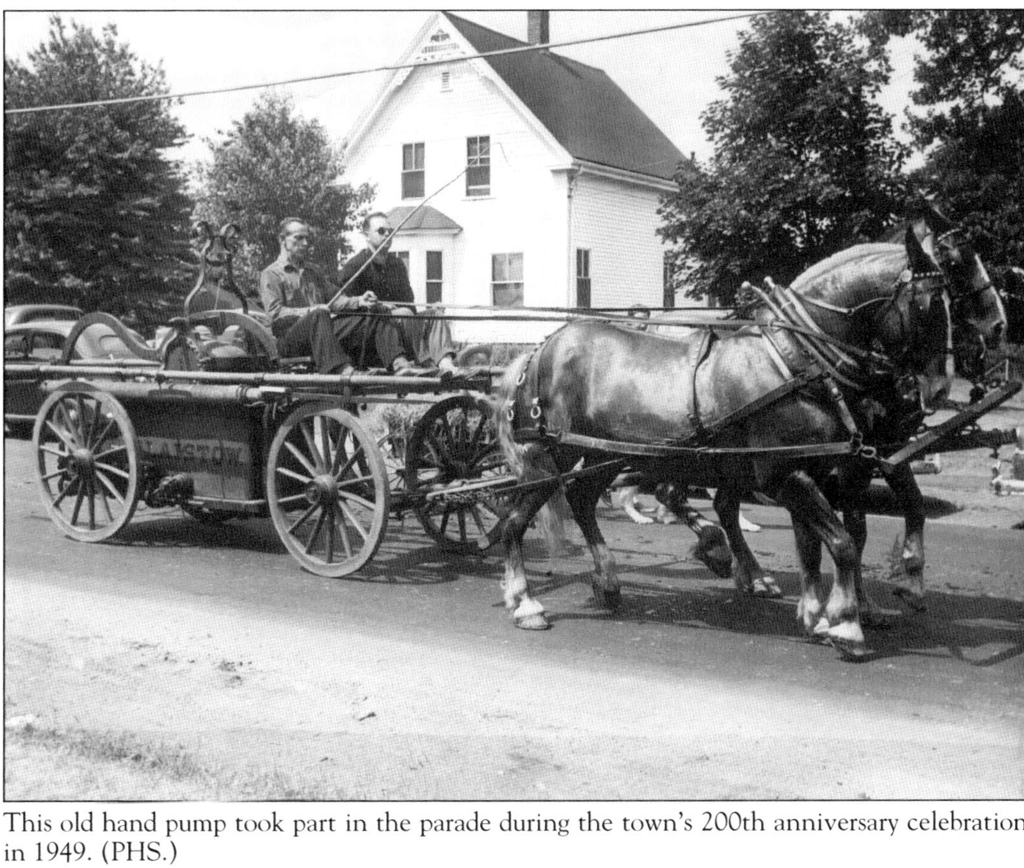

This old hand pump took part in the parade during the town's 200th anniversary celebration, in 1949. (PHS.)

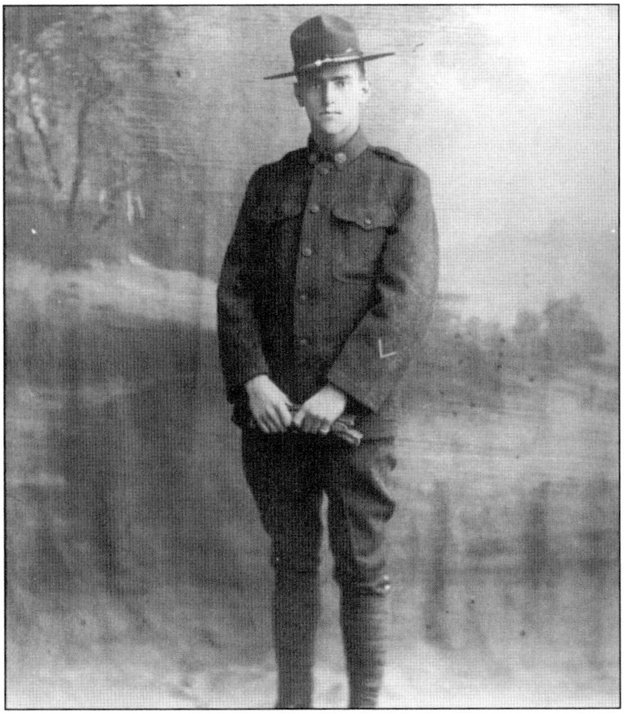

Albert "Vic" Geary (1891–1975) was a veteran of World War I who organized Plaistow's local chapter of the American Legion in 1931. Geary also deeded land on Greenough Road to Post 34. In the 1970s, Legion officer Ralph Stone created a community center bearing Geary's name to serve the area's elderly citizens (CHC.).

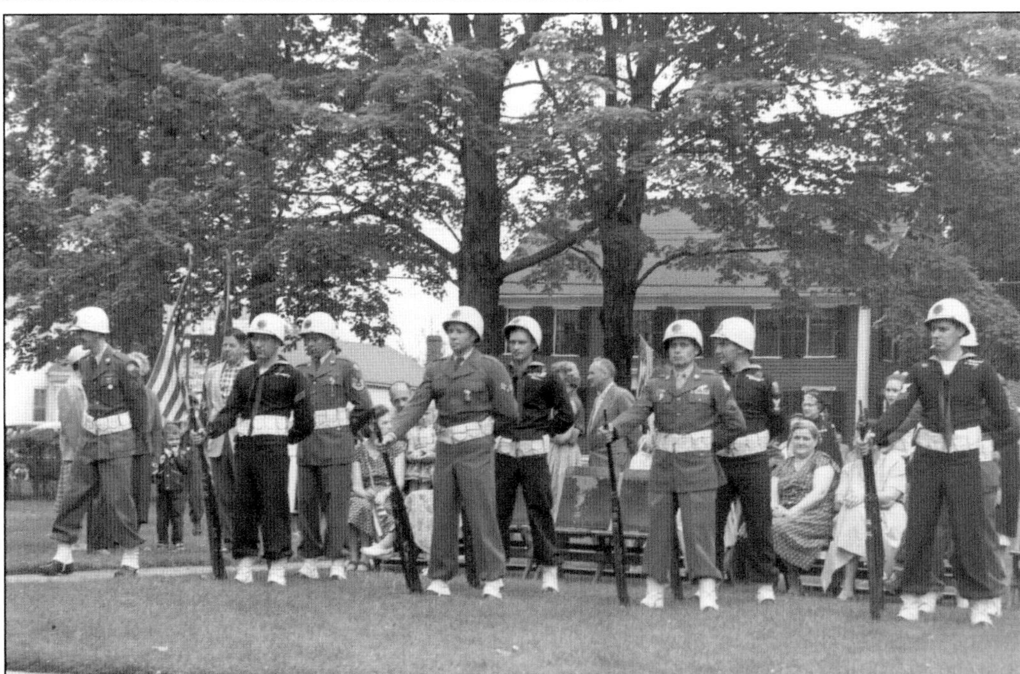

The American Legion participates in the Memorial Day Parade *c.* 1955. Since its founding, Post 34 has been an integral part of Plaistow's Memorial Day ceremonies. Under the leadership of Vic Geary, Post 34 rallied to establish a civil defense unit for Plaistow that became a model for surrounding communities. (CHC.)